White Collar Productivity

White Collar Productivity

Edited by
Robert N. Lehrer, P.E., Ph.D.
Consultant

Nonresident Associate, The American Productivity Center

Director Emeritus and Professor Emeritus
School of Industrial and Systems Engineering
Georgia Institute of Technology

McGraw-Hill Book Company

New York   St. Louis   San Francisco   Auckland
Bogotá   Hamburg   Johannesburg   London   Madrid   Mexico
Montreal   New Delhi   Panama   Paris   São Paulo
Singapore   Sydney   Tokyo   Toronto

Library of Congress Cataloging in Publication Data

Main entry under title:

White collar productivity.

   Includes index.
   1. Labor productivity.   2. Organizational
effectiveness.   3. White collar workers—Labor
productivity.   I. Lehrer, Robert N.
HD57.W49   658.3'14   82-118
ISBN 0-07-037078-8   AACR2
ISBN 0-07-037077-X pbk.

1234567890   KPKP   898765432

ISBN 0-07-037078-8

ISBN 0-07-037077-X PBK.

The editors for this book were Diane Heiberg and Esther Gelatt,
the designer was Richard Roth, and the production
supervisor was Teresa F. Leaden. It was set in Baskerville
by Bi-Comp, Incorporated.

Printed and bound by The Kingsport Press.

Dedicated to the APC and the IDL Team
Myers Hand
Paul Anderson
Michael J. Cissel
Michael W. Johnson
James Patton
Carl G. Thor

Contents

Preface

This book is written for those who want to understand better how white collar productivity can be improved. It should be of interest to any reader who seeks increased understanding of the subject. However, it is aimed principally at individuals who have direct and indirect responsibility for the productive use of white collar resources. These individuals include those who supervise white collar work and those who are ultimately responsible for the effective use of an organization's resources at successively higher organizational levels (levels of management above the supervisor, extending to top management and the board of directors). It also includes many nonline people who have both direct and indirect responsibility for improving the efficiency with which white collar organizational resources are used.

The message applies to small as well as large organizations and to both not-for-profit and profit-making organizations. Not all approaches are equally applicable, but there is common ground within every organization for adaptation and application of selected concepts and methods for enhancing white collar productivity. Readers who have direct responsibility for white collar productivity, both line and staff, are encouraged to read the book with a critical eye toward their own setting—using an imaginative approach to what is presented as potentially insightful in loosening their own organization's Gordian knot of white collar productivity.

This volume is the result of effort on the part of many individuals. I, as the editor, have shaped the organization and have been assisted quite generously by an outstanding group of contributors. They have shared their insights and experiences in chapters which list their names as authors. I acknowledge their contribution with extreme appreciation.

ROBERT N. LEHRER

White Collar Productivity

CHAPTER ONE

Introduction

ROBERT N. LEHRER
Consultant

White collar employees, including individuals who are managers and administrators, knowledge workers, professionals, technical specialists, and clericals, have increased in number at a much more rapid rate than blue collar employees. The two groups reached equality in numbers within the U.S. labor force during the 1950s. White collar employees now outnumber the blue collar groups by three to two, and are projected to continue their growth in the foreseeable future.

Rapid increase in white collar employment has been reflected within most organizations and is increasingly being recognized by management as cause for serious concern. Can the rate of increase be curtailed, without adversely affecting organizational performance? (Yes.) How productive are white collar employees? (Usually, not very.) Can white collar productivity be improved? (Yes.) What approaches have been used successfully to enhance white collar productivity? (Many.) Can these successful approaches be used effectively in other settings? (Yes.) This book will discuss each of these issues and will elaborate on a variety of approaches which can be used to successfully enhance white collar and knowledge worker productivity.

These concerns were voiced in a variety of ways and with considerable authority by advisers to the American Productivity Center (APC)[1] during its initial period of organization, resulting in initiation of a research project devoted to indirect labor productivity (IDL).[2]

1

The project initially focused on employee groups considered by most organizations as outside the "direct" worker category. This focus was progressively narrowed to exclude "indirect" blue collar workers, to deemphasize attention on the clerical group, and to concentrate on the broad category frequently referred to as knowledge workers. The procedure used involved interaction with APC founder organizations in order to obtain an assessment of their concern for and approaches to indirect labor productivity, literature search, fishing for leads to identifying individuals and organizations which had actively and successfully addressed the white collar productivity issue, contacting these organizations and individuals to obtain information about their approaches and results, conducting a workshop devoted to further assessment of productivity improvement approaches and to presentations detailing various successful ones, field visits to selected organizations to further investigate promising approaches, and integration of information and insights gained during earlier stages. All organizations and individuals were candid and open in sharing information and insights and were sincerely interested in contributing to the project.

Conclusions from one year's intensive effort were:

1. Few organizations were formally and directly addressing the broad aspects of improving white collar productivity.

2. Concern for white collar productivity enhancement is increasing. Many chief executive officers recognized the significance of white collar productivity potential—but few had arrived at a position of comfort in knowing what to do about the situation.

3. The most significant barrier to enhancing white collar productivity was lack of an adequate conceptual framework for dealing with the many facets of the problem.

4. There are many useful and proved, though restrictive, approaches to improving white collar productivity. Unfortunately, there is lack of knowledge about how these approaches can be used *selectively* and *integratively* to address the totality of white collar productivity. A conceptual framework is needed.

NOT MUCH BEING DONE

Probing discussion with upper management representatives of some 80 founder organizations indicated little action of a *comprehensive* nature directed toward measurement or improvement of white collar indirect and overhead employee productivity.

The importance of controlling the rate of increase and cost associated with these employees was recognized, and many organizations were doing something of a limited nature to improve their situation. In almost all instances, these approaches were judged to be beneficial but also inadequate and lacking. None of the organizations contacted were satisfied with their approaches.

Within organizations which had made little progress in dealing with white collar productivity there was evidence of a searching for useful new approaches along with an optimistic and hopeful, but skeptical, attitude—let us know what you come up with, if you manage to come up with anything.

The organizations which had made progress in dealing with white collar productivity were proud of their accomplishments, and generous in sharing information and experience. None of them were satisfied with their accomplishments. They were aggressively seeking and searching for additional useful approaches to broaden their coverage of productivity enhancement and measurement, particularly in the managerial, professional, and technical areas.

Only one organization had made broad gains, across the board, in controlling and enhancing white collar productivity. One subsidiary of a multinational corporation with over 25,000 employees falling in the nonmanufacturing, nondirect category had experienced an average annual increase in white collar employees of 2.6 percent from 1970 to 1977. Since then this subsidiary has managed to not only eliminate the 2.6 percent growth but to achieve a 1.3 percent reduction. At $40,000 per year direct and indirect cost per white collar employee, this 1.3 percent reduction equates to $13,520,000 saved and an annual cost avoidance due to eliminating the established 2.6 percent growth rate of $27,040,000, a total saving of $40,560,000! These gains were made in a constructive way which has enhanced not only productivity but morale as well.

A GROWING CONCERN

It is doubtful that there is even one chief executive officer (CEO) who does not worry a bit about indirect and white collar personnel costs. Most do, and many periodically issue edicts to tighten up on these costs. Hiring freezes, staff reductions, budget cuts, zero-based budgeting, and reorganization are some typical approaches. There is conviction, often a gut feeling, that fat is present in the system and that it can be excised without hampering organizational performance. But organizational performance is almost always hampered by these approaches. Organizational realities being what they are, clever managers find ways to justify overcoming imposed reductions, and the situation often regresses toward its earlier state, usually with loss of key employees, damaged morale, and considerable individual resolve to beat the system.

These no-nonsense approaches to controlling white collar costs are frequently desperation moves associated with a crisis situation, are often regarded as temporary fixes, and are coming to be recognized as less than desirable. Concern is shifting toward more proactive approaches which recognize that the white collar productivity problem is real, is of sizable proportions, can be managed, and deserves to be managed with the best talent and attention available.

Recognition by the CEO that white collar productivity can and should be addressed does not come quickly or easily. For example, one large organization which had just recently initiated a broad and formal program was 5 years in the process of gaining top management and board recognition of the magnitude of the problem and the associated opportunities. High-level staff had been "talking" the problem for over 5 years but perhaps were not saying the right things, or what they were saying was not being heard, or top management was not ready and/or receptive for various reasons. They became ready very rapidly when they finally realized that 52 percent of their 127,000 employees were white collar and accounted for 70 percent of personnel costs. A resource commitment of this magnitude, once recognized, does demand attention—particularly when one knows that some progress has been made in enhancing white collar productivity within various other organizations. Even knowing these things, one must be optimistic that the problem can be dealt with constructively and that the potential benefits are significant.

Various estimates have been made, based upon somewhat objective analysis and from experiential judgments, that within a "typical" organization, white collar personnel—particularly those regarded as knowledge workers, including managers—are only 40 to 60 percent productive. Unfortunately, this is likely to be a valid estimate—and it should cause considerable concern for everyone with managerial responsibilities. "Is this the case within *my* organization?" Perhaps not. But *any* chief executive officer can be confident that his or her white collar workers are not as productive as they could be. The opportunity range for productivity enhancement within a very well managed organization may be only 10 or 20 percent, but even a 5 percent improvement would have a major impact upon successful performance of the organization.

While there is a broad and growing awareness that white collar costs are oppressive, conviction that substantial savings can be achieved at the same time that overall organizational performance is improved is slow to develop. This is a difficult area with which to work. Organizational realities tend to encourage inefficiencies. But the greatest barriers to getting on with the job are lack of management conviction and lack of a conceptual framework. The two are intricately intertwined. We have arrived at our current situation because of lack of imaginative and strong management leadership in managing white collar productivity improvement. This is so mainly because no conceptual framework has been available to provide a structure for systematically evaluating various options for enhancing productivity related to specific organizational settings.

Many improvement techniques have been developed and have been used to achieve useful improvement results. There is no lack of available "tools" for productivity improvement. But there has been a paucity of information about how these diverse tools can be selectively used for supporting productivity enhancement related to opportunities for productivity improvement within a specific organizational setting at a particular time.

The APC study of white collar productivity clearly indicated the nature of the problem within a large and representative sampling of leading U.S. organizations. It also provided insight into what might be done to assist in focusing attention and efforts on improving white collar productivity within any organization. The message clearly is one of optimism and hope, and it should help to destroy the myth that white collar/ knowledge worker productivity cannot be dealt with. Lack of productivity is due not to lazy white collar workers but to lack of management attention to providing a setting which encourages valid, effective, and efficient performance from each and every white collar worker.

We will build upon the work of the APC team, and extend it. A conceptual framework will be developed in the next chapter, and each main portion of this framework will then be further elaborated in terms of proved, useful approaches in subsequent chapters.

NOTES

[1] The American Productivity Center, located in Houston, is a nonprofit, nonpartisan, independent organization committed to the understanding that productivity is essential for maintaining the American economic system, countering inflation and unemployment, and improving our standard of living. It is supported by contributions and grants from corporations, foundations, and individuals. With its permanent staff and with associates assigned by founder organizations, APC seeks the best knowledge available on productivity in public and private sectors; distills the knowledge; and creates new ideas and disseminates these in seminars, conferences, tapes, slides, publications, databanks, learning aids, packaged audiovisual training programs, custom programs, and advisory services.

[2] The IDL project team, under the guidance of Carl Thor, vice president, measurement, consisted of Myers Hand, project leader (APC associate from American Can Company), Paul Anderson (APC associate from International Multifoods), Michael J. Cissel (APC associate from Shell Oil Company), Michael W. Johnson (APC associate from Phillips Petroleum Company), and James Patton (APC associate from Gulf Oil Chemical Company). The editor was loosely associated with the project during his time with APC, while on sabbatical from Georgia Tech, serving as an associate and visiting senior adviser. It became his lot to summarize, extend the concepts and findings, and report the results of the team's accomplishments. Chapter 2 is, in essence, the summary report of the IDL project team effort.

CHAPTER TWO

A Conceptual Framework

ROBERT N. LEHRER
Consultant

We have not viewed the totality of overhead and indirect activities in a way that encourages us to see the range of useful approaches available and how these approaches can be used selectively and tailored to our own needs. Fundamental to this point is confusion concerning the internal and external dimensions of individual productivity.

People, truly, are the key to productivity. Most individuals want to do a good job and to contribute to the success of their organization. For various reasons they may not use their full potential. Good management practice can provide leadership and motivation, which will unleash at least some of this unused potential. Even when this is done, however, full productivity is unlikely to be achieved, for it is not likely that individual efforts will be directed only to those activities which will make a maximum contribution to the achievement of organizational objectives.

Individuals, ultimately, have control of their own efforts on behalf of the efficiency[1] of their activities, but they have only partial control of the effectiveness[2] of these activities. A job well done which does not contribute to achievement of the organizational objective is not done productively. Even though individual performance may be *efficient,* it would not be *effective* in contributing to accomplishment of the organizational mission. It would lack *validity.*[3] Lack of effectiveness and validity is at least partially beyond control of the individual.

Surely, most white collar workers have some latitude in determining what they do and how they do it, but various *structural* constraints ensure

6

that a substantial element of individual effort will be misdirected and will not be *valid* in relation to contribution to achievement of organizational objectives.

Successful efforts to capture the productivity potential of white collar indirect and overhead employees require that the organization be viewed in terms not only of individual workers and those things which enhance or inhibit their efficiency and effectiveness but also in terms of the various structural elements which have a direct impact upon the validity of their accomplishments relative to contribution to achievement of organizational objectives. This can be done by considering each structural element in turn:

- The *organizational* structure
- The *functional activity/work* structure
- The *service interchange* structure
- The *information* structure
- The *physical resource/technology* structure
- The *human resource* structure

TECHNIQUES AND APPROACHES

An amazing number of approaches to enhancing white collar productivity are available and have been successful in specific applications: clerical work measurement, budgetary/manning standards, paperwork simplification, direct time study, use of statistical methods to establish standards by regression analysis, overhead value analysis, predetermined time systems, work sampling, common staffing system, management by objective, organizational analysis, quality circles, goal setting, methods improvement, value analysis of management practices, overhead function analysis, human resources accounting, etc.

Each of these approaches (techniques) has achieved useful results in a particular setting. However, each has been found lacking when applied in other settings and within other organizations. Each one tends to approach one facet of the overall problem without due regard to the unique characteristics of the organizational setting and without due consideration of selective and synergistic application of other techniques to a conceptual framework depicting the broad nature of white collar productivity for a specific organization and organizational entity. In order to further develop the needed conceptual framework, each structural element will be described.

ORGANIZATION STRUCTURE

Every organization has a mission. It is its reason for being. Strategies and objectives are developed to guide the organization toward fulfillment of its mission. Conceptually, strategies and objectives are the basis for determining a set of functional specifications which are necessary and sufficient for accomplishing a mission. These specifications define the functional organization, which is translated into the formal organization by adding the physical dimensions—mainly the human resources needed to perform the functions required to achieve organizational objectives, following the appropriate strategies. Thus the mechanism for accomplishing the mission of the organization is defined. In addition, policies or guidelines for conducting the affairs of the organization are developed to aid in translating the more general beliefs of the organization into specific standards of conduct.

The formal structure, built upon the functional organization, helps to define worker power requirements for specific activity levels for each functional activity, and the mode of interaction between functional elements which will allow the organization to perform and to accomplish. Worker power requirements are converted to positions, with necessary skills and abilities and performance requirements, and the "fit" of each position within the overall structure is determined. Individuals are then associated with the specified positions.

Each individual within an organization is tied to organizational mission. Unfortunately, in many cases this tie is not clear or direct. The basis for relationship through the network of the organization is the goals for positions and individuals. Unless each individual's efforts are supportive of this network and contribute to achieving organizational mission, those efforts are not productive because they lack *validity*. This lack of validity may be the result of the individual's not attempting to relate his or her efforts to organizational mission or not wanting to do so. But more likely the matter is, at least partly and in many cases largely, beyond his or her control—because the structure itself has less than perfect validity. Even though he or she may have well-formulated goals and objectives, the structure of the network itself may ensure that those goals and objectives do not have complete validity relative to those of the organization.

Improving the validity of organizational structure is the first and most important consideration in enhancing white collar productivity. Two approaches will be considered.

A Top-Down Approach

One approach to enhancing the validity of organizational structure is by means of an abbreviated organization analysis, focusing on management and supervision, in order to uncover opportunities for increasing the effectiveness of the knowledge worker work force and to refocus emphasis on work which supports organizational objectives, goals, and strategies.

There are many ways to perform an organizational analysis. The most useful ones tend to be limited in time required for individual input, involve local management as "principals" in the process of data gathering and analysis, and are supportive of line management helping themselves to recognize and capture improvement opportunities. They tend to bring out into the open a series of questions and issues which should be addressed—such as allocation of time, cost, and effort to functional areas; distribution of functions; and contributions of functions and individual activities to achievement of organizational mission. Addressing these issues leads to enhancement of validity.

Even in those rare cases where an organizational structure is designed very well, with a high degree of validity, it is unlikely that it will continue to maintain this validity over time *unless* it is continually monitored and modified to keep pace with changing conditions. This is seldom done well. There is need within all organizations to assess validity periodically and to modify the organizational structure to enhance its validity.

A Bottom-Up Approach

The use of specific statements of goals and objectives for individuals is another useful approach to tying individual orientation to organizational objectives, strategy, and mission. This approach has been widely applied and can be extremely useful. However, not all organizations have had happy results with it. When the approach has failed, it is not the basic concept which lacks validity but the manner in which the concept is applied.

Based upon the functional organization, each position has a specific role to play within the organization in support of functional requirements. The role is modified, expanded, or contracted by the characteristics of the individual assigned to the position and by a variety of organizational interactions. Use of specific statements of goals and objectives for individuals formalizes the individual's principal intended contributions to the organization; provides a framework for integrating these contributions with organizational objectives, strategies, and mission, ensuring that the functional organization is adequate; provides opportunity for individual commitment; and serves as a basis for evaluating individual performance. The use of specific statements of goals and objectives for individuals, properly integrated with the behavior of an organization, can make a major contribution toward ensuring a reasonable validity for white collar efforts. Even where it is effectively used, further consideration of structurally imposed barriers to the validity of white collar efforts, by systematically assessing the entire network, is useful and advised.

Summary

The first structural element which should be considered in a comprehensive effort to enhance white collar productivity is the network of organization interactions which link individual efforts with organizational mission, the organization structure:

- Mission
- Strategies
- Objectives
- Functional organization
- Formal organization
- Positions
- Individuals, goals, and objectives

Two specific approaches have particular utility in dealing with organizational structure: an abbreviated organizational analysis, and the use of specific statements of goals and objectives for individuals. Both concentrate on clarification of individual contribution to organizational mission. The abbreviated organizational analysis approaches the matter more or less from the top of the structure down. The use of specific statements of goals and objectives for individuals tends to start from the bottom, that is, with individuals and their goals and objectives, and work up the structure and then back down. Both approaches are complementary and can be used together or separately. Each will be discussed in detail in Part 2.

FUNCTIONAL ACTIVITY/WORK STRUCTURE

The next structure or network which is a useful point of departure for enhancing white collar productivity is elaboration of the functional organization. Each function previously defined is embodied within a portion of the formal organization, and usually one or several functions are the responsibility of an organizational entity.

Accomplishment of assigned functions usually requires that these functions be subdivided into subfunctions, some of which may be highly similar or identical to subfunctions required to accomplish functions assigned to other organizational entities.

Accomplishment of subfunctions requires identification of necessary activities and/or positions, and delineation of the associated tasks, operations, and actions required for each activity. Typically, individuals are associated directly with the specified positions, tasks, operations, and actions but seldom very directly with functions, subfunctions, or activities.

The functional activity/work structure is derived from the functional organization portion of the previous structure:

- Functions
- Subfunctions
- Activities
- Positions ⎤
- Tasks ⎟ Individuals
- Operations ⎟
- Actions ⎦

It will serve as a point of departure for three analytical approaches:

1. Measurement of worker power resources allocated to accomplishment of specific operations, jobs, and tasks, evaluated relative to specific performance standards for these tasks, jobs, and operations—a bottom-up approach

2. Measurement of worker power resources allocated to accomplishment of tasks, activities, and subfunctions (or perhaps projects), evaluated relative to a statistically based predictive formula—an in-between approach

3. Measurement of worker power resources allocated to subfunctions and functions across the organization, evaluated relative to work causes—a top-down approach

Before the specific approaches are outlined, some discussion of the nature of white collar and knowledge work is necessary.

Functions *should* have a high degree of validity. Some loss of validity may be introduced in dividing functions into subfunctions, and considerably more loss of validity may be incurred as activities for accomplishing subfunctions are defined. Elaboration of the structure into activities and beyond introduces opportunity for loss of effectiveness and efficiency as well as additional loss of validity.

Individuals become involved directly relative to their work at the activity level, usually by execution of various actions which lead to accomplishment of various operations. These are parts of tasks which are required in order to accomplish position requirements, which are part of the activities which have been defined as necessary to accomplish the subfunctions. The subfunctions are necessary parts of the functions, which are dictated by the strategies and objectives defined as appropriate for fulfillment of organization mission.

Efficiency is individual-based and is evaluated by how well individuals do what they do when they do it, based upon a standard of performance. It is independent of effectiveness and validity. It is tied directly to actions.

Effectiveness is also largely individual-based but is also influenced by imposed constraints of two kinds: one is by misdirection of effort toward doing things which should not be done or are not necessary, and the other is by preventing individuals from doing what they should do. These constraints may be self-imposed or imposed by the organization and by others.

The essence of effectiveness is doing the right thing. It is independent of efficiency but related to validity. However, considering effectiveness to be independent of validity is useful, and it will be so treated. Validity is defined as a measure of the relationship of defined activities, subfunctions, objectives (exclusive of individual objectives), and strategies to contribution to organization mission. Improvement in validity can come only from strengthening these relationships.

Lack of validity is imposed upon individuals by the way in which mission is elaborated within the structure, from mission on down to those defined activities with which individuals are involved by virtue of their position or job assignment.

Effectiveness is measured by how well individual actions, operations, tasks, and positions contribute to defined activities relative to a standard or norm necessary for achievement.

All activities, tasks, operations, and actions within an organization are intended to be either direct in their contribution to producing the products or services of the organization, or indirect and necessary in order to facilitate accomplishment of direct contribution activities, tasks, operations, and actions. White collar and knowledge work is characterized by a high proportion of facilitative work and by being once or twice removed from activities which directly contribute to production of the products or services of the organization. It is usually even further removed from making a direct contribution to achieving organization mission. In addition, it differs substantially from direct work in three significant ways: it is less routine; there are many *different* or alternative actions, some of which are observable but many of which are not, which may lead to activity accomplishment; and there may be substantial time delays separating actions and their impact upon contribution to organization mission.

A Bottom-Up Approach

Direct labor activities have long been the subject of rationalization studies in order to improve and measure efficiency, effectiveness, and validity. Extensive use of various work-measurement approaches is common within most manufacturing organizations, and not unusual within service organizations. Should one elect to approach white collar productivity from the bottom up, it would be prudent to learn lessons from the successes and failures associated with the bottom-up approach in the direct labor area and in the indirect blue collar area, and to carefully evaluate adaptation of these approaches to the white collar area. It may be an appropriate approach, but it should be considered as a last resort alternative and should be adopted only after careful consideration of other approaches.

The work-measurement approach concentrates on designing job methods such that they are efficient, and measures the time required for execution of the standardized job actions or motions against a normalized performance rate. This is done either by direct observation or by use of predetermined time values. Allowances are provided for various nonwork times, such as breaks, personal time, and interruptions. The resulting standards, usually expressed as time per so many units of work or number of units per hour or day, are used for planning, scheduling, assigning, and controlling worker activities, and occasionally as the basis of financial-incentive pay schemes.

The actions required to perform an operation are defined, standardized, and measured. Efficiency is measured by comparison of worker performance with standard performance. Effectiveness is dealt with in three ways: frequently, but not always, the process or procedure of which the individual operations are a part is analyzed in a search for more effective ways to accomplish the end result; the individual actions required for performing the operation usually are specified such that they are the most effective and efficient way to accomplish the operation; and allowance is provided for anticipated amounts of nonwork time. Assuming that these things have been done on behalf of effectiveness and that conditions do not change, effectiveness is controlled by controlling worker efficiency. However, conditions usually do change, with some adverse effects on job effectiveness. Also, effectiveness has not been adequately treated beyond the process or procedure, which may itself be ineffective.

The logic of work measurement is very tight, *if* necessary work actions can be defined, are repetitive, and have a direct relationship to accomplishing a necessary unit of work. However, work measurement requires a very detailed procedure for establishing standards and an involved process for using the standards. It can be very expensive to install and expensive to maintain.

There is a growing recognition that even though traditional work-measurement approaches to productivity have yielded substantial accomplishment and benefit, there are dysfunctional side effects which may compromise productivity gains and result in eventual losses. People are, all too frequently and perhaps not with intent, treated as mechanistic entities which are expected to be reactive elements in a totally mechanistic and bureaucratic scheme. They are expected to do what they are told to do, in the fashion specified, according to predetermined standards for performance—without having understanding of why this may be necessary and/or desirable or having any say in determining the structure which is imposed upon them. Reaction of white collar workers to these conditions can be quite severe and negative.

Management literature is rich in analysis of worker dissatisfaction, both blue and white collar, and in prescriptive recommendation for approaches to achieving better performance by means of motivation-based involvement. Individuals tend to perform better when they have had some participation in determining what they are to do, how the thing they are to do is done, and how these activities relate to organizational mission, strategies, and objectives. Thorough participation causes a sense of ownership, commitment, and motivation. In addition, participation provides opportunity and capability for individuals to contribute to improving not only their own efficiency and effectiveness but also the validity of their efforts relative to the network of organizational structure leading to mission and back to individual efforts.

Many of the negative aspects associated with traditional work-measurement approaches to white collar productivity can be alleviated by good management practices, including use of a participative approach. In many situations an employee-manager negotiated performance standard is at least as useful as one established by formal work measurement. This is particularly so where interchange defines mutually acceptable measures for achievement, and where continuing improvement of effectiveness and validity, by innovation involvement, are built into the working environment.

In summary, various work-measurement approaches which have been borrowed and adapted from direct labor applications can be successfully applied to selected areas of white collar activity. The most likely applications would be to routine or semiroutine clerical work and to routine repetitive elements of the work of other white collar employees. Even though these applications can be made successfully, work measurement should be considered as a last resort alternative. The costs are high, only a portion of the white collar group can be covered, and other approaches which are likely to be less costly and more effective are available.

An In-Between Approach

One substantial difficulty associated with work-measurement application to white collar work is that actions, which are the basis of traditional work measurement, are not always directly related to results, which is what we really would like to measure. If actions are not directly the basis of results, we cannot measure results by measuring actions. An alternative approach must be used. Many of the "actions" associated with white collar work, particularly with knowledge workers, are mental and not directly observable, and their impact on results may be delayed. In addition, a large portion of the results of white collar work can be achieved in a variety of ways and with a variety of quality levels.

One way to deal with these difficulties is to approach measurement independently of specific "actions" and individual operations. This can be done by aggregation of actions, operations, and perhaps tasks, focusing on results for activities, projects, and subfunctions. This is often an appropriate approach where results can be adequately defined and measured. This is the case for many sales, office, and white collar and knowledge worker functions but may not be applicable to research workers, development engineers, and other such positions where results are not expressible in specific and measurable terms.

If desired results for an activity, project, or subfunction can be specified in measurable terms, it is likely that various identifiable conditions or factors associated with the activity, project, or subfunction determine the amount of time to accomplish the result. If this is so, a cause/effect relationship exists. The various conditions or factors "cause" the time required for accomplishment. Variation in the conditions or factors is likely to cause variation in the time required. If the conditions or factors and their variations, as well as results, can be measured, the relationship between the conditions or factors and their variation and required time can be expressed as a quantitative model describing the relationship. This model can be used to predict the time required to achieve results for specific conditions and factors.

As the various factors which are believed to influence the worker power required for accomplishment are identified, they can be counted or measured for each repetition of the task. The data collected in this way can then be statistically analyzed by multiple linear regression. This is a powerful technique which provides simultaneous estimates of the contributions of the several factors. The result is a model of the system, an equation which can be used as an analogy of the physical system. The technique allows the analyst to judge the adequacy of the model and the data set from which it is derived.

The various related descriptive and influential factors which are examined for use in the regression model are called "predictors." The worker power used (or "required," if this distinction can be made) for the task is the "response." The multiple regression analysis estimates the amount of association each of the predictors has with the worker power used. By suppying future values of the predictors to the model, the model can be used to predict the amounts of time which can be expected to be used for future similar tasks. The adequacy of this prediction process can be judged during the analysis phase, with the possibility of collecting more data or introducing additional predictors into the model whenever the model is judged inadequate.

The multiple regression approach is based upon past performance, so that if a satisfactory prediction equation is obtained, it will predict the expected use of worker power for the same average levels of efficiency and effectiveness that existed when the data were generated. This may not be satisfactory.

Several things can be done to account for the levels of efficiency and effectiveness in the prediction model. Efficiency and effectiveness can be evaluated for each task and corresponding adjustments can be made to the response variable to reflect normal or desired levels. The adjusted data can then be analyzed to obtain an adjusted model. When this is done, the worker power needs will be predicted at the normal or desired levels of efficiency and effectiveness. Note that what is regarded as normal or desired must be specified by people (a value judgment) and is not a result of data analysis. Regression models are predictive but not prescriptive. The worker power required to perform the operations, tasks, activity, project, or subfunction at the normal or desired levels of efficiency and effectiveness will be predicted by the multiple regression equation.

A Top-Down Approach

If one could define the basic functional responsibilities within an organization, define the activities associated with these functions, and identify either direct or indirect measures of what causes these activities, one could gain insights into where further analysis to improve worker power utilization might be useful, by analysis of the relationships between work cause and worker power variations.

This approach has been used, quite successfully, with dramatic results. One organization has developed and applied this approach to measurement using 14 functional definitions and some 115 activities which include all indirect worker power, with 60 quantitative and measurable work cause indicators which relate worker power requirements to defined "functional" activities. Periodically, worker power allocation to each activity and the associated work cause quantities are reported and analyzed. Productivity indexes are developed for each activity and are tracked over time and compared across organizational location. Base levels or norms are developed for these productivity indexes, and deviations from the norms are analyzed by activities regardless of where they occur, as well as by location, by functional groupings, by organizational entities, by plant and location, and by major business unit groupings.

Indirect labor productivity is "measured" not by individual workers but in a grosser sense as resources associated with the defined activities and functional definitions. The productivity tracking over time and comparisons within the organization are made openly available to all individuals and are carefully reviewed to identify opportunities for further analysis which may lead to productivity improvement, to establish priorities for improvement, to stimulate intraorganizational interaction, as the basis for reorganizing and streamlining productivity programs, and as the basis for white collar worker power planning.

Conceptually, this approach addresses the issue of resource allocation by functional activity and provides a "measurement" base for questioning validity and effectiveness of these allocations and for subsequent investigation of ways in which validity, effectiveness, and efficiency can be enhanced. The measurement is approximate and has increasing utility as data are accumulated over time and across organizational entities so that the organizations or functions which have deviations from the norms or averages can be analyzed to gain understanding of why favorable and unfavorable deviations exist, and to develop insight regarding what can be done to move performance in the desired directions.

This approach is a top-down one, starting with the functional organization and measuring "functional" activities. It measures activities, not people, and can be useful in identifying efficiencies as well as inefficiencies and as the basis for planning to improve validity, effectiveness, and efficiency of white collar work.

The dramatic results achieved with this approach are at least in part "situation-specific"—a reflection of the organizational climate and style of the organization involved. However, the concepts have universal applicability and can be tailored to the specifics of almost any organization. The strategy of development is a top-down initiative (by top management), a bottom-up design of the system (through involvement and participation), and provision of a strong supportive structure to make it easy for line management to use the resulting information constructively. This strategy is a good one.

Summary

The second structural element which should be considered in a comprehensive effort to enhance white collar productivity is an elaboration of the functional organization, the functional activity/work structure. Three approaches have been suggested: a bottom-up approach, starting with analysis and measurement of worker actions in order to standardize job methods and to establish job or operation performance standards using work measurement; an in-between approach, measuring an aggregation of individual operations and tasks, focusing on measured indicators of results as the basis for predicting worker power requirements; and a top-down approach to an approximate measurement of all white collar/indirect labor activities relative to various work causes, which develops productivity indicators for all functional activities.

All three approaches can be useful. However, they should be considered for possible use in the reverse order—functional activity measurement first, activity work measurement last. These approaches will be discussed in detail in Part 3.

SERVICE INTERCHANGE STRUCTURE

Many organizations which have been highly successful in productivity enhancement have built into their internal structure and operating philosophy the concepts of marketplace and enterprise economics. Each organizational unit is a cost, profit, and responsibility center with an appreciable degree of operational autonomy. It "purchases" goods and services from other organizational elements and "sells" its goods and services to other organizational elements. Each unit is expected to compete, and profitably survive, and frequently each has the option of obtaining goods and services from alternative sources, even from outside the organization, if this would be more cost-effective. Such schemes are usually applied to production units and supported by transfer pricing standards and standard cost systems.

These same concepts of autonomy and enterprise economics can be applied, with modification, to white collar activities. Each organizational unit can be considered as a service interchange center—purchasing services from various other organizational units and in turn providing services to other units. The only justification for either purchasing or providing services is that these services are necessary and contribute, either directly or indirectly, to accomplishment of organizational mission.

Rather than establish standard cost systems to evaluate the flow and costs for various services, it is more appropriate to obtain a profile of services used and services provided by each organizational unit over a period of time. Each service can then be priced by the providing unit and evaluated relative to value by the receiving unit. All services can then be evaluated in terms of validity and effectiveness, and "standards" for cost/benefit relationships for necessary services can be developed. Various techniques can be used to encourage or force identification of alternative ways to provide necessary services such that they are more valid and effective, and to identify opportunities for innovation which will enhance efficiency in the work required to provide the service. Frequently, an improvement target for all units is used to force identification of a range of alternatives, with specification of benefits and risks or disadvantages. Both "buyer" and "seller" units participate, and they agree not only on cost/benefit relationships but also on priorities for various improvement targets. Determination of which alternatives are to be implemented is made by representatives of the next higher organizational level, frequently involving the chief executive officer. Seller-buyer relationships are evaluated in terms of cost/benefit interaction, supported by a systematic search for more valid "needs" specifications and more effective and efficient ways to satisfy validated needs.

The service interchange structure is conceptually an elaboration of the formal organization, to profile and evaluate the services provided by and furnished to each organizational unit:

- Demand
- Services required
- Services provided
- Interactions—cost/benefit relationships

Approaches within this structure will be described in Part 4.

SUPPORTING STRUCTURES

Three vertical, hierarchical, and derivative structures of a conceptual framework for dealing with white collar productivity have been presented. Each has been developed by deriving the logical hierarchy of elements which support the ultimate or top element. The first is an elaboration of the organizational structure, starting with mission and ending with the individual members of the organization. The second and third structures have been developed as expansions of two elements of the first structure: the functional activity/work structure as an expansion of the functional organization element, and the service interchange structure as an expansion of the formal organization element. We now shift our attention to three supportive, horizontal structures: information, physical resource/technology, and human resource (see Fig. 2-1).

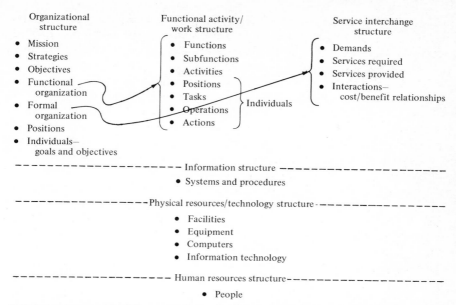

FIG. 2-1. **A conceptual framework for dealing with white collar productivity.**

INFORMATION STRUCTURE

Information provides the signals which enable an organization to function. Our concerns are primarily but not exclusively with formalized aspects of information which are designated as systems and procedures, which represent the acknowledged correct ways information is to be processed, reports are to be prepared and used, and systems are to function.

Systems and procedures may be implemented manually or in various degrees by mechanization or computerization. In either case, the sole justification for any system or procedure is to help workers in the performance of their jobs. It is critically important that individual job performance be effectively supported, that the job which is supported is valid relative to its contribution to organizational objectives and missions, and that the system or procedure is internally effective and efficiently accomplished.

Systems and procedures analysis is the approach used to design or redesign systems and procedures in order to improve efficiency, effectiveness, and validity. Where computerization is involved, typically an expert or group of experts assist in definition of specifications which establish user needs, and the experts prepare the detailed system or procedure and the programs and routines which are required for computer use. The skill of the experts *and* their attitudes toward supporting others are determinants of the validity, effectiveness, and efficiency of systems and procedures. Even when systems and procedures are initially highly valid, effective, and efficient, things tend to change over time and these characteristics tend to diminish. Restudy is in time justified but may be delayed with periodic patch-ups.

The efficiency and internal effectiveness of mechanized or computerized applications of systems and procedures is appropriately the responsibility of the experts and those in charge of computer services. However, these experts should not be the ones to define systems and procedures structure. This should be done by the users, with advisory support from the experts, not in terms of systems and procedures but relative to the problems of computer interface. This approach permits the design of systems and procedures which reflect the user's needs, style of operation, and opportunity to improve validity as well as efficiency and effectiveness.

It is obvious that many improvements in white collar productivity which are achieved within the information structure focus may be the detailed development of improvement options identified or visualized by a cost-benefit analysis within the service interchange structure, as previously discussed. This is appropriate, but systems and procedures analysis independent of analysis of the service interchange structure is also appropriate and worthwhile.

One highly successful approach to white collar productivity in the information structure is participative work simplification. User groups are trained in systems and procedures analysis and then critically analyze selected systems or procedures. With advice from computer experts on computer interface which is eased or complicated by user design, the group develops more efficient, effective, and valid systems and procedures which are then, when appropriate, computerized by the experts. All those nice things associated with participation and involvement are associated with this approach, and it has been highly successful for many organizations. It will be discussed in more detail in Part 5.

PHYSICAL RESOURCE/TECHNOLOGY STRUCTURE

Technology has been the major contributor to productivity improvement for many years. Capital investment in better tooling, equipment, processes, and products has been the main source of productivity enhancement—but has had little impact on improving white collar productivity. With the exception of the computer, technology has had only a minor influence on white collar work. Even the impact of computers is questionable in regard to improving white collar productivity.

There is no doubt that computers have had a huge impact upon almost all organizations. Substantial repetitive clerical work no longer need be done by humans. Many reports and analyses which would be impossible or impractical to obtain by manual procedure are rather easily obtained by use of computers. Management and other knowledge workers can be better served and do things which previously they could not do as a result of these many reports and analyses. However, in most situations a full understanding of costs and benefits involved and issues of validity in regard to organizational objectives and mission remains unclear. Even so, computers and information technology remain an area of high potential for enhancing white collar productivity, ranging from clerical activities to supporting knowledge workers and managers. A vast array of office technology is currently available, and more is on the way. The "office of the future" and the "paperless office" are more than concepts. At least in experimental form, they are actually in being.

Appropriate exploitation of technology should be a major aspect of any effort to enhance productivity. Many organizations formally track technological developments and systematically assess potential application within their organization. Developments which seem to offer promise for useful application are further evaluated, potential application areas are identified, and information is provided to individuals who might be affected. Unfortunately, efforts to exploit technology are usually limited to product and process improvements and are seldom directed to potential white collar productivity enhancement.

Technology monitoring and evaluation and a clearinghouse function relative to technology are appropriate and will become increasingly important in the white collar areas as a flood of new technology becomes available. Every organization that is serious about enhancing white collar productivity should formalize this function and assure that its charter extends beyond just monitoring and evaluating new hardware technology to encompass the process of facilitation of useful application in various parts of the organization, in proper relationship to efforts directed to the other structural approaches.

Appropriate physical resources and technology range from dictating equipment, to minicomputers, to word processing, to computer application to teleconferencing, to automated and paperless information systems, to workplace and office design innovations.

An all too typical view of office technology is that it is directed only toward improving clerical productivity, and sight is lost of potential benefit in the knowledge worker area. Frequently, potential application is not systematically analyzed, possible application beyond one area is not considered, individual behavioral inclinations are not adequately considered and catered to, and adequate cost/benefit analyses (return on investment) are not made. Consequently, many white collar technology investments are made on a slipshod basis, and frequently either useful applications are not seen to be justifiable or investments are made without adequate consideration of user acceptance, only to have equipment underutilized or not used at all shortly after acquisition.

Most of these difficulties can be overcome by formalizing responsibility for office technology monitoring, evaluation, information dissemination, *and* facilitation of adoption. Proper discharge of this functional responsibility requires organizational vision and a "systems" view of the organization, coupled with behavioral skills of the change-agent nature. Some useful applications tend to be almost all-encompassing. Others tend to be almost exclusively individual in scope. In both extreme cases individual behavior must change, and such changes should be at the initiative of the affected individual(s) for best results. We will discuss the process of monitoring and adapting technology in Part 6.

HUMAN RESOURCE STRUCTURE

Again, I repeat the statement that people, truly, are the key to productivity. We have mentioned people in conjunction with each of the previously discussed structures. They are intimately involved in all and cannot be considered in isolation from these structures. However, it is useful to have an additional structure for human resources, for emphasis, and to provide a framework for specific approaches.

All those "good management" practices which foster high-performance individuals and organizations could appropriately be mentioned. My preference is to draw a few summary comments from others.

Drucker,[4] in specifically addressing the knowledge work segment of the white collar group, concludes that we do not know how to measure either the productivity or the satisfaction of the knowledge worker but that we do know quite a bit about how to improve both. I am inclined to disagree about not knowing how to measure, for useful aggregate measurement approaches are available. Specific measurement approaches will be discussed in Part 3. Agreement or disagreement is mainly a matter of how "to measure" is defined. I fully agree that we know a great deal about how to improve knowledge worker productivity. Drucker states it well: Demand responsibility from them. Determine what can be done to facilitate their performance, to help them do what they are being paid to do—by providing time, information, and tools for doing the job, and by removing barriers. Do what is necessary to gain their recognition of what their efforts contribute to achieving organization objectives and mission. Require that each have a program of goals and objectives, and plans for achievement. Direct them toward contributions to objectives and mission. Make sure they are able to appraise their own contributions. Effectively manage assignment control, and staff from strength.

Mali[5] advocates seven strategies:
1. Develop productivity-mindedness.
2. Use equipment aids.
3. Increase discretionary content of jobs.
4. Replace performance appraisals with productivity appraisals.

5. Provide time-management training.
6. Motivate.
7. Manage productivity by objective.

These are all approaches which are useful in most situations.

So much for general approaches and comments. We will conclude with brief mention of two specific approaches which are not sufficiently known and used, and one very general approach which is well known but underutilized.

The first specific approach is to evaluate investment in human resources in much the same way that investment in capital facilities and equipment is managed—on the basis of return on investment and return on net assets.

Most organizations are rather sophisticated in their evaluation of capital investments, particularly on marginal or additional investments being required to have a known potential rate of return. Less sophistication is evidenced in the management of capital productivity once investments are made. However, a growing number of organizations "manage" largely on the basis of attempting to achieve a desired rate of return on net current value of their capital assets.

These same approaches can be used to manage rate of return on marginal investments in human resources and rate of return on total net current value of human resource assets. Additionally, such approaches yield valuable insights into the relative benefits which can be achieved by resource substitution—varying the allocation of investments in both human and capital resources in order to achieve desired performance results.

The second specific approach is one of resource management, taking advantage of opportunities to staff at a minimum people level. Organizational realities being what they are, work loads vary and managers tend to staff in order to be able to meet maximum anticipated work load. In some cases work loads are difficult to predict, and backlogs develop when loads are heavy and people are underutilized when loads are light. In other cases managers and supervisors have learned that it is "safer" to be able to handle additional imposed or requested services, and "justify" staffing to be responsive even though extra resources are known to be excessive.

The alternatives to overstaffing are various approaches to load leveling by developing a flexible staffing resource. This may be done in several ways: overtime, flexitime, and a variety of well-known techniques—and by use of part-time, temporary talent or purchased services.

Temporary talent can be used, obviously, to fill in for absent people who are ill or on vacation. It can also be used, obviously, for peak loads due to specific projects or seasonal variations imposed on top of normal loads. These things are old hat. Newer approaches go beyond these, and fill the valleys of work load above the minimum staffing requirements with temporary personnel, who are used only when work load exceeds the minimum and are not employed when not really needed. Going further, some of the regular minimum work load may be more productively done on a purchased basis, at lower costs than can be achieved by company personnel. In addition, "problem" jobs can frequently be "sold" to someone else, at a profit.

The general approach, which is well known but underutilized, is participation and involvement of employees in devising ways to perform their jobs better and to contribute better to the successful performance of their organization. These approaches will be presented in Part 7.

NOTES

[1] Efficiency is how well you do what you do (in employing resources, output per input).

[2] Effectiveness is whether what you do is what is prescribed or not.

[3] Validity is whether what is prescribed contributes to meeting the objectives and missions of the organization.

[4] Peter F. Drucker, "Managing the Knowledge Worker," Chapter 26, *People and Performance: The Best of Peter Drucker on Management,* Harper's College Press, New York, 1977.

[5] Paul Mali, "Managing White-Collar Workers," in *Improving Total Productivity: MBO Strategies for Business, Government and Not-for-Profit Organizations,* Wiley, New York, 1978.

PART ONE

Measurement

*I often say that when you can measure what you
are speaking about, and express it in numbers,
you know something about it; but when you
cannot measure it, when you cannot express it
in numbers, your knowledge is of a meager and
unsatisfactory kind; it may be the beginning of
knowledge, but you have scarcely, in your
thoughts, advanced to the stage of science,
whatever the matter may be. —Lord Kelvin,
1883*

*The role of measurement in dealing with white collar productivity
improvement is greatly misunderstood. Measurement is important,
and Lord Kelvin's quotation is thought-provoking. However,
measurement is not an end objective; it is a means to an end. Our end
objective is to achieve improvement.*

*Measurement does, in many cases, help us to understand the
situations we are dealing with and to determine useful courses of
action toward our objective of productivity improvement. However, in
many other cases measurement as such may be of little or no use.*

*The common interpretation of measurement related to work
activities and productivity improvement is that of time study or work*

measurement. This view is much too restrictive and includes only a small part of the measurements which are useful in dealing with productivity issues. Additionally, the terms "time study" and "work measurement" have unfavorable emotional overtones for many individuals.

The objective of this part is to provide a perspective of measurement, as related to the broad scope of white collar productivity enhancement.

Chapter 3, by Carl Thor of the American Productivity Center (APC), addresses the issue of productivity measurement as an essential element in an improvement cycle, and discusses measurement from the perspective of a person who has been deeply involved in development of the APC system for total productivity measurement at the firm level. His presentation discusses fundamental concepts of productivity measurement, stresses the use of a collection of partial measures, involving a participative approach, addresses the desirability of having measurement systems which address the needs of both top management and operating people, and advocates starting with analysis of outputs rather than activities, with attention to formal objectives.

Presentation of the details of the APC total productivity measurement system is beyond the scope of this book. However, such systems are an important part of organization-wide productivity programs, and conceptually they provide a productivity measurement system which parallels and complements the more usual financial and accounting measurement systems. They differ in terms of providing diagnostic ability to reflect the contribution to profitability of changes in productivity and price recovery associated with the various inputs required to produce an organization's products and/or services. The partial productivity measures suggested as particularly appropriate for white collar activities are particularly useful by themselves and also provide the basis for more comprehensive productivity measurement systems.

Chapter 4, by Marvin E. Mundel, approaches measurement from the point of view of a very experienced and innovative industrial engineer who started with traditional work measurement in manufacturing and built upon this restrictive approach those additional approaches needed to measure results at higher levels within an organization, encompassing not only production but also service outputs.

His hierarchy of work-units starts with individual motions (1st-order work-unit) and progresses in an integrative manner to those which deal with aggregate results (8th-order work-unit). He presents his work-unit structure along with an illustrative application for an industrial service function, starting with the mission statement for the organizational entity and its definitive characteristics (8th-order work-unit), and then he progressively defines the lower-level work-units required to achieve total results. Such an approach uses work-unit definitions to identify what services are produced at various levels so that rational planning, improvement, and control can be based upon logical analysis and measurement. A second example is presented which illustrates application of work-unit analysis to municipal government service activities.

Mundel's approach is unique, and powerful. It is one of the few which provides opportunity for linking individual actions with organization mission, identifying the measurable outputs throughout the functional activity/work structure. It is supported by various measurement techniques which are more fully described in his other writings.

This part is intended to provide a broad perspective of measurement, particularly to encourage the reader to think beyond the usual intrepretation of work measurement and to recognize that various forms of measurement have utility in dealing with white collar productivity enhancement. Measurement will be involved substantially in subsequent chapters, particularly in Chapters 7, 8, and 9.

CHAPTER THREE

Productivity Measurement in White Collar Groups

CARL G. THOR

Vice President, Measurement, American Productivity Center

Measurement of productivity is sooner or later required in any balanced productivity improvement effort. It is sometimes said that productivity improvement can stand on its own, that an analyst does not need to know productivity history in order to recognize where improvements could be made and to proceed to make those improvements. This can be true in the short range, but ultimately it becomes necessary to control the assets devoted to productivity improvement in the same sense that control is required everywhere in the business. Only organizations with unlimited resources can afford to undertake productivity improvement everywhere it is needed, regardless of assessed cost and importance.

At the other extreme, productivity measurement specialists sometimes prescribe very detailed and painstaking programs to develop the exactly appropriate measurement system in an organization which must be completed before a productivity improvement program is allowed to begin. This is also an error. Measurement is not the goal; improvement is the goal. A measurement system is a tool to direct scarce resources to the targets where the most benefit can be obtained from those scarce resources.

Figure 3-1 illustrates the relationship of measurement to other key stages in an improvement cycle. First comes *awareness* of productivity. Most alert citizens of the United States are now aware of the national and international implications of declining productivity growth rates. But

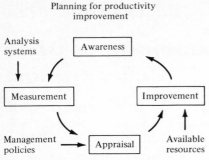

FIG. 3-1. **Measurement is an integral part of the improvement cycle.**

productivity at the firm level is still sufficiently misunderstood that it is wise to be explicit about what a particular organization means by "productivity" in its individual context. It is also necessary to recognize that productivity awareness is required to different depths in different functions and levels of the organization. It is not sufficient simply that those who direct the organization be aware of the productivity opportunity.

Being aware of the challenges of productivity improvement and resolving to undertake a planned improvement effort, the next step is to understand productivity *measurement* in conjunction with the other measurement and analysis systems that are already present within the organization. There is often a great deal that these other systems can contribute to developing or strengthening a productivity measurement system. A basic set of measures is required that will direct attention to parts of the organization that are in a stronger or weaker position for productivity analysis and improvement. The bulk of the chapter will be directed toward discussion of productivity measurement systems.

With measured results in hand, there is a diagnosis or *appraisal* step that needs to be taken. This can range from a formal and structured diagnosis to a very informal, rapid checklist approach. The appraisal must take into account the basic needs and policies of the organization. For example, a productivity improvement effort might be wasted in a part of an organization that will be downgraded in importance or where substantial management changes will occur in conjunction with a newly adopted company strategy. The productivity analyst and the operating manager (if they are not the same person) must sit back and make an arm's-length review of the problems and opportunities that are found in the part of the organization under study. Results from productivity measures provide part of the required information, but existing goals and objectives along with management style and limitations must also be considered.

Having gone through a process of appraisal, located problems and opportunities in certain areas, and analyzed resources available to make changes, the manager must then investigate and employ the appropriate *improvement* techniques. This is not a linear process. If some success in improvement has been accomplished, it is wise to publicize this to further feed employee awareness, which in turn will stimulate better measures, more thorough appraisals, and so on in a circular manner.

TYPES OF MEASURES

There are many elements of a definition of productivity that must be considered separately. Productivity is widely defined as output divided by input. This is a good starting point. Productivity is the relationship between the use of resources and the results of that use.

Important, but not explicit in most definitions, is that the output and the input must be from the same general process. It is not very meaningful to talk about a productivity measure of tons of steel per typist employed. Though a steelmaking organization has tons of steel as an overall output and also has typists deep in its organization, there is not sufficient relationship between that one input and the overall corporate output to make the ratio meaningful. To analyze the whole organization, something much closer to the totality of inputs is required to be matched against the tons of steel output. An appropriate intermediate output can be found that is of the same process and location as the input represented by the number of typists.

Some productivity measures are direct reflections of an input and output of a process; others have surrogate components. For example, neither sales nor parts handled is the exact output of a plant production scheduler. The "true" output is a series of reports, conclusions, and decisions. However, a ratio that compares either sales or parts handled with number of production scheduling employees or hours will give a fair indication of the relative effort required by production schedulers.

A productivity measure that compares an input with an output is useful only if that productivity measure in turn can be compared with some other measure. The simple expression that the productivity of a process is 15 does not alone give much useful information to the analyst. However, if the analyst can compare that 15 with either past performance, a standard of current performance, or the current experience of some other entity, then the 15 becomes meaningful. For example, if it is known that last year the entity achieved a productivity level of 14, then the 15 represents a quantified improvement over the previous year. If through engineering or other means, a "standard" has been set that the entity should produce 16, then the actual performance of 15 can be represented as a 94 percent of standard, also useful information. If it is known that another reasonably comparable plant, whether belonging to the same organization or to a competitor, has produced 18 or 12, then the 15 also takes on substantial meaning. Thus a definition of productivity as being output over input is not complete without a clear indication of the form of comparison that is intended to take place.

It is also necessary to specify what inputs are being considered in the analysis process. The traditional means of measuring productivity has been to compare the output of a process with the labor input. There was a time when labor was the dominant input in virtually all industries, and in effect labor could be used as a surrogate for all inputs. This convenient assumption is still valid in certain industries, particularly those of a service variety where the dominant cost is still labor. However, it is also easy to find examples of industries, such as petroleum refining and aluminum reduction, where labor is a relatively small part of the total cost.

Other factors of production can usually be divided into capital, energy, and materials. Economists have always recognized capital, as represented by buildings, land, and equipment, as being a factor of production. Materials need separate consideration (as long as materials have not been deducted in calculating the output, as in value added output analysis). Similarly, energy often needs separate consideration. Energy was until recently considered a minor submaterial.

The form of measure that compares the output of a process with only one of the inputs is called a partial productivity measure. This is clearly deficient in a situation where there are many important factors of production interacting over time. For example, a great deal of the improvement in labor productivity over the years has come from the substitution of capital for labor. Automation of this sort often results in relatively automatic increases in the labor partial measure, without recognizing clearly that this improvement may be largely offset by the extra capital cost associated with automation. The ideal approach is one in which all the factors of production are combined in the same denominator, so that trade-offs between factors are all captured in the expression. This approach to measurement, called total productivity, is the one most often advised for overall corporate analysis in industries that have many key factors of production.

In the white collar context, it is often not necessary to pay much attention to inputs other than labor. In the traditional office, the great bulk of cost has been incurred for labor. Increasingly, however, costs are now being incurred for data-processing equipment, specialized office automation, special materials, supplies, and even air conditioning, all of which have become important in the overall calculation. It is certainly wise to make a quick review of the importance of nonlabor costs before assuming away the need to analyze other than partial labor productivity. If these nonlabor costs are important, they should be explicitly recognized in whatever measurement system is developed.

Another important distinction in productivity measurement, and perhaps the one in which the most mistakes are made, is that between physical productivity measures and cost or financial productivity measures. The clearest form of productivity measure is the physical productivity measure. Both outputs and inputs are expressed in physical terms such as tons of steel per employee hour or number of claims settled per claims adjustment employee in an insurance company. This form of measure is simple and easy to explain and is not affected by the inflationary trends in today's economy. The weakness of this form of measure is that few real-life processes are so simple as to have one output and one input. It is usually necessary to combine unlike outputs and/or unlike inputs. Thus claims settled in an insurance office can be counted, at the first order of approximation. But upon further analysis, it may be determined that business claims and consumer claims each occupy a distinctly different amount of time and effort or that there is some other distinction between claims that invalidates simple adding of number of claims. The same sort of thing is true in a production environment. Most plants produce a great many products, and it is only with some sacrifice of accuracy that combinations are made in physical terms, such as pounds or units.

To get around the problem of combining unlikes, it is often necessary to use cost or price data to combine (or "weight") unlikes. Thus the different products of a production process may be combined in terms of their relative dollar value. It is similar in the area of inputs. Counting employee hours of input is relatively easy and for many purposes is sufficiently accurate. But if there has been a very substantial difference in the level of employees doing certain work, the true productivity effect has not been captured unless a weighting system is introduced in the input analysis that recognizes the relative "skill levels" of different employees. This weighting system may well be something as simple as relative salary level.

Introducing dollars for the convenience of combining unlikes also introduces the problem of relative inflation contained within the dollar data. As long as an analysis is being made of current *level* of productivity, this is no problem. But usually a *trend* analysis is desired, and then care must be taken to ensure that the same mechanism for combining unlikes is used in each year of the comparison. Thus, a simple sales to payroll ratio, while meaningful in the context of any given year, can become dangerously misleading in trend analysis if there have been changes in the relative inflation associated with different types of labor and/or different products of the organization.[1]

Finally, another key distinction between different types of measures has to do with the basic intended use of those measures. Much is made in the literature of the distinction between top-down and bottom-up approaches in all realms of management theory. In the area of productivity measurement, there are adherents to each phrase as shorthand for the appropriate approach to setting productivity measures. In the complex business organization of today, it is necessary to recognize and accept that both approaches are almost always necessary in the typical organization. Measures should be selected and developed largely for their relevance to the manager who is going to use those measures. Thus, for the top managers of an organization, who are mainly concerned with the generalized picture and the longer view, an approach to productivity is required that is fully integratable with long-range planning and with financial profitability measures. That is the language of their daily thinking, and productivity measures must also be in that language. This means that an overall company might well measure itself on the basis of its two or three most important outputs and rather general aggregations of the various inputs. So the model being used might be quite sophisticated in the links made with other information systems of the organization, but it might be almost primitive in its ability to pinpoint problems in any detail.

At the other extreme, the operating managers of an organization, be they line or staff, need day-to-day and month-to-month productivity measures to keep their attention firmly riveted on the need for productivity improvement in their specific organization. Many line organizations and virtually all staff organizations should have a key output indicator that is *other than* the appropriate indicator for the whole organization. Staff areas do not produce tons of steel. Though they contribute to the production of steel (with leads and lags) their true outputs are decisions, reports, transactions, documents, and any number of other elements for the support of the organization. Even the line managers often have outputs of their particular shift or plant that are different in some character from the total output of the organization. This should not stop them from having measures that are relevant to their own needs, in terms of both what output is used and the input factors that are included. This bottom-up approach to productivity measure setting is equally valid and equally necessary for an organization.

Aggregating upward, the results of a varying collection of typically partial measures from operating and staff units will obviously reach the group manager with somewhat different productivity trend information from what a top-down planning model might provide. This is not nearly as important an issue as the fact that a complete planning system with both sorts of measures gives everyone in the organization productivity guidance that is badly needed. A thoroughly documented and well-run productivity measurement system will provide enough subordinate information so that the group manager is fully able to sort out any differences in signals that he or she might receive between a bottom-up and a top-down approach.

A FIRM-LEVEL TOTAL PRODUCTIVITY
MEASUREMENT SYSTEM

The preceding discussion considered the advantages of a total productivity measurement system and the need for a top-down productivity planning model that links with profit performance. The American Productivity Center (APC) has developed such a system, which can serve as an effective complement to the specific, operationally oriented measures of staff department performance discussed below.

Corporate management analyzes its various divisions on a profitability basis. Any other form of measure other than profitability is in danger of being sidetracked if it is not reconcilable directly with profitability planning data. It would be futile (and unnecessary) to suggest that there is anything wrong with profitability as a basic measure of business performance. However, financial accounting has not evolved in a way that assures complete faith in current dollar financial statistics. One of the adverse effects of inflation has been to erode confidence in the financial accounting system. An important feature of total productivity measures is to offer an inflation-free look at overall business performance.

The connecting link between profitability analysis and productivity analysis is the relative inflation of input unit costs and output unit prices. Most approaches to total productivity measurement make price and cost information of subordinate interest or reject it entirely. General-purpose deflators are used to adjust dollar data into constant dollar or physical equivalent data. But these deflation indexes in general do not directly reflect the experience of an individual corporate entity but rather indicate results based on some surrogate macroeconomic compendium. If a company does have its own cost and price information and can put it into usable index form for profitability-productivity analysis, it is then possible to fully complete the link between profitability and productivity. Inflation adjustment can be of most value when based upon actual company experience rather than broad national economic indicators.

The key elements of the APC performance measurement system are profitability, productivity, and price recovery. The relationship is illustrated in Fig. 3-2. Reading across the output and input rows, it can be seen that it all starts from the equation, value = quantity × price. For any output and for any input, the dollar value expressed on the income statement can be said to be made up of a physical quantity multiplied by a unit price or unit cost. Reading vertically, and thinking in terms of relationship over time, the relative change of output value compared with the relative change of one or more of the input values can be defined as change in profitability. This profitability can be expressed as a rate of contribution to "economic" earnings from the operation being analyzed.

The relationship between quantity of output and quantity of input at a

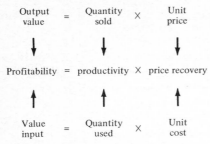

FIG. 3-2. The relationship of productivity and price recovery to profitability.

point in time and over time is called productivity. These quantities are expressed in physical terms, or alternately in constant dollar terms, which is the best available surrogate. The third columnar relationship, price recovery, is defined as the relationship between change in unit price and change in unit cost over time. It is an index of relative inflation, or in other words, an index of the ability (or desire) of an organization to pass on its unit cost changes to unit price changes.

The APC performance measurement system results in a matrix that connects change in profitability, productivity, and price recovery with each of the input factors as demonstrated in Fig. 3-3. The change is

Inputs	Change in profitability	Change in productivity	Change in price recovery
Labor 1			
Labor 2			
Labor 3	_____	_____	_____
Total labor			
Materials 1			
Materials 2	_____	_____	_____
Total materials			
Capital, leases			
Capital, depreciation			
Capital, return	_____	_____	_____
Total capital			
Energy 1			
Energy 2	_____	_____	_____
Total energy	_____	_____	_____
Total all inputs			

FIG. 3-3. The APC performance measurement system results in a matrix that connects changes in profitability, productivity, and price recovery with each of the input factors. Results are expressed in both rate of change and dollar effect.

expressed as both an improvement ratio and a dollar effect. Both are necessary, because an organization is typically interested not only in knowing which factors show the largest percentage changes but also in identifying factors that provide the biggest net impact in dollar terms.

The data required for the APC performance measurement system are value, quantity, and price for each time period for each output and input of the entity being analyzed. For each data element, having two of value, quantity, and price obviously gives the third automatically. This system can treat two time periods, actual versus budget, or any other two-element comparison. The two-period ratios can be linked to other pairs of periods to trace changes over a time span.

The only major departure from normal accounting practice is that the capital input includes not only lease expense and the depreciation of fixed assets but also a return component (opportunity cost) represented by denying the entity that capital's alternative use. This covers both fixed assets employed and whatever working capital is appropriately charged to this entity.

Using this performance measurement system, it is possible to distinguish readily between the performance of the two organizations shown in Fig. 3-4. Normal profitability analysis would consider them to be identical. However, organization A has improved profitability through productivity improvement. It has apparently done a good job of controlling

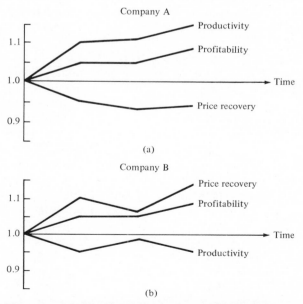

FIG. 3-4. **Total productivity measurement provides for tracking, over time, changes in the component effects of productivity and price recovery on profitability.**

and improving internal operation. The decline in price recovery may, in fact, serve to broaden the market in the long run. Organization B, however, has done a poor job of controlling its operations. Its profitability was saved by aggressive price recovery, something that can rarely be maintained in the long run because of price controls, heavy competition, or consumer resistance. Any organization badly needs to know whether it is an A or a B.

WHITE COLLAR PRODUCTIVITY

White collar, professional, or knowledge workers, however defined, are working in a different environment from the rest of the organization. The principles stated above concerning productivity measurement apply to white collar departments or groups as well, but besides there are some special characteristics that need to be considered. White collar workers often find that they are providing an output that is not easy to quantify. Though the typing pool has a quantifiable output, most white collar workers, and particularly those who would be classed as "professional," are in a position where the output is intangible and has other analysis problems. The work is often nonrepetitive, and therefore, by definition, a standard for doing it has not been established. Work in these areas also tends to be interdependent. It is much harder to associate the performance or nonperformance of a particular task with an individual, because there is usually the need to receive upstream input and/or to deliver into a downstream time schedule that is not of the individual's making.

It is also necessary to recognize the sensitivity of professional workers to productivity measurement. This is not to say that blue collar workers are not sensitive to productivity measurement also. However, blue collar workers rather expect to be measured, since there is a long history of their being measured both individually and in the aggregate. There is no such history for most white collar workers, and since many corporate training and orientation programs emphasize they are hiring the "brain power" of these people, it is rather natural that such professionals view some of the more primitive forms of productivity measurement as being totally irrelevant or, worse, antipathetic to the thoughtful subtlety that characterizes their specific job. Another difference in blue collar and white collar work is that white collar work is often controlled by and closely related to a set of widely recognized objectives, but these objectives are often fairly fuzzy and have a quality and/or timeliness element in them besides an efficiency element. Though objectives exist in blue collar work, they often are not widely publicized and have to do with very tangible and countable things.

One of the major challenges of productivity measurement is to separate the effects of productivity, quality, and timeliness. All three are typically important, and it is no denigration of quality and timeliness to suggest that there is a need to measure pure productivity (and for that matter pure quality and pure timeliness) before they are lumped together in some grand performance indicator.

In approaching measurement of white collar productivity, the first question to ask is what is the output of the processes for which an employee is responsible. Every employee works within a process, although it is not always fully recognized. It is thus advisable to try to connect the output of these processes with personal objectives or the objectives of the group as set by whatever formal objective-setting mechanism there is within the organization. This will clearly distinguish between "activities" and true objectives. For most situations the objective is to complete certain jobs and not merely to complete pieces of a job. Thus, in an insurance claims adjustment area, the output is "fully adjusted claims" rather than phone calls or pages typed. In the larger view, at least, main management interest should be in how many claims are settled (within quality parameters) rather than how a claim is settled.

Given that most solutions start with an analysis of outputs and objectives, consideration is needed of different methods of developing appropriate measures. The common approach has always been that an "expert" will view the process and make recommendations. Although this is sometimes appropriate in difficult-to-measure situations in the factory, it is a fairly dangerous approach in professional areas where the professional workers feel (often correctly) they know more about the process than the so-called expert.

Another approach would be to have the expert interview different members of the organization and solicit their ideas as to appropriate measures. This has the advantage of getting some employee input, and it allows the analyst's previous experience to be tempered and adjusted by the special circumstance of the particular organization.

A technique that is coming into general use in this context is the nominal group technique. This technique employs a structured process for task analysis and is essentially a group participation method using the knowledge and experience of the group to analyze work processes, create productivity-improving ideas, and of particular interest, design productivity measures. It has been widely used in knowledge worker environments, providing a method of exploiting the specialized knowledge the group has of its individual workplace. It has the additional advantage of leaving the participants, as representatives of the whole work force, generally quite satisfied with the measurement system that results. Their influence on their coworkers may well be decisive in ensuring acceptance of the improvement ideas generated or the measurement system that has developed in this process.

The nominal group technique not only identifies improvement or measurement ideas but also includes voting and ranking to obtain the

Measure	Range	Weighting	Measure value		Scaled value		Weighted and scaled value	
	Worst to best		Last quarter	Current quarter	Last quarter	Current quarter	Last quarter	Current quarter
Downtime	40–15	0.3	20	17	80.0	92.0	24.0	27.6
Meet user deadline	58–98	0.3	87	95	71.8	92.3	21.5	27.7
Rerun time	500–200	0.2	221	250	93.0	83.3	18.6	16.7
Repeat complaints	30–10	0.1	13	11	85.0	95.0	8.5	9.5
On-line response	4.0–2.0	0.1	2.3	2.7	85.0	65.0	8.5	6.5
Composite index							81.1	88.0

FIG. 3-5. A sample performance report for a computer center, showing the 5 performance measures and their relative weightings as developed by the nominal group process. The actual range over which each measure varies, from "worst" to "best," is converted to a 100-point scale so that the worst value equals zero and the best value equals 100. The "raw" measure values for last quarter and for the current quarter are listed under "Measure value." The scaled values, the raw values converted to the 100-point scale for each measure, are listed under "Scaled value." These listings show that relative performance for each measure on its own 100 points equal 100 percent scale. The final columns present the weighted and scaled values on a composite basis, whereby 100 percent performance for all individual measures adds to a composite index of 100 points or 100 percent.

group's opinion as to which of the alternatives is best. Applying simple weighting methods to the results can give an overall, composite productivity measurement index that can be tailored to reflect many nuances of the group's overall activity. Whereas no one measurable activity will fully describe the activity of the group as a whole, an aggregation of several measures, each chosen to be a partial descriptor of the entire process, can result in full representation of the variety of activities that take place. Some of the components of the overall index might be representative of quality, effectiveness, timeliness, and other factors that cannot be included in a raw efficiency measure.

Figure 3-5 presents an example of the combination of five measures derived from a nominal group process that initially generated dozens of measure suggestions. These five were selected for their collective coverage of the main activities of a computer center. They simultaneously give some coverage to each of the elements of productivity, quality, and timeliness. Each component can be analyzed for its particular trend, and then the combined trend can be used as a basis for determining the overall "performance" of the center. This sort of measure can become the basis for a widely accepted improvement yardstick, because the derivation of the measure itself was a participative exercise of group members.[2]

Whether or not it is desired to go through a participative process of this sort to derive measures, it is quite reasonable to judge the overall productivity of a white collar group on a collection of measures rather than on one single measure. The imprecision associated with any one measure does not dominate the productivity trend for the whole organization. A certain smoothing of results will occur if elements of the overall index have a "checks and balances" effect on each other. For example, the apparent progress shown by an all-out drive for rapid processing of output, which would improve a productivity indicator, would be partially offset by any decline in quality that might result. Overemphasis on quality, on the other hand, leading to overly slow processing, would yield a decline in the productivity component.

In conclusion, productivity measurement can be applied to white collar and professional environments just as it has been in the past to blue collar and plant production environments. A great many of the principles of productivity measurement are common to both settings. Special elements of care are required in ensuring that the uniqueness of the white collar environment is respected, but this should not stop an organization from analyzing white collar productivity. Most approaches to white collar analysis will start with a careful analysis of the true output, rather than activities, of an organization and will pay careful attention to the overall formal objectives of the group in question. Much success has been derived using participative techniques where employee "buy-in" adds a new very positive element to what otherwise might be a sterile and possibly objectionable exercise.

NOTES

[1] Weighting and deflation techniques are addressed in: Leon Greenberg, *A Practical Guide to Productivity Measurement,* Bureau of National Affairs, Washington, D.C., 1973; John W. Kendrick and Daniel Creamer, *Measuring Company Productivity: Handbook with Case Studies, Studies in Business Economics Number 89,* Conference Board, New York, 1965; Irving H. Siegel, *Company Productivity: Measurement for Improvement,* W. E. Upjohn Institute for Employment Research, Kalamazoo, Mich., 1980.

[2] Use of the nominal group technique is covered in: André L. Delbecq, Andrew H. Van de Ven, and David H. Gustafson, *Group Techniques for Program Planning,* Scott, Foresman, Glenview, Ill., 1975; William Stewart, *Performance Measurement and Improvements in Common Carriers,* Purdue University, Lafayette, Ind., 1980; William T. Morris, *Implementation Strategies for Industrial Engineers,* Grid Publishing, Inc., Columbus, Ohio, 1979.

Work-Unit Analysis*

MARVIN E. MUNDEL, P.E.

M. E. Mundel & Associates

Work-unit analysis is a methodology for identifying service outputs and their components. It provides a conceptual structure for working with service outputs in the same manner that drawings and bills of material assist industrial engineers and managers in working with hardware outputs. Work-unit analysis assists with planning service outputs, budgeting for them, improving them, and applying "management by objectives," providing a chart of accounts for cost accounting, a basis for measuring labor productivity, and so forth.

This chapter will define the necessary terms, give some illustrations of work-unit analysis, and show some of the results obtained. Of course, the results are not the direct results of work-unit analysis; the results are from the application of classical industrial engineering techniques, with work-unit analysis providing the vehicle for adequately identifying what is being produced. One must first identify what one is trying to improve before improving it.

DEFINITIONS

A Work-Unit[1]

A work-unit is an amount of work or the results of an amount of work which it is convenient to identify as an integer, an "each." "Convenient"

* Reprinted with permission from *AIEE Spring Annual Conference Proceedings,* 1977. Copyright American Institute of Industrial Engineers, Inc., 25 Technology Park/Atlanta, Norcross, Ga. 30092.

Numerical designation	Name	Definition
8th–order work–unit	Results	What is achieved because of the outputs of the activity.
7th–order work–unit	Gross output	A large group of end products or completed services of the working group, having some common affinity.
6th–order work–unit	Program	A group of outputs or completed services that represent part of a 7th–order work–unit but are a more homogeneous subgroup in respect to some aspect of alikeness.
5th–order work–unit	End product	A unit of final output; the units in which a program is quantified; a convenient–sized output which is produced for use outside of the organization and which contributes to the objectives of the organization without further work being done on that output.
4th–order work–unit	Intermediate product	A part of a unit of final output, the intermediate product may become part of the final output or merely be required to make it feasible to achieve the final output.
3d–order work–unit	Task	Any part of the activity associated with, and all of the things associated with, the performance of a unit of assign-ment by either an individual or a crew, depending on the method of assigning.
2d–order work–unit	Element	The activity associated with the performance of part of a task which it is convenient to separate to facilitate designing the method of performing the task or determining some demension of the task.
1st–order work–unit	Motion	The performance of a human motion. This is the smallest work-unit usually encountered in the study of work. It is used to facilitate job design or dimen-sioning and never appears in control system above this level of use.

FIG. 4-1. The 8 orders of work-units.

in the above definition means that the identification method aids in planning, control, analysis of method, and so forth.

An examination of the definition of work-unit will suggest that one could have large and small work-units; hence another definition:

An Order of Work-Units

An order of work-units is a complete list, at a uniform level of detail, of all the parts of a service. In order to provide a uniform language, eight-integer numbered orders are used, with decimals introduced to identify any orders of work-units between the integer orders. The orders of work-units are defined in Fig. 4-1. Now we may define our new technique.

Work-Unit Analysis

Work-unit analysis is the delineation, in hierarchical form, of the outputs of an organization. The analysis usually proceeds from the objective downward to lower orders of work-units, constrained by the following three criteria:

1. A clear relationship must be retained between the objective and all lower orders of work-units.

2. The list of work-units, at any order, must be both mutually exclusive and all-inclusive.

3. Unnecessary detail, predicating choices at lower orders, should be avoided at the higher order of work-unit descriptions, if feasible.

The analysis continues until the following two additional criteria are met:

1. A level of work-unit is reached which is suitable for forecasting, planning, and control.

2. A level of work-unit is reached which is suitable for some type of work measurement.

Work-Unit Structure

A work-unit structure is the final result of work-unit analysis, as described.

EXAMPLE I (AN INDUSTRIAL SERVICE)

The Work-Unit Structure

Now that we have established our terms, let us take a look at an example. Figures 4-2 and 4-3 are part of the work-unit structure for the Plant Engineering office in a fiber mill.

```
TYPE:  Output facilitative
MISSION AREA:
       1.   All physical plant
       2.   All production equipment
       3.   All materials handling equipment
INTENT:
       1.1  Maintain intact
       1.2  Upgrade as scheduled, within planned costs
       2.1  Maintain available for on-line use
       2.2  Reduce accident rate caused by machine-correctable faults
       3.1  Maintain available for on-line use
       3.2  Optimize economy of operation
DIMENSION:
       1.1  Cost of damages attributable to prior, uncorrected defects
       1.2  Conformance to up-grading schedules and costs
       2.1  Percent of time production equipment is available for use
            during prime shift
     2.2.1  Frequency of lost-time accidents per 1000 hours of direct
            labor, machine correctable
     2.2.2  Non lost-time accidents per 1000 hours of direct labor, machine
            correctable
       3.1  Percent of time available for on-line use
       3.2  Reduction of M-H costs while maintaining current service level
            to production and warehouse operation
GOALS:
       1.1  Not in excess of what prevention costs would have been
       1.2  Not in excess of ±5 percent deviation
       2.1  97 percent
     2.2.1  Reduce to 1 in 10,000 or less
     2.2.2  Reduce to 1 in 5000 or less
       3.1  90 percent
       3.2  5 percent cost reduction
LIMITATIONS:
       1.   Low educational level of labor force
       2.   Old plant
       3.   No current repair parts usage data
       4.   Rising wage costs
FREEDOMS:
       1.   Can use budget inventory money as desired
       2.   Adequate spare parts storage area
       3.   M-H equipment relatively new
```

FIG. 4-2. Work-unit structure, 8th-order for a mill plant engineering function.

Advantages

1. At the 8th-order work-unit level the work-unit structure establishes quantitative goals to measure the effectiveness of plant engineering.

2. At the 7th-order work-unit level it provides a framework for resource allocation strategy planning.

3. The 6th-order work-unit level provides both a finer level of detail for resource allocation and a "bridge" to the identification of groups of unit services, the 5.5th-order work-unit level; the 5th-order work-units relate to specific pieces of equipment.

4. The whole system provides the beginning of a chart of accounts for watching costs and comparing them with budgets.

5. It identifies outputs for a management system by objectives.

6. It identifies outputs for methods improvement.

```
7th-order work-units
01  Grounds and roadway maintenance provided
02  Building maintenance provided
03  Production equipment maintenance provided
04  Materials handling service provided
05  Material handling equipment maintenance provided

6th-order work-units
0101  Main roadway maintenance provided
0102  Feeder roadway maintenance provided
0103  Decortification areas maintenance provided

0201  Production building maintenance provided
0202  Warehouse building maintenance provided
0203  Office building maintenance provided

0301  Decortification production equipment maintenance provided
0302  Spinning shed production equipment maintenance provided
0303  Weaving shed production equipment maintenance provided
0304  Dyeing shed production equipment maintenance provided
0305  Finishing and inspection are a production equipment maintenance
      provided

0401  In-plant decortification M-H service provided
0402  In-plant spinning M-H service provided
0403  In-plant weaving M-H service provided
0404  In-plant dyeing M-H service provided
0405  In-plant finishing and inspection M-H service provided
0406  Between-plant M-H service provided

0501  In-plant push truck maintenance provided
0502  In-plant lift truck maintenance provided
0503  In-plant hoist equipment maintenance provided
0504  Between-plant lift truck maintenance provided
0505  Truck maintenance provided
0506  Maintenance equipment maintained

5.5th-order work-units for 0301
0301  Decortification production equipment maintained

030101  Supply tanks inspection completed
030102  Supply lines inspection completed
030103  In-plant tank inspection completed
030104  In-plant piping inspection completed
030105  In-plant electrical system inspection completed
030106  Decortification beater system inspected
030107  Supply tank repair completed, prior to failure
030108  Supply tank repair completed, after failure
030109  Supply line repair completed, prior to failure
030110  Supply line repair completed, after failure
And so forth
```

FIG. 4-3. Expansion of work-units for 7th, 6th, and 5th orders.

Improvements

Numerous improvements were made. Rather than cite an exhaustive list, we will give only sample illustrations of each type of improvement.

During the formulation of the work-unit structure Some improvements were made in the course of making the work-unit structure: in setting goal 2.1 it was noted that limitation 3 existed. Plant Engineering immediately set up a system to collect such data so that the achievement of goal 2.1 would not be hampered by shortages of high-use repair parts.

During the ensuing budget formulation For the first time in the memory of the present managerial team the budget discussion for Plant Engineering was essentially substantive rather than acrimonious and emotional. Much less time was needed.

During the operating year

1. Costs, kept by work-units codes, were monitored. Reallocation sessions were substantive, decisive, and cooperative.

2. Work measurement was instituted, at the 5th-order work-unit level, to improve the subsequent year's budgeting.

3. The high costs associated with work-units such as 030108, *Supply tank repair completed after failure,* in comparison with the cost of 030107, *Supply tank repair completed, prior to failure,* led to a complete revamping of the preventive-maintenance system with large savings.

Scheduling and assigning The specification of standard tasks led to a more rigorous, formal system of using the work force than did the previous informal system. However, in the absence of prior work counting and work measurement, the gain could not be quantitatively assessed. No additional cost was associated with this improvement, however.

Equipment usage Failure to achieve goal 2.1, *97 percent on-line use of production equipment,* during the first quarter led to a detailed cost study of alternatives. It was found cost-effective to have such repair done, after the work shift finished, by a small special group of production machine repairers paid a higher rate for night work.

EXAMPLE II[2] (CITY SERVICES)

Introduction

The city of Orange, California, in an effort to combat the rising cost of city services and revenue "crunch," undertook to raise the productivity of city services.

Work-unit Structures

As a pilot study, work-unit structures were made for:

1. Police, community services
2. Library
3. Management services
   a. Finance
      (1) Accounting
      (2) Treasurer
      (3) Payroll/cashier

    b. General services
      (1) Purchasing/warehouse
      (2) Garage
      (3) Reproduction
    c. Personnel

Later work-unit structures were made for:
1. Police traffic bureau
2. Building inspection
3. Water services

Work Measurement

All the work-units were subjected to work measurement. The two main methods were:
1. Time and work-unit output reporting
2. Fractioned professional estimates[3]

Part of the list of 5th-order work-units from *Finance* and their standard times is shown in Fig. 4-4. Productivity reporting (earned hours divided by work hours) was instituted and monitored.

A typical, updated, periodical productivity reporting form (in this case for *Police, Community Services*) is shown in Fig. 4-5. With all departments' attention directed at the earned value of work done, compared with hours expended, much more attention was given to:
1. The flow of work
2. The planned use of time
3. The search for new and better methods

In many ways these are similar to the types of improvements introduced in Plant Engineering. Work had ceased to be an endless flow of miscellaneous activities; it had become a productive process with identifiable outputs.

Results

Concerning the results in Orange, Mr. Sackett, Director of Management Services, City of Orange, reports:[4] "Using, for the most part, FY 1975 as a base year (bench-mark of 100%) the productivity of measured departments, through the third quarter of FY 1976, shows a value of 108%. In that this covers a work force of 78 employees, at an average of $13,645.00 per man-year, the value of the increased outputs per year, as of the third quarter of FY 1976, was $85,145.00."

CONCLUSIONS

Numerous other illustrations could be cited. Work-unit analysis has usefully preceded work applying the quantitative techniques of management and improvement with hospitals, undercover police forces, re-

ZERO BASE COMPUTATION

Agency __MANAGEMENT SERVICES__

Organization __FINANCE__

Subdivision __ACCOUNTING__

Budget [ ] __FY__

Performance [ ] from _____ to _____

Date prepared _____

Page __1__ of __6__ pages

Prepared by _____

Approved by _____

Date approved _____

Work-unit number (1)	Work-unit identification (2)	Type of work-unit (3)	Standard time Annual (4)	Standard time Period (5)	Work count Forecast (6)	Work count Actual (7)	Direct hours Budget (8)	Direct hours Earned (9)
010101	A budget prepared (annual budget)	Lin.						
010102	A budget entry recorded on computer (each line item)	Lin.	0.0620					
010103	An account opened or closed (each account opened or closed)	Lin.	0.0833					
010201	A purchase ordered checked, stamped, separated, and filed (each purchase order)	Lin.	0.0963					
010202	A computer entry made to open new vendor information (each new vendor)	Lin.	0.0244					
010203	A purchase order encumbered on the computer (each purchase order)	Lin.	0.0481					

010301	An accounts payable invoice checked for accuracy and processed	(each invoice)	Lin.	0.0533
010302	A cash bond refund payment processed	(each payee)	Lin.	0.1350
010303	A departmental petty cash reimbursement made	(each line)	Lin.	0.0292
010304	A Finance Department petty cash reimbursement made	(each line)	Lin.	0.0789
010305	A project contrast payment processed	(each payment)	Lin.	1.4167
010306	An agreement payment processed and information set up in tickler file for future payment	(each payment)	Lin.	0.8152

Subtotal for direct hours _____

Support hours, with support ratio = _____
[ ] Subtotal for _____
[ ] Total for _____

FIG. 4-4. A partial listing of 5th-order work-units for a finance organization.

Week number	Week ending	Percent performance	
		Weekly	Cumulative
1	5/9	98.2	—
2	5/16	130.8	—
3	5/23	92.6	105.9
4	5/31	111.9	106.9
5	6/7	115.7	109.1
6	6/14	115.2	110.4
7	6/21	121.3	112.2
8	6/28	112.7	112.2
9	7/5	101.7	111.6
10	7/12	105.3	110.9
11	7/19	94.4	109.4
12	7/26	102.0	108.9
13	8/2	113.5	109.2
14	8/9	93.7	108.2
15	8/16	114.3	108.4
16	8/22	106.0	108.3
17	8/29	97.3	107.9
18	9/5	106.3	107.8
19	9/12	102.9	107.6
20	9/19	103.3	107.5
21	9/26	106.0	107.4
22	10/3	110.6	107.5
23	10/10	90.5	106.7
24	10/17	97.6	106.2
25	10/24	100.6	105.9
26	10/31	106.9	105.9
27	11/7	96.5	106.4
28	11/14	98.3	105.0
29	11/21	104.2	105.0
30	11/28	101.1	104.9

FIG. 4-5. A sample of a productivity reporting form for police community services entitled, Police Community Services Performance: Weekly and Cumulative for 30 Weeks.

search groups, lawyers, and so forth. It opens the door for industrial engineering to work with service activities, the largest part of our economy.

NOTES

[1] Definitions from M. E. Mundel, *Measuring and Enhancing the Productivity of Service and Government Organizations,* The Asian Productivity Organization, Tokyo, Japan, 1975.

[2] Extracted from: C. R. Sackett, *Report, California I.P.A. Project 74-40, Productivity Standards Development,* February 24, 1975, to June 1, 1976, City of Orange, California.

[3] Details of various measurement techniques are presented in M. E. Mundel, *Motion and Time Study: Improving Productivity,* 5th ed., Prentice-Hall, Englewood Cliffs, N.J., 1978.

[4] C. R. Sackett, op. cit., p. 12.

PART TWO

Organizational Structure

Organizational Structure
- Mission
- Strategies
- Objectives
- Functional organization
- Formal organization
- Positions
- Individuals—
  goals and objectives

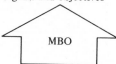

Two approaches to enhancing the validity of individual effort on behalf of contribution to organizational mission are presented. The first is an abbreviated organizational analysis, INTROSPECT. The second is the use of statements of goals and objectives for individuals, management by objectives.

INTROSPECT is a guided self-analysis of allocation of resources and effort within an organization or organizational unit. The process identifies issues for examination and questioning, which in turn can lead to insights which develop opportunities for improving the effectiveness and productivity of the knowledge worker work force through better allocation of effort and resources, and for refocusing effort in support of objectives, strategies, and mission of the organization. It is a proprietary program developed by the Corporate Consulting Services Group of the General Electric Company, based upon earlier work of Jim Hendrick. The approach is presented by Ralph A. Johnson, drawing upon his and his group's extensive work with its development and application to some 140 organizations both within and outside GE. I have called the approach a top-down *one, for it addresses basic issues of relationship to mission of individual effort as these efforts are influenced by organizational structure.*

INTROSPECT, as presented, makes use of skilled consulting services and utilizes computer programs for data manipulation and presentation in various formats which aid examination and analysis. The details of these programs are not presented, for they are proprietary and would be lengthy, but input and output are illustrated, and sufficient illustration is provided to allow knowledgeable individuals to proceed on their own or, if appropriate, to secure the services of a consultant who has access to the programs and experience in application of the procedure.

The second approach to improving the validity of individual efforts on behalf of organizational objectives, strategies, and mission is management by objectives (MBO). I have called this approach a bottom-up *one, for it usually starts with the individual and a statement of his or her goals and objectives. The process requires an interation up and down the organization and if executed well will result in validity of the organizational structure relative to individual goals and objectives contributing to organization mission.*

The MBO approach has been around for quite some years and has received a great deal of attention and use since Peter Drucker's endorsement of the concept in 1945. Many organizations have achieved good results with MBO, but many others have not. Dr. George Odiorne has, over the years, been an outspoken advocate and critic of MBO and is a recognized expert on how to avoid the various pitfalls which hamper effective use of this potentially valuable managerial process. He shares his insights in the chapter on MBO.

CHAPTER FIVE

Organization Analysis by the INTROSPECT Process*

RALPH A. JOHNSON[1]
Program Manager, Corporate Consulting Services, General Electric Company

INTROSPECT (to look into oneself, self-examination) is the designation for an abbreviated organizational analysis developed and used by General Electric. An INTROSPECT study provides recommendations for improving organizational structure and organizational productivity by means of:

- Reducing the cost of managing
- Reducing duplication of effort
- Reducing fragmentation of effort
- Adjusting span of control to correct for underspanning or overspanning
- Redirecting effort toward organizational objectives, strategies, and mission
- Providing a rational plan for adjusting work force size and assignments in keeping with changes in business volume and mix

More than 125 INTROSPECT studies have been conducted since 1975 covering all major sectors of GE and some dozen or so outside

* I wish to acknowledge the contributions of all the consultants in Manufacturing Management Consulting, each of whom contributed in some way to the development and refinement of the INTROSPECT process, and Jim Hendrick, whose brilliant, original thoughts led to the formulation of the process. Inquiries about INTROSPECT should be addressed to Manufacturing Management and Quality Control Consulting at General Electric.

organizations. The units involved have included those with profit responsibility and those with only cost responsibility, have ranged in size from 100 to as many as 5500 people, and have included production and service organizations, with structures of line and staff components, functional, multifunctional, and matrix organizations.

Results within General Electric have totaled well over $100 million savings. The procedure is a disciplined, structured, and mature one which has earned credibility and acceptance seldom accorded other programs, techniques, and processes within the company. It involves people high in the client organization—those who understand the goals, objectives, and thrusts of the business—in a joint study coordinated by representatives of the Corporate Consulting Services group.

Typically, an INTROSPECT study is originated at the request of a unit chief executive officer (CEO) or manager when the unit has or anticipates substantial expansion or contraction of business volume, a new manager, a substantive change in line of endeavor, or a new system, or when a general organizational reappraisal is desired.

Approximately 14 to 18 weeks is required for a study, involving 1 or 2 consultants (from Corporate Consulting Services), 2 or so coconsultants from the client organization (about ¼ time), interface with the unit manager, and about 2 to 3 hours' time from each manager and supervisor within the client organization. The study team analyzes organizational data provided by top management and all managers and supervisors, aided by computer manipulation and presentation of data, identifies issues to be considered and alternative means for achieving improvement, and develops a set of recommendations and an action plan for implementation.

INTROSPECT, as a process and as described in the following materials, can be applied to any organization—if one has available the required skill resources to parallel our approach. Even if these skills and resources should not be available, many organizations do have the ability to modify our approach and to borrow from it for developing their own version of introspective organizational analysis.

PRINCIPLES

Most organizations have too many managers. Our experience indicates that as much as 40 percent too many is not unusual, and typically the excess is greater than 25 percent. In order to place the management structure in better perspective, the following principles or concepts guide the use of the INTROSPECT process:

1. *Managers are hired to provide direction and guidance to an organization and, as such, should spend most of their time in managing the component.* Managing includes leading, guiding, directing, training, measuring, and otherwise interfacing directly with the personnel in the organization. Our

experience has shown that the most effective managers generally spend about two-thirds of their time performing these activities. The remaining time is spent by the manager on management support work, which is not related directly to any one person in the group but is performed for the group as a whole. These activities include planning, organizing, budgeting, financial analysis, and similar activities.

2. *Managers should have a span of control which is large enough to require their full attention in managing the component, and yet small enough to enable the manager to adequately cover the group.* Overspanned managers frequently lack effectiveness and underspanned managers drift into excessive individual contributor work and thus neglect the management part of their jobs, i.e., the necessary planning, guiding, and monitoring of work. When this happens, the manager becomes underutilized as a manager and the need for the position has to be questioned.

3. *Organizations should have a minimum number of layers of management.* Excessive layers reduce effective two-way communication and make it very difficult to obtain understanding of goals and objectives at the lower echelons. Reduction of managerial layers can provide quantum savings in managers while increasing productivity at the individual contributor level.

Individual contributors, mainly salaried personnel but with some consideration of hourly people, are also examined, using the following principles or concepts:

4. *Individual contributors should focus their efforts on a few well-chosen activities which contribute directly to the objectives of the organization.* We have found all too often most personnel do not have their work highly focused and are therefore fragmented over too many activities. This is particularly important when it involves highly skilled people who do an excessive amount of work which could be done by lower-paid employees. Fragmentation also tends to indicate duplication of effort with activities performed, more correctly, by other people in the organization.

5. *Misplaced work occurs when the mission for certain activities is assigned to one component and yet the work is also performed by another component.* Where this occurs, duplication of effort is the result and is usually in evidence in support operations such as equipment maintenance, expediting, office supplies, and contacting customers. It seems that these activities are most susceptible to misplaced work, and the result is costly duplication of effort.

6. *Objectives are sometimes blurred by ineffective communications.* As objectives, goals, and action plans are communicated through the various layers of an organization, they become modified and sometimes altered such that individual contributors as well as lower-level managers perform work which they honestly believe is necessary but which in fact may be slightly off target. Sometimes when communication is difficult, the cause lies in an excessive number of layers of management. The result is re-

duced capability for making changes, attacking problems, and addressing opportunities.

CONCEPT

INTROSPECT projects are conducted by a joint study team, in six steps. These will be presented briefly here and then elaborated upon.

Step 1: Initiation

The first step is organizational, involving selection of coconsultants, team training, development of project objectives, and compilation of a work dictionary.

Step 2: Data Gathering

Two forms are used: the Position Analyzer and the Organization Memo. Each is completed by all managers and supervisors, requiring about 2 to 3 hours.

The Position Analyzer (Fig. 5-1) obtains information about the nature of each managerial position (similarity of functions managed, geographical proximity, coordination, planning, etc.), evaluation judgments on performance, and availability of a replacement.

The Organization Memo (Fig. 5-2) is used to gather information about organizational structure, identifying to whom the position reports, who reports to the position, and the allocation of individual effort in 5 percent increments of time (according to the work dictionary definitions) for the individual manager and any individual contributors reporting to him or her. Only managers report data, and each is briefly interviewed by a team member at the time the data are gathered to obtain supplementary information about the manager's organizational mission in order to classify each reported activity as being either prime to the organization's mission or in support of the mission.

Step 3: Data Processing

The collected data are processed by computer and combined with payroll information, and various data output displays are produced:

a. Organization chart (Fig. 5-3). Based on data calculated by the computer, an organization chart is drawn on a plotter. This chart is constructed in a horizontal mode rather than the vertical mode that is usual for most other types of organizational charts. The advantages in portraying an organization in this manner are several. The chart can be produced accurately and updated very quickly, since it is computerized. In addition, the chart is compact and includes a substantial amount of data, which makes it easy to understand and analyze the organization. Each segment of the organization being studied is portrayed in a configuration roughly resembling a house. The summary house data are listed

POSITION ANALYZER

COMPLETED BY: _____

FOR THE POSITION OF: _____

Chart No._____Pos. No._____

PLEASE COMPLETE TODAY!

I. REGARDING THE WORK MANAGED BY THIS INDIVIDUAL:

A. The functions managed are:
1. ☒ Identical
2. ☐ Similar and related
3. ☐ Dissimilar but related
4. ☐ Each distinctly different

B. The people managed are located:
1. ☐ In the same office
2. ☒ In the same building
3. ☐ In the same complex but different building
4. ☐ Beyond a 10—mile radius

C. If more than one person is supervised, coordination between them is:
1. ☐ Never required
2. ☐ Sometimes required
3. ☒ Generally required
4. ☐ Constantly required
5. ☐ Only one is supervised

D. Planning the work of people should require:
1. ☐ No managerial time
2. ☒ A nominal amount of time
3. ☐ 50 percent of time
4. ☐ 100 percent of time

E. Directing and controlling the work of people managed requires:
1. ☐ No managerial time
2. ☒ Limited supervision
3. ☐ Frequent and continuing supervision
4. ☐ Constant close supervision

F. The type of work supervised is:
1. ☒ Repetitive and simple
2. ☐ Routine
3. ☐ Varied and complex
4. ☐ Critical, skilled, highly complex

G. The work output managed is:
1. ☐ Identical to the work of one or more other direct reports
2. ☒ Similar to the work of one or more other direct reports
3. ☐ Different from the work of all other direct reports
4. ☐ Totally unique

H. The people managed are:
1. ☒ Workers and/or individual contributors only
2. ☐ Other managers, supervisors, workers, and/or individual contributors
3. ☐ Other managers and/or supervisors only

II. REGARDING PERFORMANCE:

A. At this time I rate the manager's performance as:
1. ☐ Excellent—Far exceeds expected performance in accomplishing all objectives and position requirements.
2. ☒ Good—Accomplishes objectives and position requirements as originally anticipated.
3. ☐ Fair—Accomplishes only the minimum objectives.
4. ☐ Poor—Does not accomplish objectives or position requirements.

III. REGARDING POSITION BACKSTOPPING:

A. If this position had to be filled by another employee:
1. ☒ We could fill it from within our department organization in time to avoid serious operating delays.
2. ☐ We could obtain a replacement within the company in time to avoid serious operating delays.
3. ☐ We would have a temporary but serious delay in operations, and have to recruit outside of our department.
4. ☐ We would have a sustaining and/or critical delay in operations, and have to recruit outside of the Company.

PLEASE RETURN THIS FORM IN A CONFIDENTIAL INTEROFFICE ENVELOPE TO:

FIG. 5-1. The Position Analyzer form used to develop a profile of the work being accomplished in all functions.

Confidential

INTROSPECT

Organizational memo

To: __L. Erickson__

From: __R. Davis__

Date: __7-22__

Month __07__ Day __22__ Year ____

STEP 1

Job	House	Room

Report to:

Last name	First name	Initial
Davis	Ron	B.

Manager Engineering
His/her title

Job	House	Room
		Function—Cal. comp./text
		Location/shift—cal.comp.

STEP 2

My name is:

Last Name	First Name	Initial
Erickson	Len	L.

Manager Process Engineering
Title

Location	Bldg.	Tel. ext.
San Fran B - 223		
		Title—text only

STEP 3

The people below report directly to me and they do supervise others.

Note if there are "open" positions. Write "open" as the name and specify title, etc.

Last name	First name	Initial	Last name	First name	Initial
Glenz	Jack	J.			
Chief Elect. Engr.			Title		
San Fran - B			Location—building		
Hable	Bill	L.			
Chief Mech. Engr.			Title		
San Fran - B			Location—building		
Winarski	George	M.			
Chief Mech. Eng.			Title		
San Fran - B			Location—building		
	Title			Title	
	Location—building			Location—building	
	Title			Title	
	Location—building			Location—building	
	Title			Title	
	Location—building			Location—building	
	Title			Title	

FIG. 5-2. The Organization Memo form completed by all managers and supervisors.

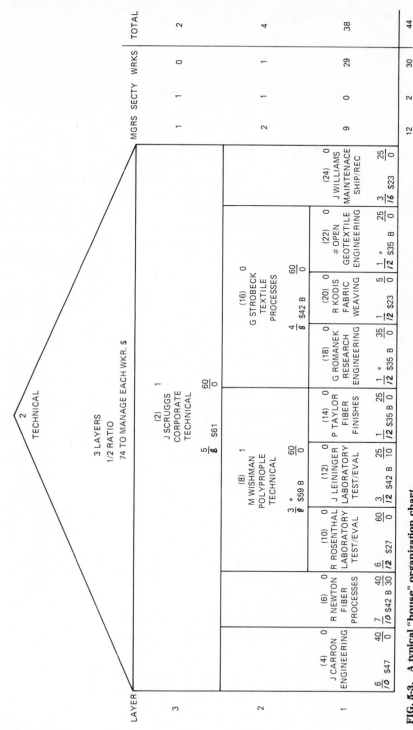

FIG. 5-3. A typical "house" organization chart.

61

at the apex of each house chart and are identified as follows:

- Function of the organization, for instance, "Technical."
- Ratio of managers to workers (30 workers divided by 12 managers produces a ratio of 1 manager per 2 workers, or ½ for the house).
- Cost to manage each worker dollar (the total of all managerial salaries, $471,000, divided by the total of all worker salaries, 636,000, is 74 cents for this house).

Within the house each manager's organization is described in a separate box, or room, which portrays the organizational data as follows:

- Manager's name and subfunction title are identified in the center of the room.
- Room number is located at the upper center.
- Number of secretaries is at the upper right corner.
- Manager's annual salary (thousands of dollars) is at the bottom center. If an esterisk appears above the salary number, it is in compression (within 25 percent of the superior's salary).
- No backup replacement for the position is indicated by a B code.
- Poor performance by the manager is indicated by a P code.
- The span of control fraction is given at the lower left corner (the numerator is the actual number of people reporting to the manager; the denominator indicates the derived potential number of direct reports).
- The management time fraction is at the lower right corner (the numerator is the percent of time the manager spends managing) the denominator is the percent of time which the manager receives in management assistance from direct reports).

Adjacent to the right side of the house chart is additional information identifying each layer of management in the house and the number of managers, secretaries, workers, and total people for each layer. All layers are totaled at the bottom. At the beginning and the end of the organizational chart, which includes all the houses, is still more data summarizing the entire organization as follows:

- Total number of houses.
- Total number of managers and workers and grand total of all employees.
- Summary ratio of managers to workers.
- Total cost of manager salaries, worker salaries, and total payroll.
- Summary cost to manage each worker dollar.

    b. Work Distribution Report by Employee Name (Fig. 5-4).
    c. Work Distribution Report by Postion/Activity (Fig. 5-5).
    d. Cost Panel (Fig. 5-6).
    e. Work Distribution by Organization (Fig. 5-7).
    f. 80/20 Viewer (Fig. 5-8).

PERSONNEL REPORT BY EMPLOYEE NAME

REPORTS TO HOUSE	POSITION	THIS HOUSE	POSITION	DEPARTMENT	SEQ	MGR	LAST NAME	INIT.	TITLE	EMP. ID	SALARY
17	2	17	12	PRODUCTION	4		WALLIS	D	REPAIR 3	442567667	19800
17	12	7	14	MAINTENANCE	14		WALTERS	W	ELECTRICIAN	421641962	22000
7	12	7	16	MAINTENANCE	8		WALTERS	M	ELECTRICIAN	260285321	22800
17	2	17	12	PRODUCTION	13		WALTERS	R	UTILITY 3	376606285	19600
17	2	17	12	PRODUCTION	12		WALTON	B	UTILITY 3	447286320	19600
28	8	8	34	MAINTENANCE	0		WARNER	W	FOREMAN	436845397	24500
28	8	8	30	MAINTENANCE	6		WATKINS	R	ELECTRICIAN 3	447644255	23000
4	8	8	62	MAINTENANCE	8		WATKINS	B	MECHANIC 3	441321301	22700
32	9	9	42	MAINTENANCE	15		WATSON	K	MECHANIC V	397463242	23400
6	9	9	18	MOLD SERV	8		WATTS	B	MNT MECH MFV	321365644	23400
6	9	9	10	MOLD MAINT	3		WEBB	R	ASST M INSP	390346112	23400
6	9	9	10	MOLD MAINT	13		WEBER	J	H F V R	390422352	23100
2	9	9	52	ELECTRICAL	4		WEBSTER	P	SR ENGINEER	399569335	25000
18	2	18	10	PRODUCTION	22		WEESE	D	REPAIR&CENTER	394404775	21300
18	2	18	16	INSP & FINIS	8		WEIBERG	D	INSPECTOR V	389506607	21300
32	9	9	40	MAINTENANCE	17		WEICHERT	M	MACH MAINT V	390546734	23400
28	8	8	30	MAINTENANCE	1		WELCH	J	MECHANIC 3	443444367	22700
6	8	8	52	MAINTENANCE	1		WEST	R	ELECTRICIAN 2	444587445	23000
2	17	17	10	PRODUCTION	8		WESTON	P	INSPECTOR 3	443526454	19700
4	8	8	60	MAINTENANCE	16		WHITE	C	MOLD REP 2	444268920	22700
32	9	9	34	MAINTENANCE	12		WOODS	W	ROUT ELECT V	392226143	23400

FIG. 5-4. A typical Work Distribution Report by Employee Name, alphabetically, to make it possible to locate any employee when the only information available is the employee's name.

WORK DISTRIBUTION BY ACTIVITY

ACTIVITY NAME	ACTIVITY CODE	THIS HOUSE	POSITION	LAST NAME	INIT	MGR	PRIME/ SECONDARY	PERCENT	ACTIVITY COST
PROCESS IMPROVEMENT	102	8	64	HAYS	B		1	20	5220
PROCESS IMPROVEMENT	102	8	64	JACOBSON	K		1	20	6000
PROCESS IMPROVEMENT	102	8	64	PATINO	M		1	20	6000
PROCESS IMPROVEMENT	102	9	46	TERMAN	T		1	5	1395
PROCESS IMPROVEMENT	102	9	46	RAY	J		1	5	1245
PROCESS IMPROVEMENT	102	9	46	THOMAS	M		1	5	1095
PROCESS IMPROVEMENT	102	9	46	DIAS	D		1	5	1095
PROCESS IMPROVEMENT	102	9	48	GLENN	E	X	1	20	5900
PROCESS IMPROVEMENT	102	9	52	JOHNSON	L	X	1	10	3340
PROCESS IMPROVEMENT	102	9	52	HYMANN	R		1	20	5020
PROCESS IMPROVEMENT	102	9	52	KUNTZ	H		1	30	7740
PROCESS IMPROVEMENT	102	9	52	PIROL	E		1	15	3150
PROCESS IMPROVEMENT	102	9	52	WEBSTER	J		1	35	8750
ACTIVITY TOTALS								745	199295
FEASIBILITY ENERG	103	5	28	BLAIR	R	X	2	5	1650
PROD FEASIBILITY ENERG	103	9	48	GRIMES	T	X	2	5	1475

FIG. 5-5. Work Distribution Report by Position/Activity. In the analysis process, the activity report by employee name is used to identify those performing each work activity.

64

COST PANEL

ACTIVITY DESCRIPTION PLANNING:MFG (CONT)	PEOPLE EQUIV.	ACTUAL	TOTAL $(000)	JOB % TOTAL	PERCENT FRAGMT.	PERCENT SECOND.	MISPLACED $	QUARTILE $ 1	PRODUCTIVITY	TOTAL $(000)
100 PLANT ENERG. SUPPORT	1.1	9	29	0.1	11.7	4.0				
101 NEW PRODUCTION SYSTEMS	0.5	5	12	0.0	9.0	21.0				
102 PROCESS IMPROVEMENT	7.4	35	199	0.6	21.3	0.0				
103 PROD FEASIBILITY ENERG	0.3	5	6	0.0	5.0	39.0				
104 CONSTRUCTION (WAGES ONLY)	51.4	138	1165	3.6	37.2	0.0				
105 ENERGY CONSERVATION	2.3	31	56	0.2	7.3	10.0				
106 ENVIRON PROTECT-FACILITY	2.3	18	54	0.2	12.5	4.0				
107 MAINTENANCE-SCHEDULING	7.6	74	195	0.6	10.3	5.0				
108 MOLDS & EQUIP RECORDS	1.5	11	30	0.1	13.6	7.0				
109 SAFETY	9.5	143	223	0.7	6.6	100.0				
110 MAINTENANCE-ROUTINE	250.6	171	5660	17.5	53.2	0.0				
111 MAINTENANCE-PREVENTIVE	79.1	366	1782	5.5	21.6	2.0				
112 ALIGNMENT CHECK	22.8	171	507	1.6	13.3	3.0				
113 WASTE TREATMENT	1.6	13	36	0.1	12.3	0.0				

FIG. 5-6. Cost Panel, on which all information relating to an activity is summarized. Potential productivity cases are identified on this display.

WORK DISTRIBUTION BY HOUSE

ACTIVITY	HOUSE 1 #	$(000)	HOUSE 2 #	$(000)	HOUSE 3 #	$(000)	HOUSE 4 #	$(000)	HOUSE 5 #	$(000)	HOUSE 6 #	$(000)
76 CAPITAL INVT. PLANNING	68	4									14	1
78 OPER.EXPENSE CONTROL&RPTG.							43	7				
79 INVENTORY ACCOUNTING							43	7				
80 PROGRAM ACCOUNTING												
81 TRAVEL VOUCHERS												
82 PAYROLL & TIMEKEEPING	11	4	15	5	6	2			2	5	7	2
83 BUDGETS & FORECASTS	50	2							1	2		
84 BUS. PLANNING:LONG RANGE	54	9										
86 STRATEGY/OPERATIONAL PLAN.	64	82										
87 ADV. MFG. TECHNOLOGY												
88 BUILDING TOOLS & JIGS	20	25							5	11	46	59
89 COST IMPROVEMENT-EQUIP.			15	37					32	7		
90 COST IMPROVEMENT-PRODUCT									12	24	1	3
91 DESIGN TOOLS & EQUIPMENT												
92 EQUIPMENT DEVELOPMENT												
93 EQUIPMENT & FACILITIES PLAN											29	24
94 EXPEDITING	60	34							7	9	1	
95 MAKE VS BUY STUDIES											2	2
96 TIME EVAL. ON NEW EQUIP.												
97 OFFSHORE MFG TECH TRANSFER	100	275										
98 PLANNING & METHODS												
99 PLANT LAYOUT	95	20										
100 PLANT ENERG. SUPPORT	30	4									5	1
101 NEW PRODUCTION SYSTEMS	10	19	1	2	1	1			49	6	11	1
102 PROCESS IMPROVEMENT											33	66
103 PROD. FEASIBILITY ENGRG.					25	2	36	2	17	1		
104 CONSTRUCTION (WAGES ONLY)												
105 ENERGY CONSERVATION									5	3	42	24
106 ENVIRON. PROTECTION-FACIL.											50	28

FIG. 5-7. Work Distribution by Organization: coconsultants work with the consultants to identify activities which are being performed in areas other than where they were intended to occur. All misplaced work is identified by activity.

80/20 VIEWER FOR TOTAL JOB

HOW IS THE MAJOR PORTION OF YOUR $32,381,600 PAYROLL SPENT ?

ACTIVITIES	PEOPLE ACTUAL EQUIV.	TOTAL DOLLARS	PERCENT OF TOTAL	ACCUM. PERCENT
110 MAINTENANCE-ROUTINE	471 250.6	5660855	17.5	17.5
147 INSPECTION-FINAL	360 257.7	5096365	15.7	33.2
2 MANAGE DIRECT REPORTS	192 70.8	1803205	5.6	38.8
111 MAINTENANCE-PREVENTIVE	366 79.1	1782775	5.5	44.3
160 REPAIR NON-CONFORMING PTS.	101 79.7	1630925	5.0	49.3
156 HOUSEKEEPING	128 62.3	1236050	3.8	53.1
104 CONSTRUCTION (WAGES ONLY)	158 51.4	1165895	3.6	56.7
153 INSPECTION&TEST-IN PROC.	138 51.4	1165895	2.9	59.6
180 WARRANTY ADMIN.(INC.R&A)	72 46.2	924800	2.3	61.9
159 MANUFACTURE PARTS	48 37.6	751990	2.2	64.1
141 QUALITY AUDITS	87 34.1	711050	2.2	66.3
152 CALIBRATION	112 31.0	647705	2.0	68.3
149 TROUBLESHOOT MFG.& PROD.	171 22.8	507010	1.6	69.9
112 ALIGNMENT CHECK	40 22.1	505000	1.6	71.5
162 MOLD CHANGE	25 20.2	486255	1.5	73.0
114 POWERHOUSE	20 18.1	494020	1.4	74.4
161 STORES REQUISITIONING	259 10.3	417945	1.3	75.7
196 CLERICAL & FILING	188 17.0	354235	1.1	76.8
146 QUALITY REPORTING	112 14.7	326200	1.0	77.8
30 DRAFTING-E&M	30 9.6	225445	0.7	78.5
24 CHECK LAYOUT DRAWINGS	85 9.2	223445	0.7	79.2
109 SAFETY	143 9.4	223120	0.7	79.9
140 NON-CONFORM. MATL. SYS.	34 9.9	215805	0.7	80.6

80.56% OF YOUR PAYROLL DOLLARS ARE SPENT ON THESE 23 ACTIVITIES.

FIG. 5-8. The 80/20 Viewer lists the cost of activities in descending order. Normally, 20 percent of the total number of activities include 80 percent of the total payroll dollars.

Step 4: Analysis

The various output displays and other data are analyzed by the team to identify potential improvements:

    a. Structural analysis: Each house and room is critically analyzed to identify opportunities for structural change.

    b. Work activity analysis: Opportunities for obtaining better allocation of individual effort are identified.

Next, additional information is obtained from the client manager concerning relationships between activities and priorities, which is used to facilitate the following:

    c. Organizational mission analysis.

    d. Organizational focus analysis.

    e. Misplaced work analysis.

    f. Fragmented work analysis.

Step 5: Report Preparation

Opportunities for improvement are analyzed and evaluated by the team, and agreement is reached concerning what options should be recommended and how they should be pursued. These recommendations are presented by the team to the client manager authorizing the study.

Step 6: Follow-up

The team monitors progress by the organization in order to provide clarification and impetus to implementation.

DETAILS OF PROCEDURE

Step 1: Start-up

After the preliminaries of initiating the project and obtaining the general guidance of the client manager, several coconsultants are selected by the client manager to form the INTROSPECT project team. The coconsultants bring to the team an intimate knowledge of the business, organization, past practices, and future thrusts of the organization. They are selected on the basis of:

- Knowledge of the organization
- Respect and credibility within the organization
- Analytical ability, creativeness, and open-mindedness
- Ability to handle confidential information
- Availability 25–30 percent of the time
- Position in the organization as direct report to the client manager if possible

The role of the coconsultants is to:

- Help develop the work dictionary, and tailor it to the objectives of the project
- Assist in collecting the data
- Analyze the data
- Develop recommendations
- Present recommendations to the client
- Assist in implementation

The corporate consultants provide direction for the project, knowledge of the INTROSPECT process, normative data from past projects, analytical techniques, experience in developing opportunities for improvement, and basic instruction in the process for the coconsultants.

The team, informally, also includes the client manager as a key member. The manger discusses the objectives for the project with the team and is kept informed of key issues and the direction of development of the project as it progresses. The guidance of a manager is critical to determining the level of detail for defining work activities in developing the work dictionary, which is used as the basis for obtaining input data.

Step 2: Data Gathering

Basic data are obtained from all managers, starting with the client manager and working downward through the organization, using the Position Analyzer and Organization Memo forms, as described in the preceding discussion (Figs. 5-1 and 5-2).

Step 3: Data Processing

Various computer presentations are produced, as described above.

Step 4: Analysis

There are two analysis phases: organization structure and focus of individual work. The structural analysis phase assesses the utilization of managers and identifies opportunities for combining underutilized or underspanned managers, while still maintaining the same level of managerial coverage.

Structural analysis Each house is systematically analyzed as follows, using the technical organization (house) of Fig. 5-3 as an example:

Average span of control is calculated by averaging the desired potential spans (shown as the denominator of the fraction in the lower left corner of each room). In this example the average is 10.

Theoretical number of managers required is determined by dividing the number of worker personnel by the average span of control ($30/12 = 2.5$). Assuming that rooms contain similar activities and that there are no geographical impediments to combining managers, the minimum number of managers required with no overspanning would be 3 (2.5 rounded up).

Determination of underspanning or overspanning is indicated by comparison of actual with theoretical number of managers (12 actual compared with the theoretical of 3), indicating a major opportunity for restructuring the organization. This organization will therefore be subject to very close scrutiny for structural improvement.

Structural analysis is then directed to each individual room in order to determine which ones are candidates for combination. The span of control fraction, in the lower left of each room, indicates a fully spanned manager if the fraction equals 1, underspanning if less than 1, and overspanning if greater than 1. Detailed room analysis is usually performed when the fraction is 0.20 or less, as follows:

A mission statement for each manager and his or her organization is developed. The following example is extracted from Fig. 5-3.

Maintenance Supervisor—Room (24): To repair, maintain, and service all the test equipment and the processing equipment used in the prototype production Test Building of the company. Responsibility includes mechanical, electrical, pipe fitting, and machinist trades. Work requirement is to plan and prioritize work, assign jobs, and help troubleshoot technical problems. Also responsible for receiving and delivery of all inbound materials for the Test Building and arranging for all outbound shipments.

Each managerial position is analyzed, and additional data are added to the house presentation. In the actual example above, the maintenance supervisor's room looks like this:

(24)		0
	J. WILLIAMS MAINTENANCE SHIP./REC.	
$\frac{3}{20}$	$23	$\frac{25}{0}$

J. Williams is manager of Maintenance, Shipping, and Receiving for the Test Building and occupies position or room 24. He has no secretary, has 3 individuals reporting to him (span), and earns $23,000 per year. He spends 25 percent of his time managing, and receives no managerial assistance from workers under him. The absence of the exception code B indicates there *is* a backup or replacement person available for this position. Also, the absence of the exception code P indicates that his superior *does not* consider Williams a poor performer. If an asterisk had appeared above his salary ($23), this would identify the fact that Williams' salary is in compression with his manager's salary, or within 25 percent.

The additional information added manually is to the lower part of the span of control fraction. In this case the "derived potential span" for Williams is 20. This is developed by analysis and on a judgmental basis by the team as appropriate for this position.

The upper half of the managing time fraction (25 percent) shows the direct management time spent by the manager on management activities, including managing his own direct reports and others who may report to him on a dotted line basis. The lower half of the fraction indicates the time, in this case 0, spent by the manager's direct reports (workers) on direct management activities, helping him perform the managerial function, such as giving technical direction and following up on projects. The total direct management time for this room is only 25 percent, which is typical where managers perform considerable nonmanagement work.

Fully spanned professional managers will utilize approximately 65 percent of their time on direct management activities, and the remainder (35 percent) in management support activities such as planning, scheduling, and controlling. Where this occurs, managers should not require any management assistance from people who report to them.

The span ratio, using a more meaningful derived potential span, is used to determine underspanning, overspanning, or correct spanning. In the example, the ratio of 3/20 indicates that J. Williams is underspanned by 17 people.

If a room is overspanned, restructuring should be considered. A search is generated within other management positions for candidates for combination. It may be possible to shift some workers from the overspanned manager to other underspanned managers. If several rooms are significantly underspanned, however, an opportunity may exist for a multiple combination. To combine or redistribute managerial positions, the following criteria must be met:

- Span: Room must be overspanned or underspanned.
- Compatibility: The missions of both positions must be similar or compatible.
- Geographical: It is helpful if the positions are contiguous.
- Work activities must be similar in nature; however, they do not have to be exactly the same.
- There are no other limitations (i.e., special management positions such as training).

Additional information from the Work Distribution Reports and Cost Panels is useful in analyzing potential organizational changes, particularly in identifying specific work activities which are involved in the positions being considered, and how these activities might better be allocated. For example, consider the following four positions (from Fig. 5-3).

Room number	Managers	Percent management time	Percent management[2] support time	Percent management assistance time	Percent total managerial time
8	M. Wishman	60	20	0	80
10	R. Rosenthal	60	25	0	85
12	J. Leininger	25	20	10	55
14	P. Taylor	25	35	0	60
	Total	170	100	10	280

Since the theoretical number of managers here is 1,[3] the total managerial time required is 100 percent, leaving 180 percent (280 percent minus 100 percent) or 1.8 equivalent managers who might be assigned elsewhere. Comparing basic data for all four managers:

	Wishman	Rosenthal	Leininger	Taylor
Span	3/8	6/12	3/12	1/12
Mission	All performing laboratory evaluation work			
Location	All located together in the same laboratory			

a combination seems possible. The missions are similar, the location is common, and the combined span would be 10/12. Details of time allocations are then analyzed as shown in Fig. 5-9 and resolved as follows:

A. Absorbed by combined manager (department reporting)
D. Delegated to workers (laboratory analysis)
E. Eliminated (forecasting)
R. Retained by combined manager (manage direct reports)

When two or more managers are combined, the amounts of time spent directly managing are not additive. The numbers are synergistically combined to approximate the amount of time which the combined manager is expected to require in order to manage the combined organization. In the case described, the combined manager (Fig. 5-10) is expected to require 65 percent of the time managing based on the fact that he or she will be fully spanned with 12 workers.[4] The theory is that fully spanned managers should require about two-thirds of their time directly managing and the balance performing management support work.

Management support work is identified as activities which managers have to perform for the organization because they are managers and which relate directly to the organization as a whole. Examples are budgeting, long- and short-range planning, communications, financial analysis, and worker power development. These activities become functional work activities when the manager performs them for the entire

Room (8)

M. Wishman

Disp. code	ACTIVITIES	Percent time
R	Manage Dir. Reports	60
A	Department Reporting	5
R	Long-Range Reporting	10
R	Product Planning	10
D	Laboratory Analysis	5
E	Forecasting	5
R	Manpower Develop.	5
	Total	100%

(0) Workers

Room (10)

R. Rosenthal

Disp. code	ACTIVITIES	Percent time
A	Manage Dir. Reports	60
R	Short-Range Plan.	15
E	Product Selection	5
D	Product Testing	10
D	Process Analysis	5
R	Salary Planning	5
	Total	100%

(6) Workers

ACTIVITIES	Percent time
Product Testing	150
Process Analysis	75
Machine Design	200
Equipment Develop.	125
Prototype Develop.	35
Specifications	15
Total	600%

Room (12)

J. Leininger

Disp. code	ACTIVITIES	Percent time
A	Manage Dir. Reports	25
E	Assistance in Manag.	10
D	Machine Design	15
D	Process Analysis	25
D	Equipment Develop.	25
	Total	100%

(3) Workers

ACTIVITIES	Percent time
Report Writing	15
Chemical Analysis	125
Process Analysis	50
Machine Design	40
Equipment Develop.	70
Total	300%

Room (14)

P. Taylor

Disp. code	ACTIVITIES	Percent time
A	Manage Dir. Reports	25
A	Product Planning	10
D	Process Develop.	15
D	Process Analysis	10
D	Machine Design	20
D	Equipment Develop.	20
	Total	100%

(1) Worker

ACTIVITIES	Percent time
Process Develop.	45
Process Analysis	20
Machine Design	15
Equipment Develop	20
Total	100%

Disposition code

A - Absorbed by Combined Manager
D - Delegated to Workers
E - Eliminated
R - Retained by Combined Manager

FIG. 5-9. Analysis of time reallocation for combining positions.

Combined manager		Combined workers	
Activities	Time, percent	Activities	Time, percent
Manage direct reports	65	Product testing	180
Long-range planning	10	Process analysis	200
Product planning	10	Machine design	300
Short-range planning	5	Equipment development	265
Manpower development	5	Prototype development	35
Salary planning	5	Specifications	15
		Report writing	15
		Chemical analysis	125
		Process development	60
		Laboratory analysis	5
Total	100	Total	1200

FIG. 5-10. Allocation of activities to combined manager and his or her direct reports.

organization including peer managers as well. For example, the personnel manager performs worker power development work for the whole company. In this instance worker power development work is a functional activity rather than management support.

The combined manager's support activities are also synergistically derived. The requirement is that the combined activity total has to be at least as much as any of the detail percentages but does not have to be the sum of them. The theory is that performing a management support activity for a fully spanned organization may not require any more additional time than it does for a partially spanned organization. It depends on the extent to which the managers are underspanned.

If the criteria for combination or redistribution are satisfied and time allocations are satisfactory, it can be concluded that a portion of time may be eliminated. Where the reductions can be turned into whole numbers of people, the house and room charts are marked to indicate the potential changes by crossing out the eliminated room, indicating with an arrow how the rooms are to be combined, and indicating a (−1) if the manager is to be eliminated (Fig. 5-11).

The likely impact of combining or restructuring is then evaluated. The analysts consider the resulting span of control for the combined room and evaluate the change in span at the next higher level. They also establish the activities for the new position. The latter is done by listing the major activities for the new organization, developing an appropriate mission statement, evaluating the managerial activities and how they would be redistributed, and assigning appropriate responsibilities to other managerial and/or individual contributor positions which may be required but are not part of the new position responsibility.

An example of lateral and horizontal restructuring is provided by refer-

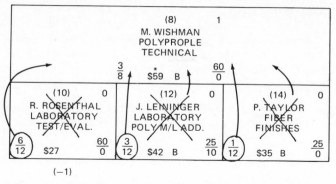

FIG. 5-11.   Documentation of room combination possibilities.

ence to the technical house (Fig. 5-3). The analysis previously outlined is applied, and it seems desirable to do the following: combine the three rooms managed by Rosenthal, Leininger, and Taylor horizontally and then merge the combined managers vertically with Wishman. In this case, M. Wishman becomes the combined manager of all workers, R. Rosenthal is eliminated, and J. Leininger and P. Taylor are converted into full-time individual contributors. This results in the establishment of a fully spanned manager (Wishman) and increases the work performed by individual contributors by two (Leininger and Taylor). One individual (Rosenthal) is eliminated along with a layer of management represented by the three managers reporting to Wishman. (Accommodation of displaced individuals will be included in the implementation plan, which will be discussed later.) In addition, the worker activities are more closely focused, and several activities actually increase beyond the sum of the present workers (i.e., Product Testing, Process Analysis, and Machine Design) (Fig. 5-10).

The room combination possibilities are documented as shown in Fig. 5-11, and the revised room is shown in Fig. 5-12. The analysis and restructuring would have been supported by mission statements and data from Work Distribution Reports.

```
┌─────────────────────────────────┐
│            (8)      1            │
│        M. WISHMAN                │
│        TECHNICAL                 │
│        LABORATORY                │
│      12      *        65         │
│      ──             ──           │
│      12     $59   B   0          │
└─────────────────────────────────┘
```

FIG.   5-12.   The   revised   technical-laboratory room, reflecting changed organizational structure, which would be supported by a revised mission statement.

When all houses and rooms have been analyzed and various appropriate organizational changes determined, these are summarized and case material is prepared for presentation to the client manager, documenting the rationale for restructuring and the expected benefits to be gained. This completes, at the moment, the structural analysis phase—which continues after the quartile analysis (which will be explained later).

Work activity analysis The second phase of the INTROSPECT data analysis procedure is designed to analyze individual contributor work activities in order to:

- Combine similar work elements to achieve a synergism which contributes to effectiveness.
- Eliminate misplaced and/or duplicated work elements being performed by individuals in different organizations or outside the job classifications.
- Reduce secondary work which is not coupled to the prime mission of the organization.
- Reduce work fragmentation by individuals.
- Correlate salary dollars to the priority of the function being performed in order to identify opportunities for improved allocation of resources.

During this analysis phase the coconsultants must think in a business overview manner and be sensitive to cause and effect relationships, input and output links, and organizational interface activities. It is very important to understand that although INTROSPECT data are not precise, past studies have shown that the activity data taken as a whole are generally quite accurate. However, in recognition of the inherent nonpreciseness of the data, recommendations should be based not solely on one data point but rather on findings which come from several data sources or analyses.

The following are several different approaches to analysis, which are not intended to be inclusive but which suggest some of the flexible ways that the data might be adapted to the study needs of the particular component. Work activity analysis usually entails the tenacious following of threads of data, which are symptoms of the problems, to identify the suspected root causes. The use of various data is described.

- Work Distribution by Employee (Fig. 5-4) shows the specific activities that are reported for each individual, manager and nonmanager alike, with each activity coded as to whether it is prime or secondary in accordance with the mission of the particular organization, the percent of time which the activity is performed by each individual, and the activity cost. This report is used mainly as a reference in evaluating the time and actual work performed by each individual.
- Work Distribution by Activity (Fig. 5-5) shows in numerical order

each of the activities, together with the personnel who reported time spent against the activity. Since the focus here is on the activity itself, all the people performing any specific activity can readily be identified, along with the time spent and relative cost. Organizational positions are identified so that the location of any individual in the organization is easily determined. This report is used also to examine fragmentation by activity, since it indicates the total number of people together with the percent of time performed by each for all activities.

- Cost Panel (Fig. 5-6) is used mainly to identify both activity and personnel fragmentation and to evaluate the relative value of the activities to the total payroll. The report summarizes data by activity within various organizational entities or functions. For instance, all the employee relations activities are portrayed together as well as each of the other functions. In addition, the levels of effort and costs together with various comparative data are also shown. The equivalent total people is merely the sum of all the individual percentages which were reported by all the personnel. The fragmentation index is calculated by dividing the actual number of people into the equivalent number of people. The percent of expense for each activity in total to the total payroll of the whole organization is presented. This is done in order to provide an idea of the relative value of the activities being examined.

- Work Distribution by Organization (Fig. 5-7) lists activities and the cost for each activity as it occurs in various houses. Where the activity is actually being performed throughout the organization is easily seen. Questions are asked as to the appropriateness of performing certain activities in various houses. For instance, if the internal auditing activity is to be performed only by Finance and yet it is also shown to be performed in the manufacturing house, this activity would be identified as possibly misplaced.

- 80/20 Viewer (Fig. 5-8) presents a Pareto listing of all activities organized by descending dollar value. Each activity is calculated as a percent to total of the payroll value, and these percentages are then accumulated numerically such that when 80 percent of the value is reached, generally only 20 percent of the activities will be included. This is important in order to select out the high-value activities for greater investigation and maximization of payoff. The 80/20 Viewer also is an input to the quartile analysis.

- Quartile analysis is a procedure which injects the business priorities into the INTROSPECT study. It provides additional insight to the team during the productivity phase of analysis. Many times the client manager can identify where the business strategies are not being supported properly at the operating level, or where excessive costs are being incurred on low-priority activities. The preciseness of the quartile analysis itself does not generally support the need for change but provides an additional ingredient which when mixed with other data tends to confirm a need for change.

The corporate consultant extracts from the 80/20 Viewer the top 20 percent of the activities which represent 80 percent of the payroll costs. Direct labor activities (if any) and other activities over which the client manager has little discretionary control are not usually included. The title and definition for the top 20 percent activities are then listed on 3 × 5 cards, one activity to a card.

The corporate consultant has the client manager separate the cards into four equal piles representing priorities from highest to lowest. For instance, if "selling" is high on the client's ranking of priorities, it would be placed in the higher-priority pile, whereas "housekeeping" might be placed in the lower-priority pile. This provides four card piles with the activities ranked as very high, high, low, and very low. To complete the quartile analysis, the consultant next constructs a 16-block quartile matrix, as shown in Fig. 5-13. Horizontal quartiles 1 through 4 are the client manager's ranking, and vertical quartiles 1 through 4 identify where the activities fall by actual cost. The blocks in the diagonal from upper left to lower right contain activities where the client manager's priorities and relative costs are in agreement.

The quartile analysis displays areas of exception between those activities which the client manager feels should be emphasized and those where actual payroll dollars are spent. The areas of greatest concern are those farthest from the line of agreement. Those activities for which it is felt the payroll dollars expended are excessive are in the upper right boxes, while the lower left-hand boxes indicate activities for which the payroll expenditure is felt to be too low. These represent areas which can be strengthened by reallocating resources to them from the activities in the upper right-hand boxes. Both areas of exception are addressed with special emphasis during both the structural and the work activity analysis.

A follow-up meeting with the client manager is usually beneficial to provide feedback from the quartile analysis and to obtain insights into why divergence from the line of agreement may exist. By this time, some key issues may have surfaced which will also be discussed.

▪ *Organizational mission analysis process.* The performance of an organization on its assigned mission is directly related to that organization's productivity. The dollars expended by each organization should match the priorities of its assigned mission, and the activities performed should be well focused in order to build functional expertise. The object of the organizational mission analysis process is to identify organizational productivity improvement while centering the analysis on the activities being performed in the organiza-

QUARTILE ANALYSIS

THEY SHOULD BE IN:

	QUARTILE 1	QUARTILE 2	QUARTILE 3	QUARTILE 4
QUARTILE 1	HIGH 147 INSPECTION $5096 2 MANAGE DIR.REPTS. 1803	111 MAINTENANCE-PREV. $1783 104 CONSTR.(WAGES) 1166 153 INSP & TEST(IN P) 925	110 MAINTENANCE-ROUT. $5661 160 REPAIR NON-CONF.PT 1631 180 WARRANTY ADMIN. 752 159 MANUFACTURE PTS. 711	156 HOUSEKEEPING $1235
QUARTILE 2	HIGH 149 TROUBLESHOOT MFG. $530 112 ALIGNMENT CHECK 500 146 QUALITY REPORTING 326	VERY HIGH 152 CALIBRATION $648 162 MOLD CHANGING 486	CRITICALLY HIGH 141 QUALITY AUDITS $711 114 POWERHOUSE 484	VERY HIGH 161 STORES REQUISING. $418 196 CLERICAL&FILING 354 30 DRAFTING-R&M 225
QUARTILE 3	LOW 142 PROD. EVALUATION $217 102 PROCESS IMPROVT. 199	LOW 140 NON-CONF.MATL.SYS. $216 107 MAINT. SCHEDULING 196	HIGH 109 SAFETY $223 1 ASST.ME IN MGMG. 194	VERY HIGH 24 CK.LAYOUT DRGS. $223 88 BUILD TOOLS&FIXT. 213 3 MANAGE OTHERS 202 91 DESING.TOOLS&EQUP. 198
QUARTILE 4	VERY LOW / CRITICALLY LOW 61 TIRE UNIFORMITY $156 89 COST IMPR.-EQUIP. 130 115 MFG.CHANGES(MC'S) 128	VERY LOW 144 QUALITY CHECKS $194 94 EXPEDITING 128 139 INCOMING INSPECTN. 127 163 PILOT PLANT-GEARS 124	LOW 64 LEGAL AFFAIRS $130	HIGH 198 SECRETARIAL $159 158 SCRAP DISPOSAL 138

FIG. 5-13. The activities on the 80/20 Viewer are ranked by the client manager to identify where payroll dollars should be spent. This ranking is then compared with where the dollars are actually being spent on the quartile analysis.

tion and how these activities are organized. Mission analysis used in conjunction with the focus analysis process, which is described next, centers on organizational productivity. The analysis is done as follows:

a. Select the organizational house to be evaluated.

b. Establish the mission of the house.

c. Examine the 80/20 Viewer for the house selected and review the activities performed by the house.

d. Compare high-value activities (80 percent of the dollars) with the mission statement. Identify activities that should not be done at all by this house. This becomes misplaced work and represents savings opportunity.

e. Evaluate high-value activities for fragmentation. If the number of equivalent people is less than 20 percent of the actual number of people, the activity is fragmented.

f. Using the activity report, examine each room within the house performing the activity, and calculate a fragmentation index (equivalent people divided by the actual number). Determine if fragmentation for this activity in the house is acceptable or not. If the fragmentation index is below 20 percent, a productivity improvement opportunity may exist.

g. Scan the balance of activities (20 percent of dollars) in the 80/20 Viewer in the same manner as above.

h. Record the opportunities for improving support of organization mission, and the appropriate revised mission statement at the bottom of the 80/20 Viewer for the house being examined.

- *Organizational focus analysis process.* The focus of the efforts of an organization is directly related to that organization's productivity. For a given worker, the focus is optimally effective when he or she is working within the normative number of activities for the particular job. The object of the organizational focus analysis process is to identify organizational productivity improvements while centering the analysis on the individuals of the organization and the work that they perform. The following process is used in conjunction with the preceding mission analysis process, to focus on organizational productivity:

a. Select the house to be analyzed and the specific room within the house.

b. Examine each individual in the room for the particular focus and extent of secondary work performed.

c. Compare the number of activities actually being performed with the norm for this particular job.[5] For instance, if the norm is 5–8 and the actual number of activities is 14, this indicates that the individual is highly fragmented and that refocusing the efforts over a smaller number of activities is likely to result in productivity improvement.

d. Examine the amount of secondary work being performed by each individual. If the amount of secondary work is over 20 percent of the total work, an opportunity may exist to refocus the individual's time more closely on mission activities.

e. Where such opportunities are identified, examine the activities for reassignment to other personnel who may have the secondary activities as their prime mission, and look for opportunities to delegate downward if the individual performing the secondary work happens to be a high-level or key individual. Finally, look for opportunities to mechanize or reduce the total amount of secondary work.

Misplaced work analysis   Work performed by a segment of an organization that is clearly beyond its mission or scope of responsibility is identified as misplaced work. This may result from changes in management personnel where the successor manager interprets the mission differently from the predecessor, or in some cases misplaced work results from lack of support between organization units. Misplaced work is usually redundant and represents an opportunity for improvement. This is accomplished by refocusing the organization's attention on its prime mission and shifting misplaced work to the unit having the prime responsibility.

House displays, mission statements, and secondary work data displays are analyzed to determine if the activities are misplaced. All misplaced activities are noted, and the dollars for both the house and the room are posted to the Cost Panel in the column marked for misplaced work.

Upon completion of the analysis and posting of misplaced work to the Cost Panel, the reassignment of these activities is performed. Where the work is not being accomplished in the appropriate house, the work will usually be found to be redundant and generally not required at all. The costs identified with redundant or nonrequired work are then collected to be incorporated in the project recommendations.

- *Fragmented work analysis.* Activities which are overly fragmented are similarly identified in order to restructure position responsibilities and to improve the job focus. Productivity may begin to suffer when an individual spends 20 percent or less time on any particular activity. Those activities being performed 10 percent or less of an individual's time are considered highly fragmented and can be reassigned to others already performing the activity a greater percentage of their time. Reassignment will free an equivalent proportion of the individual's time which can be applied to other work activity. Fragmented activities transferred to others already performing the activity a higher percentage of the time may possibly be absorbed by the latter individual without requiring additional time on his or her part, because of the increased productivity gain through the refocusing process. In cases where reassignment is not possible, the individual jobs of those performing the activity should be restructured to increase the individual percentage, thereby increasing the focus.

The data are passed through several screens to ensure that the magnitude of the productivity improvement opportunity is reasonable. These are:

a. Only activities which should be focused are considered. Some activities which should not be focused are deleted. For instance, most managers generally want everyone to be involved in cost improvements a small percentage of the time. Therefore, it is desirable to have the cost improvement activity fragmented.

b. Only individual contributors are considered. Managers should normally spend most of their time on managing.

c. No management activities are included.

d. Only activities with payroll efforts totaling at least $10,000 are considered in analyzing the data. This is to increase attention to activities having significant costs.

e. A maximum of 20 percent of the total activity cost may be reduced through improved job focus. This is true even though more than 20 percent of the activity cost is fragmented. It is not reasonable, for example, to assume that if 70 percent of an activity is performed by individuals who spend 10 percent or less of their time on the activity, those individuals performing the remaining 30 percent can absorb the total effort without increasing the time spent on the activity.

f. Activities with a potential savings of less than $5000 are eliminated, since the effort required to restructure positions would be high compared with the benefits to be derived.

Secondary work   An individual's work is usually made up of two types of activities: those relating directly to the prime mission, and the balance which are in support of the prime mission. These support activities are sometimes regarded as being secondary work. The norm for the ratio of prime to secondary work is usually 80/20. However, past studies have indicated that significant savings do not occur until the ratio exceeds 60/40. In many cases the ratio was as low as 10/90. In the more severe cases the team attempts to refocus the work of the individual to eliminate unnecessary secondary work so that the majority of time is directed toward the prime mission.

One way to identify secondary work is by using the Activity by Employee data display, which shows all the activities for each individual and indicates which ones are secondary. In addition, a total secondary percentage is calculated both by individual and for the room. This method is complementary to the organizational focus analysis described earlier.

Another method of analysis of secondary work is done by using the secondary work data display along with the secondary 80/20·Viewer and the Cost Panel. The secondary work distribution by house display identifies all the secondary activities being performed in each house. Using this panel, the secondary activity cost can be compared with the house total, either secondary or primary, in order to determine the house ratio of prime to secondary work. Where this ratio falls below the 80/20 norm, additional analysis may be warranted.

A secondary 80/20 Viewer can be used to present the effort across the total job and the secondary effort within each house in a Pareto ranking. The secondary work distribution and the 80/20 analysis provide a way of focusing on activities to determine to what extent they are performed as secondary work and what priority they have as secondary work, both across the entire organization and within each house.

Volume-related data   The cost of work activities performed by an organization often can be related to the volume of its output. For example, selling activity costs for a field organization may be compared with orders received, yielding selling costs per order. This is one measurement of the effectiveness of the organization in performing its mission. Similar organizations often can be compared to identify opportunities for productivity improvement. The cost of work activities can also be compared with appropriate measurement bases related to the service they provide. For example, the clerical support required in a shop operation's organization can be stated as a percentage of direct labor, the percentage associated with different shop operation's groups can be compared, a target for all groups as a whole can be established, and each group can be compared with the target.

In addition to comparisons within the job, comparisons can also be made with data from earlier INTROSPECT projects. These comparisons are accomplished by having the client manager select several businesses that are close enough to be similar. The corporate consultant, after disguising the data, normalizes the data to a common base such as percent to direct labor, percent to sales, or percent to payroll, and establishes a comparative base.

Step 5: Report Preparation

After analysis is complete and each improvement opportunity for structural and work activity change is documented as a recommendation, the consulting team finalizes the report for presentation. Practice dictates that the consulting team must agree unanimously on each recommendation, which we believe is necessary in order to instill confidence in the client manager that the corporate consultants have surfaced all possible recommendations and that the coconsultants have weeded out any unusable or inappropriate recommendations. This "forcing mechanism" of agreement serves also to eliminate doubts on the part of coconsultants as to the viability of recommendations.

The actual presentation to the client manager is then delivered both orally and in written form. Generally, the corporate consultants present the project overview together with the objectives and an explanation of the concepts, while the coconsultants present each of the detail structural and work activity recommendations. Client managers may elect to receive the recommendations alone or to include their staff, depending on how close they have been to the project and the sensitivity of the recommendations.

Each recommendation is presented with its own rationale. The benefits and savings are documented, and the explicit nature of the recommendation is delineated. If client managers have included their staff, it is generally advisable to have the manager instruct them to ask questions only for clarification during the presentation rather than to debate the merits of each recommendation.

Depending on the size of the organization and the number of recommendations, the presentation can require several hours. If the staff is allowed to debate each of the recommendations, it will be difficult to complete the presentation within a reasonable time. It should be pointed out, however, that the staff is not obligated for implementation at this point and will receive, subsequently, individual explanation and further rationale as to the recommendations from the team.

The team next meets with each functional manager on the client manager's staff and reviews the recommendations affecting his or her function. Sufficient time is taken to expose the manager to the concepts, fundamentals, and principles, and to explain the backup data and rationale for each of the recommendations. It is essential to get the manager's understanding and acceptance of the recommendation in order to facilitate implementation. Generally, where recommendations are not implemented, it is because of lack of understanding rather than credibility of the recommendation.

Implementation

For implementation to proceed in an orderly manner, it is critical that the team devise an implementation plan which identifies key milestones and a suitable feedback mechanism. It is expected that each of the recommendations will be reviewed by functional managers and their personnel (as deeply into the organization as possible) to gain an understanding from the appropriate personnel. Implementation of a recommendation will generally require combination of several jobs, elimination of a layer of management, or the transfer of work activities from one individual to another. Recommendations will require change, and change can come about only if the manager and the personnel affected by the change understand the rationale behind it. Even under ideal circumstances, implementation is difficult. There will be personnel moves which are difficult to effect without undue hardship. Recommendations may require the refocusing of certain activities which can be difficult to implement. It is necessary, therefore, for the functional manager to remain very close to the organization to forestall obstacles or roadblocks and reduce resistance. Client managers have to remain involved in the process and should require periodic feedback from each member of their staff.

It has been our experience that the bulk of potential savings from recommended changes (50 percent or more) will occur within 6 months after the completion of the project. The balance of the savings, up to a cumulative total of 75 to 80 percent, will occur over the next year. Therefore, it is necessary to push for implementation as hard and as fast as possible in order to obtain the benefits quickly; otherwise the data will begin to age and the credibility of the recommendations will disappear.

Step 6: Follow-up

The final step in the INTROSPECT procedure is a follow-up on implementation by the corporate consultants, generally about 3 months after the completion of the project. The corporate consultants meet with the team and the client manager to review implementation progress. This is necessary for several reasons. First, the coconsultants can advise the corporate consultants as to the desirability of implementing certain recommendations together with the problems identified that were not previously exposed. This gives the corporate consultants additional insight into the advisability of certain recommendations and the adequacy of the data analysis. At the same time, the corporate consultants are expected to probe the lack of implementation and push for stronger efforts if required. Client managers can also inject their priorities along with their assessment of risks and costs of implementation.

Another follow-up meeting is held 6 months after the completion of the project with the same procedure followed. Since the bulk of the savings have generally taken place by this time, it is normally the last formal follow-up meeting by the corporate consultants. The corporate consultants are expected to maintain adequate records for internal reporting on the progress of the project implementation but will generally update their records by telephone after the second review meeting.

BACKGROUND

During the early 1970s, as a result of the recession, General Electric found itself overextended in terms of people and identified productivity of salaried personnel as one of the company's key corporate concerns. It was well recognized within the company that considerable effort had long been applied with good success in achieving productivity in the direct labor area, but there was a noticeable lack of identifiable programs, processes, or techniques for addressing the issue of productivity of salaried personnel. Accordingly, the Corporate Consulting Office was asked to develop a technique which could be used by operating components to address this issue.

After examining several approaches and techniques, the Corporate Consulting Office selected a process which was later to be called IN-TROSPECT. The name was selected to convey the idea of self-analysis, the ability of the organization to examine itself by looking inward. This concept was strengthened by another concept, the use of coconsultants or personnel from the organization to administer the process. It is this concept of self-analysis that has made the INTROSPECT program one of the most successful programs in the General Electric Company.

The pilot project was conducted in the Central Air-Conditioning Business and proved to be eminently successful. As a result, Corporate Consulting was asked to apply the process throughout the Consumer Sector and since then to all other sectors throughout the company.

The process has been modified, improved, and enhanced considerably over the past few years as a result of the experience obtained from the various applications throughout the company. More than 125 projects have been completed to date, with savings identified in excess of $100 million, and approximately 75 percent of these savings have been implemented so far. In the last 2 years, we have had requests from several other corporations to utilize the INTROSPECT process. At this time, we have applied it in a dozen or more companies, realizing the same potential for success as within General Electric.

It is expected that the INTROSPECT program will be applied ultimately to all organizations within the company. However, it is not to be looked upon as a one-shot process. Already we are developing ways to reapply the program to earlier components where projects were completed more than 3 years ago. In this respect, the process can be looked upon as a recycled or continuous process, applicable to any component which has allowed its organization to drift from the business objective or when the growth of salaried personnel has become excessive to their needs.

APPLICABILITY

Experience with many INTROSPECT projects has helped identify several success factors in analyzing an organization. The first, and probably the most important factor, centers on client managers. They must perceive the need for improving the organization and be strongly committed to implementing improvements. If the client manager is entering into the project unwillingly, or for reasons other than to improve the organization, the chances for success are greatly diminished. This is not to say that the demand for improvement cannot come from their superiors. Where this happens, *and* the client manager sees the INTRO-SPECT process as a means to an end, the project can be very successful. To ensure positive motivation of the client and to construct the work dictionary effectively, consultants should press clients to identify their project objectives, expectations, and concerns in great detail.

In addition to perceiving the need, the client must also have a commitment for implementing improvement. The most promising recommendations in the world, if not acted upon, cannot enhance productivity. The client may want to implement but simply not know how to do so, since recommendations can be far-reaching in their impact. To offset this, the consultant should develop a detailed implementation plan, and usher the client through it step by step to gain and ensure understanding and to promote positive action.

The next most important success factor is the selection of coconsultants. If this is done casually, and marginal or inappropriate people are selected, the project will surely fail. However, where this is done well and the proper personnel are selected, excellent recommendations are developed every time. Clients, of course, select the coconsultants, and their motivation or need for improvement serves as the driving force in the selection. However, the consultant can influence the process by stressing the role which the coconsultants are to play and by identifying specific criteria for the client to use in making the selection.

Also critical to the success of the project is the construction of the work dictionary. In order to collect the proper data for analysis, not only must the work dictionary contain selective activity terms but the level of detail must be appropriate. If the right activity terms are not included, no data are collected on the task in question and, therefore, no analysis can take place. If the activities are too broad, a level of detail is missed, making analysis very difficult if not impossible. If the activities are too detailed, the limitation on the number of activities that can be analyzed becomes a problem. To ensure an effective work dictionary, the previous two success factors become very critical. The project objectives have to be clear and concise in order to obtain the right level of detail, and the coconsultants have to be knowledgeable about the business and the organization in order to be sure that all work is covered properly and the terms are worded correctly. Where these conditions are met, the work dictionary construction can be accomplished properly and provide an excellent data base for critical analysis of the organization.

In summary, the INTROSPECT process can be a very effective tool in assisting an organization to analyze itself for improving salaried productivity. To be effective, however, the client must want to improve the organization and be committed to making changes in the structure of the organization and the work force of the people in the organization. Good coconsultants must also be selected. Where this is done properly, the INTROSPECT process can be highly successful in identifying direct savings, yielding 10 to 20 times the cost of the project. Furthermore, the process will impart to the organization certain principles, fundamentals, and concepts which will provide a lasting and beneficial impact.

REFERENCES

For additional information, General Electric's Corporate Consulting Services has available a brochure titled, "Employee Effectiveness—INTROSPECT" which contains an executive summary of the process. For greater depth of understanding, the procedure is detailed explicitly in the "INTROSPECT Analysis Handbook." To obtain additional information contact:

> Program Manager—INTROSPECT
> Corporate Consulting Services
> General Electric Company
> 1285 Boston Avenue (28EE)
> Bridgeport, CT 06602
>
> Phone: (203)382-2513

NOTES

[1] Currently vice president, manufacturing, Phelps Dodge Magnet Wire Company.

[2] All data are obtained from the house organization chart except for this column, which is obtained from other data reports explained later.

[3] The theoretical number of managers in this case was calculated as follows:

Sum of derived potential spans	= 44
Total number of managers	= 4
Average span: 44/4	= 11
Total number of workers	= 10
Theoretical number of managers: 11/10	= 1

[4] This includes the 10 previous workers plus 2 additional workers converted from managers.

[5] The norm is based on a large number of studies conducted within General Electric and other companies, and is accepted or modified by the consulting team.

CHAPTER SIX

Management by Objectives

GEORGE S. ODIORNE
Professor of Management, University of Massachusetts

Management by objectives (MBO) has been highly successful for many organizations, becoming the basis for a strong managerial philosophy which encourages the entire organization to be action-oriented toward efficiency, effectiveness, and fulfillment of basic organizational mission. Many other organizations have attempted the use of MBO with less than satisfactory results. This chapter is not intended to be a complete presentation of MBO but is a highlighting of some of the fundamentals which if not properly dealt with tend to limit its effectiveness. When the fundamentals are properly recognized and the organization is properly prepared to incorporate them into its own culture, success is usually achieved.

MBO is a way of getting improved results in managerial action. It is *not* an additional element of a manager's job but is a *way of doing the management job.* It is based on observations of what successful managers *do* in many companies and organizations (General Mills, General Motors, Minneapolis-Honeywell, IBM, General Electric, to name a few).

MBO is especially pertinent in *managing managers.* Its most common and most successful applications have been focused on upper levels of management. However, it can be (and has been) successfully extended down the organization to include first-line supervision, *where* top management endorses and supports it through using it themselves.

MBO relates to several key problems in managing an organization:

- It focuses on what is expected—in terms of objectives.
- It fosters teamwork—by identifying common goals.
- It programs work—by setting terminal dates for accomplishment of specific tasks.
- It recognizes "process"—through dialogue in establishing mutual agreement on goals and accomplishment toward them.
- It facilitates salary administration—providing a rational basis for rewarding performance and accomplishment.
- It helps to assess promotability—by identifying the potential for it.

In its briefest form, MBO can be described as a managerial method whereby the superior and subordinate managers identify major areas of responsiblity in which an individual will work, set some standards of performance for good (or bad) performance, and agree on the measurement of results against those standards.

The advantages of this kind of management are in better results, lower costs, improved performance, more promotable people, improved quality of service, more businesslike management of salaries, and development of subordinates' best abilities.

COMMON CONCERN IN MANAGING MANAGERS

In managing managers some areas of concern are chronic, recurring, and although often postponable, not cancelable. They include those things which can seldom be delegated to subordinates, since they are about those very subordinates and are matters of interest to them.

- *Pay raises:* Should the pay of a subordinate be increased, decreased, or left the same? How should salary increase funds be allocated among the respective subordinates?
- *Bonuses:* Upon what basis should available funds for managerial bonuses be distributed? How can this distribution be made so as to reflect actual contribution to the surplus which created the bonus? How can windfalls be prevented? How can hard luck be taken into consideration?
- *Promotability:* What are the elements in present performance which can be used to predict success or failure of a person who is promoted to a higher-level job? How does his or her present performance stack up against these indicators? To the extent that bad performance would be a bar to promotion, how good is the most recent performance record?
- *Performance reporting:* For purposes of filing accurate records of the performance for the past period, what entries should be made about an individual's achievements and failures to achieve?

- *Coaching and improvement counseling:* What matters in an individual's recent performance should be discussed with him or her? What results areas need betterment? In which ones is he or she doing an exceptionally fine job?
- *Management development:* Is there any kind of formal educational effort which might improve performance? Seminars? Attend a course? Join an association? Be given assignments which would enlarge experience?
- *Assignment for the future:* With respect to future jobs or tasks within the present job, should any changes be made? Should new responsibility be delegated?

The one common element in all these areas of concern is that they require discriminatory judgment about an individual's job performance and professional capacity as a manager.

WHAT MBO SHOULD ACCOMPLISH

As a result of managing by objective, several normal benefits of value to the organization and the individual should be made more likely.

A natural tendency toward "goals displacement" will be alleviated. There is some research which tends to show that in human organizations, a normal and perhaps natural (at least an explainable) tendency exists for people to start out toward momentarily clear goals but shortly to become so enmeshed with activity that the goal is lost. In its most aggravated form, the "activity" management becomes a matter of deep-rooted procedures (as with salary administration, job descriptions, etc.), and attempts to revert to basic purposes meet with strong resistance. (Do it my way.) MBO from the top management perspective is a direct attempt to build into management systems an unremitting attention to purpose.

Role conflict and ambiguity between individual managers and subordinates should be clarified. There is evidence that, left to their own devices, the average manager and subordinate manager are not apt to be in agreement about the subordinate manager's responsibilities in terms of outputs for any given period of time ahead.[1] Under such a lack of agreement it becomes impossible for the subordinate to "succeed," with corresponding ill effects in pay, bonus, promotion, and recorded performance reports. Even further ill effects ensue when coaching to "improve" the subordinate probes matters such as personality, attitude, motives, background, or similar proposed explanation of "failure." MBO attacks directly the gap of expectations and directly defines "success" in specific output terms.

MBO should be causally associated with overall success of the organization. Drucker has noted that in leading corporations like General Motors, Ford, IBM, and GE, where size has required divisionalized forms of organization, "Management Is Management by Objectives."[2] My own prolonged observation in leading firms is that in more successful firms (the ones that achieve goals) more people are aware of their goals than in less successful organizations. A manager at Sears knows goals better than the failing small merchant. Participative management is not uniformly present but is perhaps more possible under MBO than under intuitive or autocratic centralized management. This style is discretionary, but in many kinds of organization (where the people have been taught to expect it) it is mandatory to avoidance of disruption. Clarity of objectives between all links of individual managers is more likely to produce cumulative clarity of objectives. Thus MBO should improve overall organization performance and increase the level of participation.

Individuals who are clear about their job objectives have improved performance over individuals who are not clear. It is to be expected that individual performance will improve when individual goals are clarified, without seeking to achieve directly other side effects, even though they might well be predicted also. Questions of motivation, attitude, enthusiasm, and the alleviation of barriers to such activating forces are left to the individual for resolution. MBO should achieve such individual improvement and growth. The assumption here is an important one. MBO should be both *functional* (gets the job done) and *developmental* (helps the individual grow). This congruence is vital to the survival of our economic system and the social and political system so intimately associated with it. If individual growth and corporate success were necessarily antithetical, the system could be self-destructing. In adopting MBO as a system, we recognize that organizations create products and produce people who are workers as well. MBO thus appeals to higher-ranking, profit-oriented chief executives. It also meets the requirements of humanistic, personnel, and development staff persons.

MBO AS A MANAGERIAL STRATEGY

Management by objectives should provide a realistic tie between immediate operational controls and long-range planning, making them different dimensions of the same process.

The entire process of management includes the following ingredients:

- A long-range plan, say for 5 years, adjusted annually. That is, when the first year is completed and reviewed, the entire process is repeated. Thus the 5-year plan is produced *every year* by dropping the prior year and adding the next in order.
- Tighter controls for the first year and *commitments* from every manager.
- Quarterly review of results of interim adjustments of activities to adhere to the year's objectives.

- Some *indicators* or criteria for decisions. These are the overall guides, such as return on investment (ROI), which are the basic decision criteria against which company performance is measured.

Management by objective is *not a top-down-only process*. That is, the top-management 5-year plan is not made rigidly without room for accommodation for operating experience. Nor is it *exclusively a bottom-up process* in which short-run goals of people are added together and thus become the 5-year plan. MBO provides that yearly goals and the budgeting for each year will meld with long-run plans through dialogue and acceptance of each other's conclusions. This often occurs at the budget-making level of responsibility.

The MBO strategy implies that the following conditions must exist over the whole matrix of management:

- The business will be stable, that is, under control during the first year, and commitments made by people in manufacturing, selling, and staff work will be observed and results used for decisions and action in managing managers.
- Deviations from standard will be dealt with by responsible committed persons to restore normality when committed objectives are not being met.
- Innovation and improvement of regular operations, as well as strategic changes which affect the character of the organization, are placed high in the system of values which are rewarded and approved.

MBO's major function in operational management in the first year of the 5-year plan is the management of managers. Thus objectives agreed upon between manager and boss become the criteria for pay, bonus, promotion, coaching, training, and selection.

Staff work, especially at the corporate level, becomes that of "making and selling intangible products to internal captive markets." The major product line produced by staff departments includes the following outputs:

- *Advice:* Case load units, billable hours, and similar indicators
- *Service:* Doing something for line departments or other staff units which they cannot do as well for themselves as can the staff service unit, which has expert know-how or special tools
- *Controls:* The production of *information* which will assist in error prevention, error correction, and restoration of norms
- *Research:* New products, new ideas, trade advantages, monopolies, cost reductions, or answers to questions requiring analytical effort

THE O IN MBO

So far we have discussed generalities: what MBO is, how it is involved with some of the common concerns of managing managers, results associated with it, successful use, and how it relates to planning and operational control. MBO is managing by *objectives,* and we now turn our attention to establishing objectives.

Strategic Objectives

Individual objectives, the basic O of MBO, have limited utility for achieving desired MBO results unless they relate to and reinforce the objectives of the organization. The objectives of the organization likewise have limited utility unless they are related to and reinforce the strategies of the organization. Therefore, the logical starting point in developing individual objective statements is with definition of strategic objectives. The following key strategy questions, and perhaps others required to address the unique characteristics of an organization, are a good starter:

- *Market orientation:* Are we market-centered or technology-centered? Do we make things for the sales department to sell, or do we find market opportunities and invent things to fit?
- *Service:* How completely do we wish to follow up our product?
- *Top down or bottom up?* Do we have the top management (board, etc.) come up with the numbers for sales and growth and work back from the numbers at lower levels? Or do we collect the bottom-up goals and cumulate them to find the corporate goals?
- *Indicators:* What is the best indicator (or indicators) of total organization success? Dollar profit? Percent profit? Earnings per share? Return on investment? Return on gross assets? Market share?
- *Pricing:* Are we a market skimmer? A price cutter? Are we in price competition or nonprice competition?
- *Ethics:* Are we a "straight arrow" company, or do we consider ourselves "rough and tough" in dealing with competitors, suppliers, employees, customers?
- *Systematic:* Do we rely more on experience and personal know-how of managers than upon systems such as computers and analytical work?
- *Incentives:* Do we aim at sharing our profits and successes widely with employees, with just a few managers, or not at all?
- *Employee growth:* Do we spend resources to grow our own people, or do we let them take care of that themselves, and hire others from outside when a new demand for talent crops up?
- *Technology:* Are we a basic inventor and exploiter of our own research, or do we wait for others and assume a second-bite-of-the-apple approach to new technology?

- *Products:* Are we a Cadillac, a medium-price, or a low-price product company, or perhaps all of them?
- *Compensation:* Where do we wish to stand with respect to the community and competitive firms? Higher, the same, or lower?
- *Community relations:* Are we a community leader or a middle-of-the-road citizen, or do we remain low-profile and silent?
- *Government relations:* Do we respond when required, do we permit some affirmative actions toward government, or do we assume positive leadership and work to affect government?

Answers to the above questions can serve as the basis for preparation of definitions of strategic objectives. I have found the form in Fig. 6-1

Format for Annual Strategic Objectives Statements

1. Should be prepared 3 months in advance of budgeting decisions.
2. Should come up from below as proposed alternative strategies.
3. Should be prepared annually at <u>half-year</u>.

OUTLINE	COMMENTS

I. Describe the present condition, statistically and verbally (add your professional opinion) on:
  1. <u>Internally</u>: Strengths, weaknesses, problems?
  2. <u>Externally</u>: What are the threats, risks, and opportunities you see?
II. Trends: If we didn't do anything differently in this area, where would we be in 1-2-5 years? (Do you like this possible outcome?)
III. WHAT ARE THE MAJOR MISSIONS? What are we in business for? Who are our clients? What is our product? What should it be?	

IV. WHAT ARE SOME OPTIONAL STRATEGIES?	What would the consequences be?		
	Contribution	Costs	Feasibility
1. Do nothing differently. 2. _____ 3. _____ 4. _____ 5. _____ 6. _____ (Press for multiple options.)			

<u>Recommended Action Plan</u>: To be turned into OBJECTIVES

FIG. 6-1. Format for annual strategic objectives statements.

useful for this purpose. The annual strategic objectives statements set the stage for goal setting and for eventual definition of individual objectives statements.

Goal Setting

The two basic tools for setting goals are dialogue and a memo. The dialogue between boss and subordinate comes first and is the basis, eventually, for a memo from the boss to the subordinate which confirms in writing that which has been agreed to in discussion—the formal statement of the individual's objectives.

Three classes of goals are pertinent:

- Routine or regular duty goals
  Measured by: exception
  When? When exceptions occur, and with an annual review
- Problem-solving goals
  Measured by: solutions as promised in time
  When? When committed
- Innovative goals
  Measured by: stages of commitment
  When? When each stage is completed

These goals should be initiated by the individual, perhaps using a work sheet such as that shown in Fig. 6-2. They should be arranged to com-

---

OPERATING GUIDE FOR THE CONSTRUCTION
OF OBJECTIVES STATEMENTS

The following pages ask you to think about your present job, with your present boss, NOW and for the coming year . . .

Three kinds of responsibilities will be discussed, and you'll be asked to think through some questions about your plans for your job in the coming year. As a start you may want to set quarterly objectives, or you may wish to set them for a longer period (no more than a year).

1. The first sheet calls for you to define your regular, ordinary routine, or recurring responsibilities, and to state the range of acceptable outcomes in each area of responsibility.

2. The second sheet grows out of the answers to the first and asks you to define two or three present managerial problems you face in your job, and your plan for solving them in the year ahead. (List only the 2-3 that are most pressing or have the highest priority in your boss's eyes).

3. The third sheet asks for your statements on what innovations, changes, improvements to present conditions, your own managerial practices, or other internal departmental management you wish to study, work on, or install during the coming year.

FIG. 6-2. **Work sheets for initial statement of individual objectives.**

CATEGORY I. List below your regular, routine (job description) kinds of
responsibilities. Refer to your job or position description
if available. List the responsibilities down the left-hand
column. Always include the trade-off responsibilities; for
example, you can't shoot for production alone, you must
consider quality.

Across the top of the next three columns you'll note that a
single goal won't do; list a range of outcomes.

List your major regular responsibilities below. Include all trade-off responsibilities.	Indications of success in results		
	Minimum permissible or acceptable	Expected average	Maximum probable
1.			
2.			
3.			
4.			
5.			
6.			
7.			
8.			
9.			
10.			
11.			
Joint accountabilities (List major ones.)			
1. For: With:			
2. For: With:			

FIG. 6-2. (*Continued*)

II. What are the major managerial problems you face in your job now? (Any indicator of success that's gone wrong is a problem.)		
List 2 or 3 of them	What are the present conditions?	What would you like it to be?
1.	1.	1.
2.	2.	2.
3.	3.	3.

FIG. 6-2. (*Continued*)

III. Innovative goals

What new ideas do you plan to work on—study, suggest, or install—in your area of authority during the coming year?

Innovation can be thought of as "a new idea from outside," which adds to results.

1. Idea:

   When:

   How:

   Results:

2. Idea:

   When:

   How:

   Results:

FIG. 6-2. *(Continued)*

prise an ascending scale of managerial excellence. Regular performance is the minimum acceptable standard. Excellence emerges when the manager begins to display problem-solving and innovative behavior, and should be reflected in the areas of concern (when decisions are being made on pay, bonus, promotion, and performance reporting).

The dialogue(s) between manager and boss is based upon the individual's proposed set of objectives. The roles of the two in the goal-setting process and dialogue are along these lines:

- The subordinate proposes a set of standards for his or her job.
  The superior insists on realistic standards which challenge ability.
- The subordinate defines measures for gauging results.
  The superior asks how they are arrived at.
- The subordinate does the detailed analysis.
  The superior questions the methods.
- The subordinate suggests alternative actions.
  The superior suggests other possible actions where germane.
- The subordinate proposes more than one course of action.
  The superior forces a recommendation from the subordinate.
- The subordinate predicts the effect of goals.
  The superior gets commitments from the subordinate and makes commitments to the subordinate.

Goals should be stated in a form that facilitates their use in measurement of results at a future time. They should be stated in a way that will probably influence behavior and results, and not simply set out in writing those activities which would be performed anyway, even if they were not discussed and confirmed in writing. They should be stated to facilitate their use during the following period, for self-guidance and self-feedback, and as a working tool which may be modified and revised by joint agreement.

PERFORMANCE APPRAISAL AND MBO

Feedback affects people's job performance. One kind of feedback subordinates receive is the information, praise, criticism, and reward given during *periodic* performance reviews. But this kind of feedback is not enough to get people performing the way they should and to keep them performing that way. This is true because subordinates receive another kind of feedback—*continuous* feedback. It comes from their coworkers, from customers, from their families, or from the job itself.

Sometimes this continuous feedback competes with the feedback provided by the boss. There are several possible reasons for this. First, there's simply more of it. The chances are pretty good that the boss will simply be outweighed by the massive amount of feedback subordinates receive from other sources. A second closely related reason continuous feedback may have more influence is its immediacy; it happens immediately after a person does something. And people are influenced more by feedback they have just received than by the same feedback when received hours, days, or months later.

A third reason continuous feedback may have more influence is that it is often in direct conflict with the goals and standards established in periodic review sessions. For example, if you want workers to conform to safety regulations but they figure out that they can make more money by violating these regulations, you may discover someday that they are systematically ignoring the rules. They can and do identify the favorable and unfavorable consequences of performing in a desired and undesired way.

To counterbalance the effects of continuous feedback coming from coworkers, the job, etc., a continuous feedback system should be established by the boss for each subordinate. And this is how feedback and appraisal fit into the management by objectives system. Once boss and subordinate have agreed upon major areas of responsibility and have established standards of performance in each, a continuous feedback system is set up by identifying some indicators both the boss and subordinate watch continuously so each can compare actual results with planned results.

Now that the boss and the subordinate have a means for knowing how the subordinate stands at all times, it is up to the boss to provide some favorable consequences when standards are met and some unfavorable consequences when the subordinate fails to meet them. If you know in advance that you cannot do this—or that the consequences you can provide simply are not strong enough to compete with those that come from other sources—recognize that the chances of getting desired performance are pretty slim. So do not set goals that fly in the face of reality.

Because both the boss and the subordinate have a way to monitor performance continuously, the annual performance review turns out not to be a review at all (you both already know how the subordinate has done). It is almost exclusively a planning and goal-setting session. The only reason to look at the past is to see what a standard was and to determine whether this standard is a desirable one to use for the future.

Appraisal forms are an extremely important aspect of this entire process. This is true for two reasons: (1) the appraisal form itself will undoubtedly affect the way people are appraised and (2) it can be one of the mechanisms which will provide continuous feedback to subordinates. It should include a clear statement of the person's objectives in terms of results anticipated. It can also specify the plans he or she will follow to meet those objectives. The form should be set up in such a way as to provide a running account—a *progress* record—of the individual's achievements. Finally, an appraisal form should not attempt to classify, categorize, label, or rate a person's performance in some abstract way. It should specify what a person agreed he or she would attempt to achieve and then record what actually was achieved.

IMPLEMENTING MBO

It is not likely today that many managers will object to management by objectives as a concept or philosophy. The question of available alternatives seems unanswerable in the face of such an eminently logical developmental system. Why, then, do people seem to have reservations about committing themselves to it? Why, indeed, do some find it impossible to make it work, while others report great success in its application and enthusiasm for its effects?

One of the major reasons for the failure of MBO in many organizations is that those in charge fail to recognize the political character of the implementation process. MBO is indeed logical and systematic, but it also must deal with a number of factors, including power and authority, the organization form, and the values and expectations of people. The MBO implementer must therefore recognize the reality of political constraints and manage them during the process of implementation.

If this is not done, MBO may start off with a flourish but gradually fade away; begin well, reach a certain level, and stall; or start well but produce a dramatic failure and be dropped, becoming a taboo subject thereafter. Success, on the other hand, results when MBO begins at a sound level of acceptance, gains from its own successes, continues to flourish and expand its influence and contributions, and is widely appreciated and supported.

Case studies of successful and unsuccessful implementation plans show that three major avenues are currently used for implementation of MBO and that all three must be modified by political constraints characteristic of every organization. The three approaches will be briefly illustrated, and then the political considerations that must guide them will be described.

Three Approaches

Methods of implementing MBO may rely on the use of raw power and direct orders, persuasion, or education. Case studies indicate that no one route is best; instead, analysis of the organizational climate and the situation will indicate the best approach—one alone or perhaps a combination of all of them. A specific set of steps in linear form would be highly desirable, but such a method would probably miss the mark and lead to an implementation that fails in one or more respects.

Authoritarian directives It is an article of faith, supported by some research evidence, that the installation of MBO must start at the top. In part, such a beginning is justified. The purpose of the business flows down and the methods for achieving the purpose flow up. The strategies of the business are chosen by persons with high-level responsibility, whereas the operational objectives are the responsibility of lower levels. This might lead to the conclusion that the power of the higher ranks must be invoked to direct implementation. This approach is founded upon the assumption that if the president issues the right directives, everybody below will obey. The concept is that of the self-executing order, a rare phenomenon.

Behavioral scientists deplore such autocratic methods, but they are used in some organizations where tight technical organization and discipline are the mode of operation. Where the following conditions exist in the organization, such authoritarian methods will indeed work:

- The leader has absolute power and is willing to use it.
- Followers need the leader more than the leader needs them, because he or she can withhold knowledge, skills, or resources which they need.
- The followers have lived under unexplained orders for some time, perhaps for their entire working lifetime, and have learned to expect them, even when the subject is MBO.
- The situation requires autocratic orders. The leader is expected to state orders quickly and clearly if he or she is in charge of a ship at sea in a storm, an airplane in distress, or a temporary work force.

Under proper circumstances, autocratic implementation of MBO has been successful. That is not to say that all situations demand it; many are not suitable for autocracy—the college faculty or the volunteer group, for example. The major limitations of the use of force to implement MBO lie in the situation in which it is applied. Where the boss has no power or has power and will not use it, the followers expect to be consulted and have something important to withhold (and will do so). Under these circumstances, the authoritarian directive will produce counterresponses that block MBO.

Persuasion   One reason for the failure of MBO to achieve its full potential has been the misguided reliance upon persuasion as a means of implementation. The guru or inspirational speaker comes to a meeting of management and through hortatory lectures persuades everyone that MBO will be beneficial. Persuasion methods ordinarily can be distinguished by their content.

First, they appear to be balanced, that is, they explain all the advantages of MBO, then turn and judiciously explain the disadvantages of not managing by objectives. This is clearly an advocacy approach designed to persuade.

Second, features and benefits are grist for the persuader's mill. A description of the features and a discussion of the usefulness of each are persuasive tactics.

Third, in this debater's form of persuasion, all the alternatives for solving some chronic problems are noted. Then each is knocked out in turn, except the MBO solution.

The *fourth* form of persuasion, incrementalism, is probably the most risky. It consists of starting with a simple segment of the whole program and selling it. "You simply sit down once a year with all your subordinates, and talk to them about their objectives" would be an incremental approach. Many instances of MBO failure have been caused by incrementalism in the introduction. The concept began as a change in the company performance appraisal system or as a salary review plan but lost favor when the full implications of the time and effort demanded were realized.

Persuasion is the favorite method of hortatory speakers and consultants. It is detested and avoided by academics who would prefer an approach that relies almost wholly upon education, particularly in the underlying theory. As a complete method of installation, it obviously leads to disillusionment. Yet it has a useful part in implementation in the early stages, if only to get people to submit to education.

Educational programs   One of the more successful patterns for installing an MBO program is a continuous educational effort which teaches the concepts, philosophy, and procedures of MBO in detail. As a training subject, MBO has many excellent features. Training should produce behavior change, and training in MBO is measurable. It can readily be determined if the training worked: Did the trainees set objectives or did they not? The quality of the results can be noted clearly. The course may suggest, for example, that a manager should establish three classes of objectives. The effect on the manager can be checked by examining sample goals statements.

MBO comprises a sound basis for relating training to the job. Some training sessions require students to set objectives on their job as part of the course; they learn by doing what they are being taught.

MBO provides a vehicle for teaching more general management education. It can be the framework for teaching motivational methods, management functions (organizing, planning, and controlling), and such interpersonal skills as coaching, counseling, and listening.

MBO can teach interpersonal skills that can be applied on the job, rather than skills which the boss will not permit or endorse when the trainee returns to the desk or plant floor. This is especially true if the boss attends the session or is used as a trainer.

MBO can reinforce company objectives rather than become, as it does in many behavioral courses, an internal reform movement to overcome the organization's autocratic or bureaucratic tendencies or to produce some new kind of organizational form.

MBO is capable of maintaining a high level of trainee interest, since it deals with the real world of work and work problems, and with interpersonal and group relations problems. Conceptually, it is easy to learn, for MBO training courses ask people to "talk shop"; they have a tendency to do this whether they are in training or not. Except for courses in which the trainers have worked hard at obscuring the obvious, the language is operational and practical.

The basic framework of MBO permits it to take a behavioral or logical systems direction without appearing contradictory or mutually exclusive. This means that it can appeal to the personnel and training people in the organization, as well as to the engineer, controllers, and dollar-centered managers. Both insiders and outsiders can be used as trainers. The insiders have more knowledge of the business and can deal with real world problems, and the outsiders can be briefed sufficiently to relate to the world of the trainee.

SUMMARY

The foregoing materials all explain the highlights with some specific details on MBO and how it operates, its theory and practice. Yet knowledge of such materials can be enhanced only if it is tried. The intellectual exercise of understanding cognitively is made real only by specific application, skill, and practice in goal setting and managing by objectives. Two uses of the materials in this chapter suggest themselves: first for those who use MBO and wish to do it better, and second for those not using MBO who wish to be successful in doing it well from the start.

For the Advanced Practitioner

MBO is not a static process but a dynamic and evolving one. The idea that MBO is a cookbook set of procedures which will be self-executing is of course a major fallacy. Rather, it requires some specific follow-through actions.

1. Continual study and improvement of the MBO program or procedures is needed to make it successful. When a problem arises, you must deal with the problem rather than abandon the valuable process as deficient. MBO has been abandoned more often by people who were not doing it well than by people who found it theoretically wrong or inconsequential.

2. Other subsystems of management must be results-centered. You must select by objectives, train by objectives, gear your pay systems to objectives, and budget against objectives. It is more than a simple procedure for performance appraisal: it is a way of managing, not an addition to the job of the manager.

For the Beginner

In starting to manage by objective there are some fundamental guides which this chapter has spelled out but which need reinforcement.

1. You must start at the top of the organization which is to be managed by objectives. If the program is company-wide, it must start with the chief executive. If it is plant-wide, it must start with the plant manager. It cannot survive without support and endorsement at the top.

2. Everyone who is to use the system must be trained in its basic principles and practices, with specific cases and examples being employed. Training exercises which require as part of their work the creation of actual objectives in class setting but carried back to the job will make it work far better.

3. It takes an investment of time, hours of staff and managerial energy, and patience with the problems which occur because of the unique nature of your organization. It is not a quickie program or a one-shot program. It cannot be done overnight.

4. The program must grow to meet the changes that occur in the firm, the environment, and the culture within which it is implanted.

5. It should have widespread acceptance of those affected, and that acceptance is best achieved through letting them participate in the shaping of the specifics of the program and its execution.

NOTES

[1] N. R. F. Maier, L. R. Hoffman, J. J. Hooven, and W. H. Read, "Superior-Subordinate Communication in Management," AMA Research Study 52, 1961.

[2] Peter Drucker, *The Practice of Management,* Harper & Row, New York, 1954.

SOME SUGGESTED FURTHER READING

Drucker, Peter: *The Practice of Management,* Harper & Row, New York, 1954. This is generally agreed to be the first writing about MBO. One chapter on MBO in this book defines its basic *concept.*

McGregor, Douglas: *The Human Side of Enterprise,* McGraw-Hill, New York, 1961. In this germinal book McGregor dealt with MBO as a system of humanizing management and especially the appraisal process. Combined with Druker, it was an important work in human aspects of MBO.

Odiorne, George S.: *Management by Objectives; A System of Managerial Leadership,* Fearon Pitman, New York, 1965. This was the first book with the title *Management by Objectives.* Now in its second edition (1979), it deals with both the conceptual and human aspects, and describes MBO as a *system.*

The Management by Objective Institute, Bowling Green State University, College of Business, Management Development Center, Bowling Green, Ohio 43403, is the professional organization of specialists in the field. They sell a comprehensive bibliography of some 3000 written books and articles on MBO. This reference book is the most exhaustive and comprehensive list of references on the subject.

PART THREE

Functional Activity/Work Structure

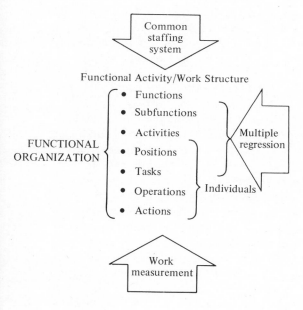

The functional activity/work structure *is an elaboration of the functional organization. Enhancement of white collar productivity which results from analysis within this structure is largely associated* with measurement *of white collar work efforts, and is based upon an assumption that the functional organization and its elaboration possess validity (in the sense that this term has been defined in Chapter 2).*

Each function is divided into subfunctions, which are accomplished by various activities. Positions and tasks are defined as necessary for accomplishing the activities. Each position is responsible for a variety of tasks, which are composed of a variety of operations. Each operation is accomplished by the execution of sets of actions.

The first approach is from the bottom up, measuring the white collar resource required to execute a set of actions which are required to accomplish a specific operation or unit of work. The work-measurement approach is presented in Chapter 7, by Robert E. Nolan, who shares his extensive experience in work measurement in the office environment. His approach is to treat work measurement, extensively and in its historical development context, as an important element of work management.

Work management implies concern for the design of jobs, work flow, and work scheduling, with emphasis on facilitating supervisory performance in the effective management of the work and people for which one is responsible.

Work measurement and work management, as presented, are most directly applicable to jobs and work activity which are structured and repetitive—and which have directly observable "actions" which result in completion of an operation or unit of work accomplishment. The approach can be extended to encompass "technician" jobs which involve creative and decision-making elements.

Anyone interested in white collar productivity should understand what can be done to measure and to more effectively manage the use of the human resources which are involved in the area of applicability presented by Robert Nolan. As you progress through his chapter it will be useful to refer back to the basic concepts presented in Chapter 2, and also to those of Chapters 3 and 4.

The second approach is an in-between one, typically dealing with an aggregation of operations and tasks, focusing on activities, projects, and subfunctions. White collar resources associated with accomplishment are related by statistical analysis with various characteristics of the tasks, projects, or activities such that a predictive equation is developed. This predictive equation allows determination of white collar resources which should be required to accomplish a desired aggregate result. This approach will be presented in Chapter 8, by Douglas C. Crocker. His approach includes presentation of the basic concepts of multiple linear regression and its application. He also presents a useful conceptual structure for white collar work activities, which encompasses a spectrum from the highly structured work for which Robert Nolan's work measurement/work management approach is particularly suited on to activities which are highly unstructured. He provides the approach of an accomplished statistician and knowledgeable measurement system designer to dealing with the realities of work "measurement" across the entire spectrum, but mainly in the area beyond "work" measurement.

The third approach is from the top of the structure down, focusing on measurement of white collar activities which support subfunctions and functions. This is done by exhaustively defining all white collar activities according to the associated subfunction and function, and then measuring these activities in terms of resources utilized and the magnitude of work-cause indicators. Partial productivity measures are developed which are useful for comparative evaluation over time and among organizational units for all white collar activities, aggregated in various ways. This approach is presented in Chapter 9 by its originator, David L. Conway. His approach is conceptually related to Douglas Crocker's but involves a less rigorous statistical analysis. Gross relationships between groupings of functional activities and indicators of work causes are developed in order to gain insights into how productivity might be enhanced.

Each of these approaches to white collar measurement has utility but is distinctly different from the others. Which approach is appropriate for enhancing white collar productivity depends upon the specific situation. It is quite likely that all three will be useful for many organizations, as they are complementary to one another.

CHAPTER SEVEN

Work Measurement

ROBERT E. NOLAN
President, Robert E. Nolan Company

The term work measurement conjures up a wide range of images—and not all are good. In the most simple terms, it is a means of establishing what a fair day's work should be. It has two main components—a measure of the volume of work, and a measure of the employee time used up. These two factors can be expressed in their only common denominator: the time required to produce one unit of work, or what we call a standard.

There are negative connotations as well, not the least of which is getting people to work harder. Another dimension of the same connotation is getting more work out of fewer people.

Positive aspects are that work measurement is essential to high performance and high productivity. It is only a tool to be used by enlightened managers and supervisors to help them to plan, organize, direct, and control the resources that they manage: the human, material, and financial resources.

Work measurement of office activities is quite different in many respects from work measurement of factory-type activities. In factories, there is usually a high volume of work, and the work is performed in short cycles. Also, the operator performs the work while in a fairly stationary position. In offices only a small percentage of the work consists of highly repetitive, short-cycle operations. Those tasks, for the most part, have already been automated. Therefore, work is generally not very routine or repetitive, and the employee can move around a great deal.

Furthermore, it is erroneous to think only of clerical work when referring to measurable office activities. The state of the art, in terms of both techniques and approaches, has enabled us to measure work beyond the clerical level—to jobs at the technical and professional level. For that matter, we can establish a form of accountability for virtually every job in the office. But more on this later.

Another term that has gained greater acceptance is work management. Where work measurement measures performance and determines proper staffing, work management takes on a much broader concept. Indeed, work measurement is an important part of work management, but it also considers the design of the job, work flow and work scheduling, and the emphasis is on how the supervisor can use the information to manage work and people most effectively.

Work management is a management tool based on the use of scientific principles with the aim of ascertaining both the cost of labor in productive situations and procedures by which that cost might be effectively reduced.

ORIGIN OF WORK MEASUREMENT

In an atmosphere of keen competition and plunging profits, business and industry seek desperately for techniques which will enable them to restore their original, logical organization. In such an atmosphere, in the early nineteen hundreds, Frederick W. Taylor outlined his solution to management's problem. He attempted to organize and clearly define work tasks. He clearly stated his basic philosophy as follows: "The greatest production results when each worker is given a definite task to be performed in a definite time in a definite manner."

Although Dr. Taylor's theoretical approach is as sound today as it was over 60 years ago, his lack of tolerance and concern for employees, coupled with management's eagerness to realize the savings immediately, gave this fresh approach its first black eye. The scientific analyst became known as an "efficiency expert," a "hatchet man." While management reveled in the spoils made possible by his work, labor condemned it. In 1912, a congressional investigation was conducted on the moral implications of "scientific" management (our quotation marks).

Paralleling Taylor's work were the studies of Frank B. Gilbreth, an engineer, and Lillian Gilbreth, his wife, who was trained in psychology. This merging of backgrounds resulted in a sound and objective approach tempered with understanding and consideration for the factors motivating employees. Rather than force employees into the pattern of a job, work was reorganized around the needs of the individual.

The Gilbreths refined methods study to an exacting discipline by breaking down complex tasks into basic elements of motion. Their studies paved the way for a major advancement in scientific measurement techniques. Analysts and engineers began to realize that methods work and time study were not distinct but rather were inseparably linked. With basic elements of motion defined, the next step, obviously, was to assign time values to these elements. However, it was not until the early forties and the work of Harold Maynard, Gustave Stegemerten, and John Schwab that a system merging time and methods techniques gained wide acceptance. These men developed a system based on elemental motion patterns, to which time values were assigned. They called this system methods-time measurement (MTM). This approach and others (like Segur's work factor) eliminated the subjective judgment of employee skill and effort so essential to stopwatch techniques and in its place provided an accurate, universal standard. Today it provides the standardized data upon which the sophisticated and complex work-measurement programs of many businesses and industries are based.

SCIENTIFIC MANAGEMENT

Management has been defined as the art and science of directing and controlling human activity toward specific goals. Therefore, a means of guiding and measuring the performance of the people involved in an enterprise is vital to management.

Good managers at any level of the organization must understand their responsibilities. As a directive force in the area for which they have responsibility, they must have factual data on which to base decisions and determine courses of action so as to produce, with the staff that they direct, purposeful results that are in harmony with the objectives of the company.

The soundest basis for a decision or for planning a course of action is knowledge derived by logically considering the relevant facts. When action is objectively planned, it may be directed toward purposeful goals. As the action is carried out, it may be continuously guided to the desired end. On the other hand, when action springs from unsupported opinion, it is unplanned and cannot be directed toward purposeful goals; efforts to control its course usually prove fruitless.

Experience amply demonstrates the pitfalls of subjective decisions and unplanned action. Enlightened leadership in business emphasizes reliance upon maximum objectivity in reaching decisions, thus minimizing irrelevant, subjective, and intuitive influences. The attainment of major goals is controlled by checking performance against objectively established standards, plans, schedules, or budgets until the goals are achieved. This has come to be known as scientific management.

APPLICATION OF
WORK MEASUREMENT

Obtaining optimum human performance—consistent with social responsibilities and moral and legal requirements—has long been a primary concern of management. This applies not only to managerial performance itself but to the performance of the entire work force: messengers, clerks, stenographers, accountants, technicians, analysts, and supervisors.

To obtain optimum performance in the office, the work must be analyzed in accordance with well-defined procedures. Account must be taken of the physical disposition of the workplace as well as of the office machines, forms, and other aids employed in the work. The exact (and when feasible, the best) method for performing the work must be defined in terms of human capability. When methods so defined are put into action by carefully selected workers who are trained under enlightened supervision, optimum performance becomes attainable.

Work-measurement techniques, then, are concerned with three basic questions. First, what is the capability of the employee in the specific work situation studied? Second, how may the employee's capacity best be applied to performing the work? And third, what is the time required to perform the individual jobs comprising the work? The moral and ethical values by which human conduct is guided and limited should be kept constantly in mind while resolving these questions.

The unequal degree of motivation of managers, supervisors, and the personnel comprising their staffs makes the establishment of uniform work standards highly desirable. Work standards establish a basis for letting all employees know what is expected of them, and of relating their individual activities to the objectives of the group and of the entire organization. Impartial administration of fair standards reduces the incidence of opinionated or prejudicial treatment of employees.

When clearly defined goals and work standards are established for a group of employees, the degree of attainment of standard performance measures the effectiveness of the group. Less than satisfactory attainment immediately indicates lack of control and the need for investigation to determine what corrective action will spur improvement. Superior attainment, on the other hand, provides a basis for recognition of performance that furthers the objectives of the organization.

Measurement of performance provides a basis for letting employees know how they are doing in relation to what is expected of them, and how they are doing in relation to fellow employees. In addition, it provides a basis for letting management know how all the employees and units are performing.

A comparison of the work load of a group of employees (standard hours required to perform the work at the normal pace of average, well-trained employees) with the actual hours worked will accurately determine any excess or shortage of personnel of various types and skills. No more reliable means exists for determining and forecasting worker power requirements.

The excess of personnel, taken at average salary rates, measures the dollar value of losses due to below-standard performance attributable to such factors as insufficient work load, poor scheduling, inadequate training of personnel, excess staff, or ineffective supervision. This dollar figure measures the value to the organization of the potential savings that might be realized if performance were brought up to standard. Excess capacity and potential savings may be related directly to worker power budgets and other financial controls established by management.

For the sake of orientation, we will pause a moment before we make the transition into various techniques and approaches. Looking briefly at past mistakes, we can make an outline of the points a work-measurement program must encompass to succeed:

1. Time standards should be accurate and based on the most efficient method of performing an operation.

2. Due consideration must be given to individuals and the factors which motivate and control their behavior.

3. Work must be organized and defined so that employees know their responsibilities and what is expected of them.

4. Any plan or program resulting from work-measurement studies should have built into it provisions for implementing possible savings without resorting to abusive and unjust labor practices.

Work measurement is a valuable tool when applied by competent analysts. The results of a sound program will provide management with the information necessary to control employment, salaries, and work loads. In other words, it will aid management in reducing costs. But "No one gets something for nothing" is an axiom especially true in work measurement. Before management can save money through work measurement, it must be willing to spend money to establish a workable plan and train competent analysts.

The minimum requirements for a successful application of work measurement to establish cost controls are an understanding of company objectives and policies; a thorough knowledge of office work, office methods, and office people; and a background of practical experience in developing new procedures and introducing innovations into the typical office situation.

When these requirements are lacking, they can be gained partly by study and training and partly by experience under skilled guidance. But they should be present in some form before an attempt is made to establish cost controls based upon work measurement.

Work management is a more responsible, scientific, and professional way to manage a business that develops the confidence and enthusiasm of workers at all levels of the organization. The bottom line is cost reduction to the tune of 20 to 40 percent of payroll costs, better service to customers, and better morale of employees at all levels.

Basically, it involves a program to improve performance through work management. Many have failed because they limited their objectives to reducing costs, and did so in a manner that was offensive to supervisors and employees. There is an approach that has proved to be successful in accomplishing the desired objectives while not offending the people. It is called "participative performance improvement." This means, simply, that employees and supervisors have a participative role in the development of standards that directly affect them.

EMPLOYEE PARTICIPATION

The employee plays a vital role in the development of a work-measurement or work-management program. Employees should have a clear understanding of what the program is designed to accomplish and how they fit in. They should be able to determine how they will benefit from standards.

The employees who perform the tasks should be considered the experts in defining tasks and evaluating how they can be improved. Also, they should have as good an understanding as possible of the standard, what is included in it, and upon what method it is based, and they should have a feeling of confidence that the time allowed is fair.

EMPLOYEE ATTITUDES

Based on attitude surveys conducted by various management consulting firms throughout the country, the most common complaint from people at all levels of the organization is, "I am not recognized for the work that I do."

If you had the proper authority to do so, you could walk up to any employee in your company and say, "I want to be sure that you are properly recognized for your contribution to this company. What are the things I need to know in order to give you the recognition you deserve?" The answer will invariably be the same. The employee will say, "If you knew how much work I do (quantity), and how well I do it (quality), you would have a good start."

People should be recognized for how well they perform their jobs. It naturally follows that their pay should be based on how well they perform their jobs. If you accept this premise, you will have a better understanding of the modern concept of work management that is being introduced in offices throughout the country.

PARKINSON'S LAW

Many managers feel their people are already producing to their optimum capacity. Are they that good? Probably not! Parkinson's law, named after the noted author C. Northcote Parkinson, states that "Work expands so as to fill the time available for its completion."

Employees quickly learn that being idle is unacceptable behavior in certain offices, particularly where a manager takes pride in running a tight ship. An hour's worth of work can become two hour's worth of work by stretching it out, double-checking things that need not be double-checked, and keeping extra records that they really do not need but now have the time to keep. Unfortunately, what happens when the work load increases is that they continue to keep the extra records and perform the unnecessary checking.

WORK MEASUREMENT—A TOOL FOR PROGRESS

Work-measurement results will enable us to quantify specific goals and let us know on a continuing basis how well we are doing toward achieving those goals. Without standards, individuals can never really reach their full potential.

Because no two supervisors operate in exactly the same style, it is hard to isolate a factor or combination of factors most responsible for successful leadership on the job. One successful supervisor may emphasize certain things, and an equally effective colleague may ignore them while stressing others.

Research has shown, however, that certain kinds of action increase a supervisor's chances of succeeding. And near the top of the list is the setting of high work standards. One leading industrial relations expert says he has never yet studied a highly productive group where the supervisor has not given special attention to maintaining high standards.

Many experiences seem to confirm this idea. Think back to the best teacher you ever had. Did he or she expect much of you or little? We can safely predict the answer. The outstanding teacher extended you to the utmost. And it was not always fun.

People are often capable of much more than they realize. Sports records illustrate this point. The 4-minute mile, the 15-foot pole vault, the 60-foot shot put, and the 7-foot high jump all seemed unattainable—until someone reached each of these marks. Then others came along and surpassed the feat. Tourist parties now scramble to the top of mountains that once seemed unclimbable.

The same things happen at work. Industrial engineers often find that their greatest problem is to convince a group that a production figure is possible. When people see that a mark is attainable, they often exceed it with comparative ease.

Sometimes in business, however, we encounter the principle working in reverse. Standards may slip to lower and lower levels. Where little has been required of people over a long period, individuals may become accustomed to a low output, unaware that they are no longer doing a full share. This may become painfully apparent when circumstances change and they are asked once again to carry a full work load.

The supervisor, of course, is not the only force working toward excellence. Nor can we assume that people are always wishing for an easier path. One experiment has shown that workers in the right climate will often set higher standards than their supervisor or an outside analyst. But, however the goals are set, the conclusion is inescapable: we can never get high performance without high standards.

WHAT IS A STANDARD?

A "standard" is defined as "any accepted or established rule, model, or criterion against which comparisons are made—that which is set up and established by authority as a rule for the measure of quantity, weight, extent, value, or quality." Golf is a good example of a standard in personal life. Par is the standard. Our measurement is the number of strokes taken. Comparing strokes with par lets us know how we are doing in relation to what is expected.

Consciously or otherwise, we measure almost everything we do. When we buy, price is our standard. In cases of extreme temperature, we look to the weather bureau to tell us how hot or cold we can expect to be. The very habits of our living we call a "standard of living."

Standards are in use everywhere. In the home, how much time is required to prepare a roast for dinner, or boil an egg, or bake rolls? How early must we set the alarm in the morning to allow enough time to rise, exercise, shower, dress, eat breakfast, and get to work on time? In recreation we refer to the team bowling average, the limit for trout, and how long it ordinarily takes to drive to the party on Saturday night. In the office we use typing words per minute, how much time it takes to walk to the cafeteria, and how long to schedule a meeting for.

THE QUESTION OF ACCURACY

If you ask the average industrial engineer or office work-measurement analyst what is most important in a measurement technique, he or she will respond "accuracy." Ask, "how accurate?" and the response will usually be, "as accurate as can be." The fact is that accuracy has little to do with measurement. It is an economic, not engineering, consideration.

The accuracy of standards, however, can be grouped in three categories: loose, accurate, and tight. Here the term accurate takes on a whole new meaning. Perhaps the best word to equate with accurate is fair. Fair to whom? Fair to the employee in terms of being realistic and attainable, but also fair to management as a fair price to pay for work. It is also called a "fair day's work pace" or "a dollar's worth of work for a dollar's worth of pay."

A loose standard is a generous standard and allows more time than is necessary to perform a function. Employees do not object to a loose standard, but it is unfair to management.

A tight standard requires a worker to work at a pace that results in undue fatigue or is simply unattainable. To reverse the point made previously, a tight standard may seem entirely fair to management, but it is unfair to the worker. If workers attained tight standards, they would be giving management more labor than management was paying for.

Workers want to know what is expected of them. If the standards are reasonable, they will produce what is expected. But if the standards are loose, will they produce more than is expected? Generally not—at least not without some form of additional or special reward or compensation. If standards are tight, they may be ineffective, because people will not even try to meet them.

The conclusions are obvious. From the employer's point of view, the tighter the standard, the lower the cost of labor, the greater is the profit. Let us say that the value of an application is $2.00. If we develop an engineered standard that equates to a labor cost of $1.00 per application, and we can encourage the employees to meet that standard, the profit can be $1.00 per application. On the other hand, if we establish a loose standard that equates to a labor cost of, say, $1.67 per application, the profit will be only $0.33 per application.

When standards are set casually or unscientifically, the tendency is to err on the high side. Whenever rough standards are developed, the standard setter will be sure to inflate the time standard to cover every possible contingency to be certain that the standard can be met.

BENCHMARKS OF PERFORMANCE

A standard is equated to a fair day's work pace, or what we can call 100 percent performance. Now, 100 percent is not the maximum; it is not perfection. We define 100 percent as "the work pace at which an average, well-trained employee can work without undue fatigue while producing an acceptable quality of work." This means that a 100 percent performance pace is one that an average, well-trained employee should be expected to maintain all day long. It is a "normal" working pace—not too fast and not too slow.

It is extremely important for people who set standards to have a good understanding of this concept of "normal." Industrial engineers usually spend weeks working with rating films to understand the concept of normal. Once a clear understanding of normal is developed in the mind of the engineer or analyst, he or she can observe an employee's work pace on any type of operation and rate that individual's performance or

FIG. 7-1. Accepted benchmarks of performance.

pace. If the pace is faster than normal, the engineer determines (usually to the nearest 5 percent) that the individual is working at a pace above 100 percent—perhaps 105, 110, or 115 percent. Naturally, the method the individual is using, as well as the amount of skill and effort the individual is exerting, are taken into consideration when performance is rated.

Figure 7-1 shows the generally accepted benchmarks of performance equated with a concept of a normal, 100 percent engineered level of performance. When we speak of an engineered standard, we refer to a standard based on good, sound methods and procedures, and corresponding with our definition of 100 percent.

50 Percent Performance

As a benchmark, 50 percent is considered the average level of performance before formal controls are applied. The range is usually 40 to 60 percent. Now, 50 percent performance does not mean that people work for an hour and do nothing the next hour, or work 4 hours and do nothing the other 4 hours of the day. What it does mean is that people accomplish about half of what could be accomplished after standards are applied to the work.

70 Percent Performance

This is generally regarded as the minimum tolerable level of performance. If employees, after a reasonable training period, cannot perform to at least 70 percent of standard, it is simply not economical to keep them in that position . . . taking up floor space, a work station, a desk, a typewriter, etc.

Let us say you have an employee who can perform no better than 60 percent of standard. Not only is management getting only $60 worth of work for every $100 of salary, but it is also getting only 60 percent return on fringe benefits, floor space, equipment being used, and so on.

100 Percent Performance

This, of course, is the fair day's work level—the level where a dollar's worth of work presumably is equal to a dollar's worth of pay. This is the goal for all employees, and it is the goal for all supervisors and managers to achieve for their section or department.

An interesting question arises when we speak of 100 percent performance: are all employees who have passed the training stage of their job capable of achieving and maintaining 100 percent performance? For example, in typing we might equate 100 percent performance with 55 words per minute. Do all people in typing jobs today possess the mental and physical dexterity to achieve and maintain a 55-words-per-minute level or better? Similarly, in coding operations, we might require employees to be able to memorize at least half the codes to perform at 100 percent performance. Do all people who perform coding operations possess that mental capacity for memorization? The answer is no, all people are not capable of performing consistently at the 100 percent performance level. Maintaining high levels of performance day in and day out requires a certain amount of concentration and perseverance. This is why we feel that 85 percent is the start of the acceptable range of performance.

120 Percent Performance

This level is usually regarded as the incentive pace, because most incentive programs are based on a 20 percent bonus. It also means that people can generally exceed the 100 percent level by 20 percent, on the average, when provided with an incentive or reward. It is not common to find people working at 120 percent or higher without some form of direct reward or compensation.

135 Percent Performance

This level of performance is called the expert level, because it can be achieved and maintained only by expert or extremely skilled workers. There are usually only a handful of employees, even in very large offices, who have the unusual mental and/or physical dexterity to perform at this pace.

METHODS, PROCEDURES, SYSTEMS

It is impossible to talk about good standards or engineered work standards without giving proper attention to methods, procedures, and systems. If we have learned anything from the combined work of Taylor and Gilbreth, it is that a method must first be established for how a task can best be performed, and that a time standard should be developed based on that method.

Methods take into consideration the desk-top equipment, the placement of materials, etc. Procedures, on the other hand, involve the sequence of events, knowledge required, and rules governing the operation. And systems includes both manual and automated systems.

JOB DESIGN

Job design is the meaningful grouping of tasks together while giving to employees the responsibility for performing those tasks. Most people are familiar with Frederick Herzberg's theories that work environments contain dissatisfiers, or hygiene factors, and motivators. Dissatisfiers include company policies, company administration, supervision, working conditions, salaries, and benefits.

Dissatisfiers add to turnover problems, rising cost, and lack of employee motivation. Companies have attacked dissatisfiers without total success with programs such as reduced working hours, longer vacations, flexible hours, increased wages, profit sharing, off-hours activities, training, and counseling.

Job design is one means of dealing with dissatisfiers. The steps required are:

- Interview employees to find out:
    What do they do and how do they do it?
    Where is work received from?
    Who is work forwarded to?
    Is work checked?
    What do employees like about job?
    What do employees dislike about job?
- Determine what can be done to eliminate the things employees dislike about their jobs.
- Determine if responsibility for final output, checking, and decision making can be handled by the employee.
- Consolidate responsibility from jobs which precede and follow the job under study.
- Delegate responsibility for routine work to lower-level positions to enrich those jobs.
- Develop a relationship between employees and customers.
- Allow employees to work independently when possible.
- Have employees report their achievements.

WHAT JOBS ARE MEASURABLE?

Standards can be applied to virtually every type of work if you want to take the time (and pay the cost) to do it. But some jobs lend themselves to measurement and control more readily than others.

Generally speaking, a job can be measured if the work is governed by fairly definite rules or procedures. It becomes uneconomical to measure some work if:

- There is not a relatively continuous supply of work.
- There is a low volume to the work.
- There is a wide variety of tasks performed by one employee.

TECHNICAL MEASUREMENT

When managers want a tool to control costs and gauge productivity of the clerical work force, they turn to work measurement. However, there is a growing segment of the office work force that has eluded objective productivity measurements—the technical-level employee.

Technical jobs such as insurance claims examiners and underwriters, bank platform officers, and personal loan officers, as well as programmers and customer service representatives in all types of office environments, are increasing rapidly. In addition, what were once clerical jobs are continually being upgraded because of improved job design as well as office technology such as on-line computer video terminal systems. Paper-shuffling tasks are being replaced with decision-making tasks.

Since today's manager is well aware of the principle that you can control only that which you can measure and the degree of your control is directly related to the quality of the measurement, the subject of productivity measurements for the technician is being met head-on in today's progressive companies.

Objections to Technical Measurement

Before a successful productivity measurement program for technical personnel can be developed, some common objections must be examined and reconciled.

OBJECTION 1: The "judgment," "thinking," and "decision-making" parts of the technical job cannot be accurately measured.

ANSWER: A closer examination of the technical job reveals that the technician does not just sit and stare into space as decisions are "mulled over." Rather, the technician gathers information by reading from source documents such as files, correspondence, computer listings, or reports. Decision making for these types of jobs also includes calculating alternatives or discussing the subject with the customer through a series of questions. Judgment definitely enters into the decision. However, this judgment factor is more a matter of the knowledge and experience of the technician than of time. Time to make the decision involves the time to read, discuss, calculate, or choose between alternatives, all of which are measurable. The training and experience of the technician influence the quality of the decision and the ease with which the decision can be reached once enough information has been gathered.

OBJECTION 2: Job elements are not routine.

ANSWER: Because of seemingly limitless possibilities, this is true. Nevertheless, the approach to reaching a decision should have some readily identifiable pattern. One example is a personal loan officer evaluating a loan application. The purpose of the loan, the amount requested, the financial condition of the applicant, all may be unique to that case. However, the analysis and eventual decision to grant the loan characteristically follow similar steps or some patterned approach.

OBJECTION 3: Record-keeping requirements reduce technical employees to clerks.

ANSWER: Cumbersome record-keeping systems for technicians must be avoided at all costs. Basing productivity measurements on three or fewer key activities will avoid this problem.

OBJECTION 4: Measurement programs for technicians take away the special status the technical employee has worked so hard to attain.

ANSWER: This objection is heard most often when the same measurement program used for the clerical-level employee is used for the technical level. Designing a separate program specifically for technical employees can overcome this objection. There are other objections. They all indicate the need to design a specific program tailored to the nature of the technical job.

The Need for a Different Approach

First and foremost, it must be recognized that the technical job is by nature different from the clerical type of position. In addition, the caliber of the employee is usually higher. Any approach, therefore, must take these important differences into consideration.

If a company already has a clerical work-measurement program, every effort must be made to design the technical program to be different. The difference must be evident in every detail, from the program name, record-keeping requirements, documentation design, reporting techniques, standard-setting approach, and most important, communications and employee participation.

Essential Ingredients

A successful technical measurement program has several essential ingredients. Ensuring that a program has all of the following will greatly enhance chances of a successful implementation.

1. Specifically designed communications: The introduction of the program as well as the communications throughout the implementation must be carefully designed and executed. While a few short meetings are adequate for explaining most clerical programs, the communications for the technicians must be more detailed and more frequent. Here is a pattern used successfully by several companies:

- Feasibility study: The analyst meets with the technical manager to explain the objectives of the feasibility study, such as determining the nature of the work, the patterns of work completion, the key output activities, and any processing problems. Results of the study are then reported along with the recommendations to management.

- Introductory meeting with technicians: The results of the feasibility study and the objectives of the program should be discussed thoroughly and well in advance of the program's implementation.

- How the study is conducted: To kick off the program with the technical employees, the analyst holds a meeting to review the objectives, explain the approach, and stress employee participation.

- Gathering and review of the task list: The analyst interviews each technician and develops a task list. Usually, the task list for a technical unit is short. The list must be reviewed with the technicians for their approval.

- Writing and review of the procedures: Through detailed interviewing of each technician, the analyst documents procedures and has them reviewed for approval. Any changes are to be incorporated at this time. It is not unusual for the technician to make suggestions for simplification at this stage. Changes that the analyst is recommending should be discussed at this time.

- Conducting the frequency study: Each step that the technician takes must be assigned a relative value expressed as a percent of the key activity. These percentages are arrived at by the technicians through a frequency study kept over a sufficient period of time to be statistically valid and representative of the normal processing cycle time.

- Presenting the standards: Using the actual procedures agreed upon and approved by the technicians, the analyst explains how the standard was set in sufficient detail for full understanding and confidence.

- Presenting the reporting system: The mechanics of the record-keeping system, how the data are captured, how the results are displayed, and the meaning and uses of the data are explained.

2. Analysts who have specific experience in the area measured: This has a tendency to increase the confidence level of the technicians. They feel that the complexities of their job are understood and properly eval-

uated. Because the analyst is familiar with the terminology and the procedures, the length of the study is reduced. The analyst is better able to keep the study in perspective for all concerned, and overall acceptance is usually high.

3. Emphasis on participation: Each technician is interviewed in detail and assists in building the procedures for the job. Differences in the way things are processed are discussed and resolved. The new procedures are agreed upon by all concerned.

4. Meaningful documentation: Technicians look at their jobs as complete procedures rather than fragmented tasks. The documentation should be in the playscript procedure format and should include all the routine steps as well as the exceptions to routine.

5. Simplified record keeping: Nothing will kill a technical measurement program faster than a cumbersome record-keeping system. Since a characteristic of the technical-level job is being in control of one's own work load, the record keeping must not reduce this freedom to act by keeping track of every minor thing that happens. Volume counts should be limited to one to three key items, preferably one. If at all possible, the clerical support personnel should keep the actual volume counts. The need to record time "off-standards" should be kept at a minimum, and only absent time, no work time, and special projects of long duration (over 1 hour) should be included. Meetings and interruptions should be factored into the standards so they need not be recorded as off-standard time.

6. Meaningful reporting period: Since most technical measurement programs will have few units of count and relatively large time standards, the reporting period should be based on the logical cycle of completing a full procedure from start to finish. This usually means a reporting period of at least every 2 weeks or monthly.

7. Proper use of results: Considering the large standards and long reporting cycle, it is meaningless to pinpoint specific performance results for purposes of remedial action. Goals should be set in terms of units per day or week, and results should be evaluated in terms of ranges. Percentages should still be calculated, but an 89 percent one month versus an 86 percent another month may not be as meaningful as achieving a performance in the range of 85 to 90 percent, period.

Benefits

Objective data for goal setting and evaluation   The technical manager is better able to set individual productivity goals with each technician, based on objective standards. The technician gets feedback on the achievement of these goals on a regular basis.

Standard costing   Without a technical measurement program, standard costing becomes less than scientific, since the cost of handling a claim or loan or whatever by the technician must be estimated. With a technical measurement program, these standard costs can be identified better and measured accurately.

Identifying training needs Performance results as well as the analysis of the individual frequency study results point out errors in handling and problems in decision making on the part of the technician.

Quality control Supervisory audits of completed work for purposes of checking quality are made easier by referring to the documentation to illustrate missing steps and indicate the proper procedure to follow.

Improving service Improved methods and procedures, better quality, and increased productivity all result in better service for the customer. In today's competitive market, this translates into increased sales if we deliver, or loss of sales if we do not.

Measurement Techniques

There are dozens of techniques for measuring work. The three general categories are informal techniques, semiformal techniques, and formal techniques. In the following discussion we will examine the strengths and weaknesses of available measurement techniques. Each measurement technique is a tool. It is wise to know the advantages and limitations of the tools you use. In this way you will not expect more than the tool is capable of providing.

Informal techniques include estimates, short-interval scheduling (SIS), and the historical data method. Whatever time values are derived from these methods cannot be considered "standards" in the true sense of the word but are rather benchmarks, reasonable expectancies, or guides.

Semiformal techniques include self-logging or time ladders, work sampling or ratio delay, and unleveled time study. The time values derived from these techniques are usually regarded as rough standards. They are a little more accurate because they are a bit less subjective, but they are still rough.

Formal techniques include leveled time studies and predetermined time data. These are very sophisticated techniques and produce what are known as engineered standards.

INFORMAL TECHNIQUES

Estimates

An estimate is an approximate judgment of amounts. Everyone is capable of estimating, although some of us are better at it than others. This immediately brings up the questions of accuracy and consistency. An estimate is an attempt to quantify the number of units that can be handled in a minute, hour, day, or week, or simply the amount of time to handle one unit of work. It costs next to nothing to do and requires no special training other than some familiarity with the jobs being estimated. Generally, it is unsupportable. If someone else's estimate differs from yours or an employee's estimate differs from a supervisor's, there is considerable difficulty proving who is right.

Take the situation where the supervisor estimates that an employee should be able to handle 50 units per hour and a particular employee is handling only 30 units per hour. If the employee says, "I'm doing the best I can" or "I'm working hard all the time," the supervisor is in a position that is difficult to defend.

Estimates are very loosely based on the method used at the time. There is seldom any documentation of the method, so that changes in method usually go unnoticed.

Historical Data

Using historical data, historical records, or past performance records is the simplest form of work measurement. It involves the use of production statistics or records compiled over a period of time—say, a month or a year—to determine how long it has taken in the past to produce one unit of work.

Consider an order-processing unit of 10 workers handling an average of 480 orders per day. This is an average of 48 orders per worker per 8-hour day, or 6 orders per hour. One order is equal to 10 minutes. A year later the same unit may have 13 workers turning out 650 orders per day. This amounts to 50 orders per worker per day, 6.25 per hour per worker, or 9.6 minutes per order.

A comparison shows a 4 percent improvement from one year to the next. In other words, historical data can serve as a benchmark, certainly not a standard, against which future production and performance are compared. They will tell us if we are doing better or worse than previously. Although the historical data method does not in itself tell us how long a unit of work should take, its value in gauging any increase or decrease cannot be overlooked.

To set up a measurement program using the historical data technique, a unit of measure is selected that is representative of the work being done and is relatively easy to capture. It can be the number of items processed or the number of hours expended for a given function.

Short-Interval Scheduling

Short-interval scheduling, usually referred to as SIS, is not so much a technique as it is an approach. However, since it is a separate, distinct method by which work can be measured and controlled, we will include it in the presentation of informal techniques.

Short-interval scheduling is defined as the assignment and control of a premeasured, predetermined amount of work with systematic follow-up and problem correction, in planned, predictable short-time intervals throughout the day.

SIS has limitations that potential users should be aware of. The program puts a great deal of pressure on employees and supervisors to meet schedules. Also, the fact that it requires a rather continuous backlog of work may have a detrimental effect on service. Another important limitation to consider is that SIS is not applicable to administration or low-volume work.

Wristwatch Time Studies

Although rarely discussed in the literature on work measurement, a common wristwatch can be used to set time standards. Particularly where company policy prohibits the use of a stopwatch, the wristwatch technique can be used effectively as a means of gathering time data.

Essentially, the procedure for setting time standards with a wristwatch is the same as that employed when a stopwatch is used. Because of the similarity in procedure, which is covered in connection with time study, a detailed description of the wristwatch approach here is unnecessary. However, two major differences between the wristwatch technique and the stopwatch technique should be noted: (1) the recording of time values in seconds rather than in hundredths of a minute, and (2) the omission of performance leveling. In practice, wristwatch studies are infrequently leveled, whereas stopwatch studies are generally leveled.

The continuous time-study sheet does not require a detailed enumeration of elements prior to the start of the study. The analyst simply describes and records the elements as the study progresses.

Summary

Informal techniques provide management with a method for evaluating the production of a unit. The advantages they have over other techniques are that they are simple to administer and quite inexpensive. But, while they are the simplest form of measurement, they are also the least accurate, because they are based on current staff and conditions and do not take into consideration the methods involved. The use of informal techniques is a first step to controlling office costs. It should not be the last.

SEMIFORMAL TECHNIQUES

While informal techniques are distinguished by an attempt to determine the average time it currently takes to process work, semiformal techniques provide an opportunity to separate the time devoted to a task from nonproductive time such as personal time, idle time, and absent time.

Work Sampling

Work sampling is based on observation of employees at work according to statistically valid observation tables. There are two kinds of work sampling: ratio delay and sampling. Ratio delay involves observing employees to determine if they are working or not working. These data can then be used to add or subtract load from a clerical unit.

Other forms of sampling involve listing some basic tasks that are performed in the clerical unit and then making random observations to determine the frequency with which they occur. This sampling is converted into percentages of time and finally minutes or hours spent on the various tasks. The volume of output for each task can be divided into the sample time to construct a standard. Because work sampling can be used to determine the amount of idle time in an area, it tends to be somewhat more accurate in rating the pace of an employee than historical data.

The basic methods of work sampling can be determined from most office administrative manuals or texts on work measurement. Work sampling, however, is limited to rather gross observation. It is normally used to evaluate a relatively small number of tasks, and then it does not usually take into account either methods or conditions.

As a measurement device, work sampling provides a means to measure work that is either uneconomical or impractical to measure by time study or predetermined time data. Therefore, work sampling can be used as a stand-alone technique to complement other work-measurement techniques. In the latter case, some applications might be:

- To establish standards on difficult-to-measure, nonrepetitive tasks such as business talking, occasional required walking, or telephoning
- To determine ratios between productive and nonproductive work in a work center
- To determine distribution of work within a work center
- To identify factors causing work delays

Work sampling can also be used to establish work-measurement standards. Sampling results can be leveled either in the traditional time-study manner or by use of a predetermined time data system.

Time-Ladder Studies

The time-ladder study, also referred to as self-logging, is a participative approach to work measurement. Employees play a major role in recording, or logging, what they are doing, when they are doing it, and the amount of work they complete during any given time period.

The only steps required to prepare for a time-ladder study are to prepare a list of the activities being performed in a unit and to explain the study to the people involved in it. The purpose of a time-ladder study is usually to determine how people spend their time, what activities or tasks they perform, and how much work is processed.

It is important that the employees involved have a clear understanding of the purpose of the study. In a work-sampling study, an objective outsider or supervisor is recording the data through observations. With a time-ladder study, it is the employee who does the recording. The employee should not feel threatened by the results or use of the results of the study. It is important to persuade the employees to report their activities honestly and completely. It should be explained that if management knows how they are spending their time and how much work is being accomplished, it can make changes in the work schedule, determine where bottlenecks occur, provide a basis for knowing each individual's contribution to the work effort, and develop time standards for the work.

A time-ladder study is usually taken over a sufficient period of time so as to accumulate valid data. How long is a sufficient period? It all depends on the normal work cycle. In some work centers, one day is like any other day. Here a 2-week period of data accumulation might be sufficient. If there is a weekly cycle, 3 or 4 weeks might suffice. If it is a department that involves a number of monthly functions, a 2-month period might be required. By taking the time devoted to any given task and the units completed by each employee, we can arrive at reasonable standards.

Generally, there are two approaches to developing standards from self-logging data: the array method and the nonarray method. The nonarray method is by far the simplest and requires considerably less time than the array technique.

With the nonarray approach, we simply total all the units of work processed in a category and all the time required to process those units, divide the number of units by the total time, and have a unit time standard. For example, let us assume that the total number of units produced over a period of time was 23,872 and that the total time for processing these units as reported on the logs was 950 minutes. Dividing the units by the number of minutes results in a unit time standard of 0.04 minute. The nonarray method does not provide any information concerning variations in processing times; it simply gives us an arithmetic mean—the average time taken by the average worker.

The array method of calculating standards provides information on the range of processing time. With this approach, it is necessary to calculate a separate time value for *each occurrence of each activity*. If the study was conducted over a long period of time and included several employees, the number of separate calculations would be quite high, not only for one activity but for all other activities.

Once the separate time values have been calculated, they are arranged in order, from the smallest value to the largest, or vice versa. From this array of time values, standards can be calculated in several ways: (1) based on the median time values, (2) based on the modal value, (3) based on the upper quartile value, or (4) based on a selected average value. Frequently, the selected-average approach is used.

FORMAL TECHNIQUES

There are two techniques in this category—time study and predetermined time data. These are considered engineered work standards—assuredly the type of standard that is required to measure individual performance and upon which to base wage incentives.

Time Study

Work measurement in its infancy was known as time study. The first measurements were aimed at determining operator performance and production levels by relating them to historical data or past performance records. These records, of course, proved to be unreliable. The need for a better and more reliable system of measurement was quite evident. Taylor took the initiative by developing the use of the stopwatch. He developed a technique for standardizing performance times by using the stopwatch to measure a specific method of performing an operation.

A short time after Taylor started his work and had become widely known throughout industry, Frank B. Gilbreth, a former bricklayer, began an intensive study of the motions that workers use in the performance of a given task. He realized that one of the greatest opportunities for cost reduction was in the improvement of production methods. These improvements did not necessarily require the installation of expensive machines and equipment but often could be secured by analyzing the operation carefully, eliminating unnecessary motions, and installing simple commonsense methods.

The Gilbreth research group was responsible for discovering and expressing the 17 laws of motion economy. They also developed the technique of using the motion-picture camera for making detailed laboratory studies. This method of filming operations for the study of motions and methods eventually developed into what is now known as "micromotion study."

The combination of the work done by Taylor and Gilbreth—the two techniques of time study and motion study—came to be known as time and motion study. The system became more formalized during the 1930s and 1940s but still had certain disadvantages which led others to develop even more effective techniques for the quantification of work.

Definition

Time study is a process of observing an operation while utilizing a timing device, and rating the pace or performance of the individual performing the operation in order to establish a standard for that operation. It involves defining a job or task in terms of its elements and making careful observations—usually using a stopwatch—to establish the time required for the element. The time-study analyst—usually someone who has had professional training and experience in this aspect of work measurement—rates the pace of the person performing the operation against the established norm as the study is being conducted. A number of observations consistent with the length of the task, its complexity, and its impact or work load are made to assure statistical accuracy.

Because this method has been used in the factory for many years, it has wide acceptance there and is considered very accurate. Unfortunately, this strength is also its weakness: time study, and the use of a stopwatch, has generally proved psychologically unacceptable to office personnel, partly because of its factory origins.

Using the Stopwatch

The most common type of stopwatch used is one calibrated in decimal minutes. This type of watch registers time on two dials. The outer dial, which is the larger one, is divided into 100 units, each representing 0.01 minute. The smaller dial records the number of complete revolutions or minutes. The capacity of the smaller dial is usually 30 minutes.

There are two timing techniques that can be used: the continuous-timing method and the snap-back method. Continuous timing involves starting the watch at the beginning of an operation, noting the time at the end of each step or after each activity, recording the time in the appropriate column, and stopping the watch at the end of the operation. The ending time of each element is subtracted from the ending time of the preceding element to determine the elapsed time for each function.

The snap-back method involves starting and stopping the watch for each step and recording the time in the appropriate column. Special (and expensive) watches for snap-back timing are available, as are multiple-watch timing boards facilitating the snap-back method. Continuous timing is the preferred choice for longer-cycle tasks, while the snap-back method is most often utilized for shorter-cycle tasks.

Performance Rating

Performance rating, or leveling, involves an evaluation by a trained analyst of the skill, effort, and work pace being applied by an operator under study. The evaluation is based on a comparison with a uniform concept of "normal." This is done to compensate for an employee working faster or slower than normal and thus distorting standard accuracy. In industrial engineering terminology, normal equates with our definition of 100 percent performance: "the work pace at which an average, well-trained employee can work without undue fatigue while producing acceptable quality work."

Therefore, while an employee is performing a task or step within a task, and while the stopwatch is recording how long it actually takes to perform the task or step, the analyst rates the pace, in terms of skill and effort being exerted:

- At 100 percent if the analyst feels the employee is performing at a pace which he or she should be expected to maintain all day long
- Above 100 percent, normally in increments of 5 (105 percent, 110 percent, and so on), if the analyst feels the employee is performing at a pace greater than can be expected of an average, well-trained employee.
- Below 100 percent (95 percent, 90 percent, and so on) if the analyst feels the employee is performing more slowly and less skillfully than should be expected of an average, well-trained employee.

Various rating films are available for training analysts to understand and apply the concept of "normal" to office work situations. Some groups have developed this capability to evaluate performance quite accurately. Nonetheless, it is a subjective judgment on the part of the analyst and has often been referred to as the "weak link" or "tragic flaw" of time study. Analyst objectivity may be influenced by irrelevant factors such as employee personality, appearance, or preconceived ideas of what the standard should be.

Terminology

Here is a list of the more common terms used in time studies.

Task: A process which is placed on one task outline and contains a step, or a series of steps, and which is determined to be a distinct operation.

Step: The process between the logical beginning and ending point of an action performed within a task. A typical task is usually performed in three steps, usually called setup step, "do" step, and wrap-up step. Complex tasks may have many "do" steps.

Item: A single entity that is identified, for a step or a task, as the key indicator that varies in direct proportion to time.

Volume: The total number of items in the sample for a step or job.

Batch: A number of similar items processed together as a group.

Timing: The observation and recording of the amount of time it takes to complete a batch or a portion of a batch of work on the timing pad.

Posting: An entry on one line of the development sheet.

Sample: The total number of postings necessary to obtain consistency in the development of a time standard.

Consistency: The agreement or harmony of parts to one another or to the whole.

Consistency deviation: The percentage difference between one cumulative time or ratio posting and another. (The time can be either on a step basis or on a total task basis.)

Ratio: The relationship between the number of items being handled in any one step and the total number of items counted for the task.

The Time-Study Procedure

A wide variety of procedures are used to conduct a time study. These vary from highly formalized procedures used by industrial engineers in direct factory labor situations to much less formal methods. We have selected an approach that has proved highly successful in an office situation. This approach can be explained in five phases as follows: (1) selecting the employee(s) to be timed, (2) interviews and data collection, (3) timing the operation or task, (4) rating the performance, and (5) developing the standard.

The customary procedure is to select a qualified employee—one who knows the proper method for performing the task, who is experienced enough to make the necessary decisions or judgments called for in a normal time frame, and who is physically and mentally capable of performing at a normal pace under timed conditions.

To time an employee who is uncertain of the procedures, method, or job requirements would make performance rating extremely difficult. On the other hand, to select a person who has exceptional mental facilities and/or exceptional physical dexterity would also be unfair and unacceptable. The key word is "normal." The closer we can get to an average, well-trained employee, the better is the chance for developing a reliable standard. If we are to develop an acceptable time standard, there are basic questions that must be answered before the timing can begin.

First, the analyst should interview the supervisor and ask:

- What procedures or steps are involved in performing the task?
- How often is the task performed?
- Are there nonroutine steps that can occur?
- What is the average batch size, and roughly how long does it take? (The answer to this question is critical in terms of establishing a batch size for timing purposes.)
- What is the maximum volume one employee can complete during the work-measurement reporting cycle? (The answer to this question is utilized as the basic component for determining an accurate standard.)

Second, the analyst should interview the employee selected to be timed and ask:

- What procedures are involved in the task?
- Are there nonroutine steps that can occur?
- What is the frequency of the task performed?

- What equipment and/or forms are utilized to perform this task?
- What is the average batch size?

The analyst should take whatever steps are required to put the employee at ease before starting the timing. This could involve conversation on non-business-related subjects and an explanation of the stopwatch and how it is used to determine standards. The analyst should explain that the watch can be turned off (stopped) if the employee would like to explain some of the procedures. Generally, the analyst might suggest that the employee work at a normal pace. Since employees are generally fresher in the morning and less energetic in the afternoon, an equal number of timings should be taken in the morning and afternoon to average out the fatigue element.

During the timing, questions concerning methods, time inconsistency, and/or procedure deviation related to the items being processed are asked at the time of occurrence. The answers may change the method of timing or be used to document the reasons for the deviations if the timing method cannot be changed.

During the course of timing a step of a task, the analyst is evaluating the employee's skill, effort, and consistency of work pace. When the step is completed, the analyst makes a rating determination. The standard is then developed using all the factors mentioned.

Advantages

Time study is a technique that has distinct advantages over other techniques:

- Except for pace rating, it is easy to explain and easy to understand.
- Time-study standards are accurate when developed by a well-qualified and well-trained analyst.
- Time-study standards can be developed fairly rapidly.
- Time-study standards can be adjusted fairly easily as changes occur in method, volume, or equipment.
- The documentation in time study provides detailed information concerning the methods and procedures employed and the equipment and materials used, which can be a stimulus for improving methods and procedures.
- Because of the degree of accuracy provided by time-study standards, they can be used for incentive purposes.
- The leveling factor, or performance rating, in time study provides for differences in pace among workers.
- Because time study usually involves timing a task a number of times, frequencies and exceptions are usually properly built into the standards.

Disadvantages

Despite the very worthwhile advantages of time study, the disadvantages can often outweigh the advantages. Here are some of the disadvantages:

- Because people generally associate the stopwatch with factory operations and consider it the tool of "efficiency experts," its adverse effect on morale cannot be denied.
- Time study usually requires timing a number of employees over extended periods of time, and therefore can put a great deal of pressure on employees and a burden on the analyst.
- Time study requires a great deal of training for analysts to learn to apply it properly, and periodic refresher training to maintain consistent rating skills. The cost of training is higher than with most other techniques.
- The subjective aspect of performance rating can lead to inconsistencies among analysts.
- Time study does not lend itself as easily to measurement of long-cycle or varied tasks as do other techniques.

Predetermined Time Systems

A predetermined time system, according to Karger and Bayha, is "an organized body of information, procedures, and techniques employed in the study and evaluation of work elements performed by human power." Specifically, these work elements are evaluated "in terms of the method or motions used, their general and specific nature, the conditions under which they occur, and the application of prestandardized or predetermined times which their performance requires."[1]

Predetermined time systems emerged on the scene in the 1930s. At that time, there were three systems: MTA (motion-time analysis), work factor, and MTS (motion-time standards). As one would expect, these techniques were developed for industrial operations. Their emergence on the industrial scene was a result of the misuse of time study and other techniques used by "efficiency experts"—people with little understanding of work measurement who did their "quick and dirty" job of cutting labor costs. It was here that the stopwatch became the symbol of the efficiency experts and fell into disrepute. Predetermined time systems were developed to overcome some of the disadvantages of the stopwatch.

One of the pioneers in the area of predetermined time systems was Asa B. Segur. He was keenly interested in physiology. In the early 1920s he became interested in the time characteristics of thinking, nerve reaction, and muscular reaction. Some of the things he discovered are:

Each action of the body is the result of some chemical reaction that takes place within the body. Since this chemical reaction takes place in a constant temperature—insofar as the chemical reaction is constant—the time for the reaction will also be constant within narrow limits.

The controlling time for human action may be defined as follows:

Average speed of a nerve reaction in the human body is 0.00045 minute per foot of distance traveled. Average number of messages that can be started over any one nerve path in the body is 5000 per minute. Average time for a single sarcostyle to complete a contraction in response to a nerve impulse is 0.00064 minute. . . . The above times apply to routine thinking, as well as to muscular reaction. These reactions, which are controlled by the brain, are becoming increasingly more important in industry than those which are controlled by the muscles alone.[2]

Segur first experimented with time equations of motion-time analysis in 1924 by analyzing micromotion films taken of experienced operators during World War I. He discovered that:

If the same motion were performed by various operators in exactly the same manner, the time for performing it was constant. This held true regardless of the type of industry in which the operator worked. The announcement was therefore made that "within reasonable limits, the time required of all experts to perform a true fundamental motion is constant.[3]

Segur expanded on Gilbreth's motion studies to prove that a person who works under a well-prescribed method gradually becomes an expert. The method was referred to as an engineered motion path. An engineered motion path has a rhythm to it. After sufficient repetition and practice, the nerve system takes over, Segur discovered. He concluded that the time required of all experts to perform a fundamental motion was a constant.

The work done by Segur and others built a foundation for what was to be one of the most widely used predetermined time systems in the world—methods-time measurement, or MTM.

According to Karger and Bayha,

The basic key to all predetermined time systems is the fact that variations in the times required to perform the same motion are essentially small for different workers who have had adequate practice. Mathematical relationships can therefore be established between motions and times, subject to predictable statistical limits.[4]

The major predetermined time systems include some that are maintained in private industry or developed for internal use within a particular organization:

- Motion-time analysis, or MTA, developed by Asa B. Segur. It is the oldest system and contains well-defined principles. The system is administered and maintained by the A. B. Segur Company.

- Work factor, developed by the Work Factor Company, based on accumulations of stopwatch studies and motion-picture and photographic studies done at RCA.
- Systems such as Get and Place, MTS (motion-time standards), and DMT (dimensional motion times). These systems were developed by General Electric from synthetic data and designed primarily for internal use at General Electric.
- Methods-time measurement, or MTM, which is a system developed in the mid-1940s at Westinghouse Electric Corporation.

While each of these systems has met with wide acceptance for use in factories, one system, MTM, seems to have the broadest application as a basis for use in offices.

Methods-Time Measurement

Methods-time measurement (MTM) is the only predetermined time system for which both data and research have been made readily available to the public. It was developed at Methods Engineering Council of Pittsburgh, Pennsylvania, by Harold B. Maynard, Gustave J. Stegemerten, and John L. Schwab after preliminary study at Westinghouse Electric Corporation.

The authors of MTM participated in the development of a nonprofit research and development organization known as the MTM Association for Standards and Research. All their data and development rights were assigned to this association. The MTM Association for Standards and Research continues to perform a valuable contribution to the field of scientific management by sponsoring research programs and training programs in this field.

The definition of MTM is the same now as it was in the original work performed by the developers:

> Methods-Time Measurement is a procedure which analyzes any manual operation or method into the basic motions required to perform it and assigns to each motion a predetermined time standard which is determined by the nature of the motion and the conditions under which it is made.[5]

MTM provides a time value for virtually every motion performed by the human body in a productive or work situation. It was developed by selecting average people (average age, size, and physical characteristics) and placing them under average conditions (average heat, light, and ventilation). The people were requested to perform series of motions, and these work sequences were filmed using a high-speed, constant-speed camera. With a constant-speed projector, the films were pace-rated by well-qualified industrial engineers until they had validated time values for all the basic motions performed.

The MTM procedure uses very small increments of time. For example, the time to release an object (MTM symbol RL1) is 0.00002 hour, or 0.0012 minute, or 0.072 second. These are unwieldy figures to work with. Whole numbers are much easier to work with and easier to remember than decimal fractions. This consideration made it advisable to introduce a new unit of measurement, called the time-measurement unit (TMU).

The speed of the camera used to develop MTM was 16 frames per second. Therefore, each frame had an elapsed time of 0.0625 second, or 0.00001737 hour. The way to avoid the use of such figures was to recognize that time units are arbitrary by nature. The MTM founders assigned the value of 0.00001 hour as the value of one time-measurement unit.

Before the MTM motions are reviewed, a discussion of some of the terms that are used is in order:

Motions: Covers the motions performed by the human body, such as reach, grasp, move, or release. Each motion is designated by a letter: R for reach, G for grasp, M for move, RL for release, and so on.

Distance: Always expressed in inches except in the instance of distances of ¾ inch or less, which are expressed as "f," for "fractional."

Case: Usually identified by the letters A, B, C, and so on. It indicates the destination where the hand or object is being directed, or the degree of difficulty.

Convention: A shorthand expression of an MTM element. For example, RfC is a convention for a reach of a fractional distance to objects which are jumbled with other objects so that search and select occur.

Continuity of motion: This refers to whether or not the motion starts from or ends at a rest position.

Office Standard Data

We have analyzed the various techniques available to measure office work. The informal techniques have a definite place in the business world as a first step. The semiformal techniques are helpful in pinpointing problem areas. And the formal techniques can be used to measure performance.

How we establish standards is a matter of choice. At this point we should be able to apply a set of criteria to select the best technique for our particular needs. Figure 7-2 shows a comparison of techniques. It illustrates the degree of accuracy, consistency, control, and savings one can expect.

One factor that cannot be ignored is the time it takes to measure office functions. Since the amount of time required to develop standards is in direct proportion to the size and number of work elements with which the analyst must deal, we must take steps to reduce the number of work

Technique	Accuracy	Consistency	Control	Savings
Formal	High Can be validated by other formal techniques.	High Properly trained analysts working independently will arrive at same standards. ±5 percent.	High Due to factual basis of information.	High (20–45 percent)
Semiformal	Moderate Will not hold up under validation.	Moderate Standards will vary ±10 percent.	Moderate Due to lack of attention to methods and work pace.	Moderate (10–12 percent)
Informal	Low	Low No consistency at all; could vary 50 percent or more.	Low Due to reliance on opinion rather than facts.	Low (1–5 percent)

FIG. 7-2. Comparison of work-measurement techniques.

elements and increase the length of time of these elements. This step is called "developing standard data."

Establishing standard data gives work analysts the opportunity to practice what they preach—to develop the most efficient methods to do their own work. In other words, it is an attempt to reduce the time to set standards without reducing standard accuracy.

The definition of standard time data is found in American Society of Mechanical Engineers Standard 106 (no longer in print; replaced by ASME Z94 Series), entitled "Industrial Engineering Terminology":

> A compilation of all the elements that are used for performing a given class of work with normal elemental time values for each element. The data are used as a basis for determining time standards on work similar to that from which the data were determined without making actual time studies.

To understand standard data, one must understand that work measurement is not an exact science. There is a judgment factor that must be applied by an analyst. In fact, the development of good data requires good analytical thinking on the part of an analyst.

According to Karger and Bayha,

> Practically all standard data are established with the "building block" concept. This concept is that, with some acceptable loss of accuracy and a tolerable reduction in methods improvement capability, progressively larger time elements are derived for more rapid and less expensive direct rate-setting usage.[6]

Description—LH	Symbol	TMU	Symbol	Description—RH
		15.2	M12C	To stapler
		14.7	P1SSd	Align
Hit	R5Am	5.3		
	G5	0.0		
Depress	mMIA	1.9		
	RL2	0.0		
Hand away	R2E	3.8		
		40.9 TMU		
	or 41	TMU		

FIG. 7-3. Standard data, staple sheets.

For example, to staple sheets of paper together may involve the MTM motion pattern in Fig. 7-3. This requires the analysis and recording of 7 MTM elements to determine that it takes 41 time-measurement units to fasten sheets of paper together with a table-model stapler. To record the same 7 elements a second time because a stapling function was required would be to reinvent the wheel.

These building blocks are combinations which always, or very nearly always, occur when a given task is performed. The principle involved is simply that once a standard is developed for a task or a portion of a task, it need not be reanalyzed for its standard time each time it occurs.

This piece of data and all standard data elements must be developed in such a way as to apply every time the operation is performed. If we can predict how the material or sheets of paper will be picked up each time prior to stapling, and if we can predict where and how the material will be set down after stapling, and if we know that the material will be picked up in the same way and set aside the same way every time one staple is affixed to the batch, then we should include these functions in the motion pattern. However, they are not wholly predictable functions. Therefore, the data set developed for stapling items together should have the following parameters:

- Start with the items to be stapled in hand.
- Include moving the items to the stapler, positioning the items to the jaws of the stapler, inserting the items, and stapling the material.
- End with the stapled items in hand.

There are essentially two types of standard data—vertical and horizontal. Vertical data are "based on actual work task elements and are therefore restricted to one kind or class of work." Horizontal data, on the other hand, "are based upon motion sequences common to many kinds and classes of work."[7]

We will explore the development of horizontal standard data because they have the widest possible application. In fact, we intend to show that a set of data can be developed to cover virtually every function involved in a work or productive situation in an office. This system is called Advanced Office Controls.

A block of data, once developed, is not economical to use until it has been coded. Coding enables it to be catalogued and retrieved from memory or from the computer when it is ready to be used. Some data systems involve such an enormous number of elements that it becomes faster to develop new data than to try to find the block of data previously developed.

Coding can be alphabetical or numerical. Perhaps the most creative work in this area was done by Richard M. Crossan and Harold W. Nance when they developed an alpha-mnemonic coding system. Their thesis was that standard data are no better than the human memory. Or, to put it another way: "You cannot economically use an element if you cannot economically find it."[8]

The alpha-mnemonic coding system is based on three practical rules:

1. No code symbol should be made up of more than three letters of the alphabet.

2. Each code letter must be the first letter in a word which describes all or part of an element.

3. No alpha letter can be used more than once in the first field or more than once in a subcategory in the second or third field.

Alpha-mnemonic coding simply means that it is an alphabetic coding system that jogs the memory (mnemonic) and thereby simplifies the retrieval of coded data.

We have identified three levels of horizontal standard data as follows:

- Level 1 comprises basic data such as MTM. It includes time values for all the basic motions performed by the human body—reach, move, and so on.
- Level 2 comprises data developed from basic MTM or similar data systems for functions performed. These can include picking up a sheet of paper, depressing a typewriter key, or writing a digit.
- Level 3 consists of data developed from either level 1 or level 2 data for complete office procedures. These can include procedures for opening mail, typing a complete letter, writing a name and address, and so on.

Office Standard Data Systems

A number of standard data systems are developed from basic MTM. For the most part, these are level 2 data systems and include, not in any special order:

- CSD—Clerical Standard Data.[9] This system was developed in 1960 by, and is available from, Bruce Payne Associates.

- MCD—Master Clerical Data.[10] This system was developed in 1958 by, and is available from, Serge A. Birn Company.
- UOC—Universal Office Controls.[11] This system was developed in the 1950s by H. B. Maynard and Company and is available from that firm.
- MODAPTS—Modular Arrangement of Predetermined Time Standards. This system was developed in the late 1960s by Chris Heyde at Unilever in Australia and is available through Price Waterhouse and Peat, Marwick & Mitchell.
- MTV—Motion Time Values. This system was developed in the 1960s by Booz Allen and Hamilton and is available from that company.
- MTM-C—Methods-Time Measurement—Clerical. This system was developed in 1978 by a consortium of MTM association members and is available from the MTM Association for Standards and Research.
- AOC—Advanced Office Controls. Developed in 1973, this system is basically a level 3 data system, but it contains enough level 2 and level 1 data so as to be able to accurately cover all functions, repetitive and nonrepetitive. It was developed by, and is available from, the Robert E. Nolan Company of Simsbury, Conn.

A system known as the Mulligan system uses motion-picture analysis (essentially level 1 and level 2 data). It was developed by, and is available from, Paul B. Mulligan Company.

Many studies have been conducted to compare one system against another. These studies often conclude that one system is vastly superior to another. And, frequently, one system may offer certain advantages, such as greater speed of application, broader range of data, more up-to-date office-equipment data, greater accuracy on short-cycle operations, or less training time required. Often, however, there can be offsetting differences.

On the basis of its acceptance and what we hope is an objective appraisal, it seems that one system does offer more advantages than any other, and we will describe that system in more detail.

Advanced Office Controls

In the past, engineered standards involved an enormous amount of detail and required considerable training in order to apply the data to office work. This is no longer the case. Economical techniques such as Advanced Office Controls (AOC) have appeared during the past 10 years that make standard setting in offices quite simple. These techniques are generally easy to understand and maintain, accurate and consistent, and economical in terms of application.

Description	MTM convention	Time units
Move opener to envelope	M8C	11.8
Opener to corner of envelope	P2SD	21.8
Insert opener in envelope	M2B	4.6
Slit open envelope	M8B	<u>10.6</u>
		48.8
	or	49 TMU

FIG. 7-4.   Standard data, open envelope.

Advanced Office Controls (AOC) is a proprietary system originally developed by Robert E. Nolan Company in 1973. It is used here to illustrate an advanced system, as it contains three levels of data under one coding system.

AOC is an analysis and measuremeni technique for controlling office costs. It is a library of engineered standard time values covering virtually every aspect of work performed in an office—and summarized onto one card. AOC is economical to apply, and is both accurate and consistent in its application. In addition to the speed of application and accuracy inherent in the system, it is easy to learn and simple to apply.

AOC was developed from methods-time measurement (MTM)—the most widely accepted predetermined time system in the world. While MTM is extremely precise, its application in the office is limited because of the lack of repetition in office work. AOC recognizes work in the office not as a series of individual motions but rather as cycles of action. A cycle of action consists of three parts: start, change, and stop. Let us look at the level 2 pattern in Fig. 7-4.

The opening of an envelope illustrates the principle of cycles of action. Start occurs with the moving of the opener to the envelope, change with the actual opening, and stop with the envelope completely open. A single AOC code PEOS records and standardizes this task. The code translates as P (paper handling) for an E (envelope) to O (open) and S (sealed envelope) and has a value of 49 time-measurement units.

This same block of level 2 data, now known as PEOS and requiring 49 time-measurement units, can be used to construct a block of level 3 data as in Fig. 7-5. This is a complete mail-opening operation which also involves the cycle-of-action principle: start occurs with the picking up of the envelope and opener; change with the opening of the envelope, removing the contents, unfolding the contents, and setting the material on the desk or table surface; and stop with putting the envelope aside. A single AOC code, GRSF, records and standardizes this block of data. The code translates a G (gather), R (receive), S (sealed envelope), F (folded contents) and has a value of 185 time-measurement units.

Description	AOC code	Time units
Get envelope and opener (later aside)	GMG	36
Open envelope	PEOS	49
Remove contents	GLG	49
Unfold papers	PU(2)	64
		198

FIG. 7-5. Standard data, open envelope complete.

Since all AOC elements are cycles of action, only 226 are required for all office work. With an average time value of over ¼ minute (more than 55 times greater than MTM), the analyst is relieved of hours of detail work without sacrificing the accuracy required for sound management control.

A standard data element cannot be economically used if it cannot be economically located. For this reason, we use an alphabetical coding rather than a numerical coding system. The alphabetical coding has a direct relationship to the words describing the basic elements. It is logical and precise, and lends itself to memorization after only the briefest of exposures.

AOC is a third-level data system that retains both level 2 and basic level 1 data within one system. Because AOC is a multilevel system, the analyst can choose the appropriate level of data to establish standards with the desired accuracy for any operation economically. AOC contains a machine data supplement that is kept up to date on all the latest office machines and equipment.

Because of the larger size of AOC elemental time values, fewer elements are required to establish standards. These elements provide precise documentation for each task, so that it is virtually impossible to leave anything out. The simplicity afforded by AOC also makes it easy for supervisors and employees to understand the basis on which the standards were developed.

AOC documentation is an excellent tool for methods analysis for simplifying an existing system or modeling a proposed system. Equipment analysis and costing can be readily accomplished also.

Automated Standard Data Systems

To our knowledge, only one automated system of standard data has been developed for office use. That system is called Auto-AOC. Auto-AOC is a complete package of computer hardware and software. It uses microcomputer technology to produce:

- Task outline—written procedures document the task, and are specific enough to use in systems analysis and training.

- Task analysis—documents how the standard was developed for each step within the procedure.
- Task summary—places each major procedure in its proper relationship with others, and calculates the standard.

Trained analysts or engineers interview employees to gather facts about how work is processed. They study task content and make improvements in methods and procedures. A procedure is written to document the approved method of performing the task. Working from the approved documentation, the analyst uses AOC to translate the work performed into the time required to perform it, and that becomes the standard for the task.

Documentation of the procedure for the user departments is then typed by clerical personnel. This documentation is retained for methods analysis, training of new employees, referral, and future audit and update.

Establishing standards for new applications and maintaining existing standards on a timely and cost-effective basis is a key concern to work management program managers. Typical analysts using AOC spend about half their standard-setting time writing procedures and developing standards. As much as 80 percent of analyst effort is spent on the standard-setting process in companies using first- or second-generation standard-setting systems.

Reduction of standard-setting time will mean more rapid coverage, easier maintenance, and a potential to utilize analyst skills better in the areas of methods improvements and human relations. Clerical support costs will also be reduced when procedure typing is eliminated.

A number of advantages are offered by Auto-AOC:

- Reduced analyst effort—20 to 55 percent less than with manual standard-setting systems.
- Mathematically correct standards.
- Storage of standards on diskettes provides easy retrieval and maintenance.
- Elimination of costly and time-consuming secretarial services for typing procedures.
- Improved analyst morale and reduced turnover result from elimination of routine work.
- No data-processing assistance is required for installation and use.

Auto-AOC utilizes the Apple microcomputer with cathode-ray tube (CRT), disk drive, and printer. The system requires no programming knowledge for use. Complete, easy-to-follow instructions allow the user to become fully trained and productive after brief exposure.

Auto-AOC provides complete flexibility, not only for setting standards and writing procedures, but also for creating and maintaining master files. This allows companies using predetermined time systems other than AOC to use the Auto-AOC technology. Comprehensive instructions supplied with the Apple allow the user to create programs easily for other uses too.

Reporting Techniques

In order to use standards effectively, there must be a method of determining how much work was processed and how much time was devoted to it. There are other considerations as well. What level of detail are you interested in seeing in a reporting system? Do you want to know how well employees perform their jobs? Or do you want even more detail such as how well each employee performs each task? Or perhaps a group reporting system is desired if you want a very simple control system that tells you how well a department or unit is performing and how many employees are needed to perform the work.

INDIVIDUAL REPORTING

A supervisor needs facts to carry out his or her responsibilities effectively in managing a section or department. This includes information on work load, staffing, and employee performance. To get the maximum benefits from a work management program, the amount of detail involved in an individual reporting system is well worth the small price to be paid for an individual reporting system. An individual reporting system involves the use of a Daily Volume Report or Weekly Volume Report, a Daily Sign Out Sheet, and a Weekly Time and Production Record.

To collect information on how many items were processed by task, this can be kept on a Daily Volume Report by the employee and turned in to the supervisor each day, or it can be kept by the supervisor or control clerk if work is precounted and distributed directly to employees. Some companies also use a Weekly Volume Report that lists each task and has a space for each day of the week so that all work performed during an entire week is on one sheet of paper.

This type of record keeping can be simple or detailed depending on the number of tasks. The more tasks, the more work counts; the more work counts, the more record keeping there is; the more record keeping there is, the more burdensome and annoying this can be to employees and supervisors.

Generally, we have found that if the amount of detail in the reporting system coincides with the supervisor's desire for detail, you have a winning situation. However, if you have people report more detail than the supervisor wants or is interested in, you will have trouble.

A Daily Sign Out Sheet usually works on the basis of management by exception. This means that employees are presumed to be on standards all day long unless there is a reason to be "off standards." These reasons can be absent time, loaned (to another department) time, no work available, or simply performing a task for which there is no standard.

A Weekly Time and Production Record is maintained by the unit supervisor. He or she posts information from the Daily or Weekly Volume Report and Daily Sign Out Sheet to the Weekly Time and Production Record. The work counts are then multiplied by the standard for each task to get standard hours.

For example, if an employee works a 40-hour week and performs only three tasks, the calculation of standard hours is as follows:

Task	Items counted	Items processed	Hours per item	Standard hours
Process invoices	Invoices	250	0.043	10.8
Process orders	Orders	310	0.051	15.8
Type checks	Checks	155	0.022	3.4
			Total standard hours	30.0

If the employee spent all week on standards with no absent or unmeasured time, the record would show that he or she accomplished 30 hours of work in 40 hours for a performance of 75 percent (30/40 = 75 percent).

The reports involved in an individual reporting system basically revolve around a Weekly Performance Report. This lists each employee in a unit, his or her time distribution (total hours, absent hours, unmeasured hours, etc.), standard hours produced, performance and coverage, or percentage of available time on standards. Other reports can be developed from this Weekly Performance Report summarizing the information to higher levels of management.

GROUP REPORTING

If management has no intention of using individual performance information, or for one reason or another is turned off or feels the employees would be turned off by it, and merely wants a means of control, group reporting can be the answer. Group reporting requires very little record keeping. Usually only 5 to 10 key volume indicators are enough to provide overall performance and staffing information.

MICRO VERSUS MACRO

It has been popular lately to describe reporting techniques in terms of micro and macro systems. Micro is a method of describing heavily detailed systems that capture information by employee, and macro indicates broader controls such as those offered by group reporting.

Companies that have achieved the most results in terms of savings and the development of effective supervisory controls have opted for individual controls because the level of detailed information on work load, time distribution, and performance was most useful.

Record-keeping systems for individual or group systems require skill and experience to develop. A well-developed individual reporting system requires from 2 to 5 minutes per day per employee to gather information, and approximately 2 minutes per employee of the supervisor's time. This extra time per employee is more than offset by the higher performance achieved and by the wealth of useful information available to the supervisor.

Time required for record keeping under group reporting systems is insignificant. By the same token, since employees are not recognized for their individual contribution to the department, overall performance is usually 10 to 15 percent lower.

Automated reporting system software packages are available that reduce the time required to perform calculations and prepare reports. Automated systems are generally cost-justified over manual systems within a 2-year period.

HOW TO DEVELOP A
WORK-MANAGEMENT PROGRAM

The usual procedure for developing a program is to designate a steering committee to develop a proposal to management. A number of factors that must be considered will now be discussed.

Consultants who specialize in office work management can be called in for presentations and surveys, and they will perform most of the preliminary investigations for a company. An alternative would be to have someone from within the organization who has experience in programs for productivity improvement conduct a survey.

Survey

A survey involves interviews with people at all levels of management to determine the type of program that best fits the needs of the organization, and the type of program that people will support. Mere approval for the program is not sufficient. Management support requires that management show an interest in the program, expect that improvement will come about, and communicate this interest and expectation for improvement to all levels of the organization.

Objectives

You must determine what you want to accomplish with your program. While cost reduction might be your primary objective, it should not be your only objective. Work-management programs with the single purpose of cost reduction are usually short-lived.

It might help you to know that the most successful programs in terms of results accomplished are designed to improve methods and procedures right along with the installation of measured controls. We generally find that half the savings come from work simplification and half from performance improvement.

While the primary objective might be cost reduction, it is accomplished by designing a program which will:

- Help supervisors and managers to be even more effective in meeting their accountabilities and goals
- Help employees work smarter—not harder, by improving methods and procedures
- Improve service to customers

Parameters

You should determine how many positions can be brought under control. We find that 75 to 80 percent of the total population of employees in an office can be brought under control.

Analyst Training

Carefully selected in-house personnel should be recruited and trained as analysts by an experienced individual or professional consultant in the best available techniques for analyzing, measuring, and controlling office costs.

Supervisory/Management Orientations

Specially designed orientation/training sessions should be conducted for each level of management so that they (1) understand the objectives and mechanics of the program, (2) have confidence in the techniques used, and (3) know how to use the information to make improvements in their respective area of responsibility.

Reporting Techniques

Reporting involves developing a scheme for collecting data at the employee level, and feedback information for supervisors, middle management, and top management as to performance, staffing, and problem areas. The reporting system must be simple to understand, operate, and maintain.

If the information in the reporting system is meaningful, and if the supervisors and managers have been trained to understand and use the information to make improvements in their area of responsibility, chances for success are good. Problems arise when there is a lack of understanding of the reporting system or where the record keeping requires an inordinate amount of counting, posting, and signout.

Participation

People at all levels of the organization should have an opportunity to be directly involved in the development of controls that will affect the way their jobs are to be performed and how they will be judged by results.

Do It Yourself Considerations

Once the framework of a program is developed, e.g., objectives, parameters, and type of reporting systems, the question of who will develop the program must be addressed. If you have no one in the organization with experience in these matters, you will have to either hire someone or retain an experienced management consultant.

PROS AND CONS

There are advantages and problems associated with any kind of program that deals with the sensitive issue of how well people perform their jobs. Perhaps we can call attention to pitfalls and how to avoid them.

The dictionary defines a pitfall as a "hidden danger." There are certainly hidden dangers in trying to achieve a successful work-management program. The most common pitfalls involve standards, record keeping, supervisory attitudes, and recalcitrant employees.

Standards must reflect the work to be done and be fair and consistent. If people do not believe the standards are fair, whatever steps are required should be taken to get acceptance without compromising the integrity of the standards.

Record keeping must be handled according to specific rules established for the program. A common term used by persons who do not believe in the record keeping is to refer to it as "Mickey Mouse." When this situation exists, you will also find work counts and time not being reported properly. Resolve this situation immediately.

Poor attitudes of supervisors toward the program result from a failure to gain their confidence during the supervisory orientations, failure on the part of analysts to gain their confidence, and failure on the part of management to convince them of the importance of the program to the organization. A poor attitude is frequently hidden. The most common manifestation of the poor attitude is simply not to participate. Supervisors or managers who do this have little time to spend with the analyst, will not contribute any ideas to change existing procedures, and will generally take a "wait and see" attitude. Immediate and direct counseling is required to bring out into the open the hostility the supervisor feels toward the program if such is the case.

Recalcitrant employees also require immediate attention. Usually their feeling of resentment toward the program is the result of a misunderstanding so that counseling is required to resolve the problem before it becomes more serious.

HOW TO RESTORE CONFIDENCE

Restoring confidence in a program can be done regardless of whether the complaints are real or imagined. If the complaints are valid, it may require changing objectives or changing the measuring technique to get better standards or changing the reporting system to reduce record keeping and provide more meaningful information—and the development of a good supervisory/management orientation program. It may also require changing the analysts. If the complaints are not valid, confidence must be restored by a well-developed orientation program at all levels about the intent of the program.

THE ROLE OF THE SUPERVISOR IN WORK MANAGEMENT

The key to a successful program is the first-line supervisors. They resist the work management program, or any program, because they view anything new as a possible threat to their security—or because they feel it may cause them more work with little gain.

Supervisors must learn that work management will help them do their jobs better. Their role must be one of active participation with a trained analyst during the study. They must have a voice in the determination of methods upon which standards are based, and they must be allowed to challenge or question any standard they feel is not valid. Unless supervisors believe the standards are fair, they will never accept the performance and staffing results.

The role of the supervisors after the program is installed is that of being in complete charge of their own area of responsibility, and guided by the information in the work management reports. They should not feel that work management runs their department.

Their responsibilities as far as the program is concerned are (1) accurate record keeping, (2) maintaining quality standards, (3) equitable distribution of work, (4) reporting job changes to work measurement, and (5) taking appropriate remedial action.

MANAGEMENT PARTICIPATION

Management must understand the objective and mechanics of the program, and actively support it. In order to do this, management must be kept informed of the progress of the program through periodic meetings and reports.

TECHNIQUES FOR
DEVELOPING ENTHUSIASM

Ralph Waldo Emerson said, "Nothing great was ever achieved without enthusiasm." Enthusiasm is also essential in work management. Furthermore, creating excitement about a program is a key executive task.

Let us now examine some techniques for developing enthusiasm for a work-management program:

1. Have the president participate directly in announcing the program to all levels of the organization.

2. Use company house organs to keep people informed about the progress of the program.

3. Spotlight supervisors and employees who have performed well.

4. Develop a method for rewarding good performance.

5. Encourage use of the program for evaluating new equipment, evaluating suggestions, designing new forms, etc., and announce these achievements to the staff, crediting the standard-setting capability of work measurement.

THE ACTION PLAN

A successful work-management program is one that achieves its objectives with the enthusiastic support and cooperation of the staff. To invigorate a program that has been less than successful requires an action plan. First, look at what is required to achieve the stated objectives:

1. Set accurate work standards.
2. Achieve good coverage.
3. Achieve accurate work counts.
4. Achieve accurate time records.
5. Provide total communication.
6. Analyze reports.
7. Discuss performance with employees.
8. Simplify record keeping.
9. Set goals (performance and staffing).
10. Maintain/improve quality.

The first four points must be accomplished. If standards are not accurate, if you do not have a high percentage of work covered by standards, and if work counts and time records are not accurate, the figures are meaningless.

Perhaps your action plan should be directed at accomplishing one or more of the above to get the program in order. The full burden should not be on the analysts, however. The supervisors should get the analyst to go over each standard with them until they have absolute confidence in them.

Getting the work measured is the supervisor's responsibility as much as the analyst's. Since we can control only work that is measured, we have no control over work that is not measured. The supervisors should examine the work employees are doing "off standard" and suggest to the analyst ways in which the work can be measured. Any kind of control is better than none at all. Reports are meaningless unless work counts and time records are accurate. Supervisors are responsible for ensuring that work counts and time records are accurate.

Point 5 can be addressed once you are confident the first four are in order. Total communication simply means that all levels of the organization must understand the objective and mechanics of the program. Do they or do they not?

Points 6 and 7, analyze reports and discuss performance with employees, are supervisory duties and reflect whether or not they are using the program.

Point 8, simplify record keeping, can and should be considered about 3 months after a unit has been placed on standards. Here again the supervisor should work with the analyst to combine tasks through a procedure called task compression. This can reduce the amount of counting and recording and make it easier to maintain the system.

Point 9, set goals, establishes a definite plan for improving performance and achieving a proper staffing level.

Point 10, maintain and/or improve quality, is a preventive-maintenance factor. Unless close attention is paid to quality problems can arise. Obviously, the first step is to quantify what the current level of quality is, determine whether or not it can be improved, and develop a plan of action to accomplish the goal set. In summary, the action plan is a plan to accomplish any goal established within a specified time frame. The support of the employees should be enlisted to accomplish the objective.

FOLLOW-UP

As with any plan, unless follow-up is made, conditions can and will deteriorate.

Wage Incentives

Work management provides a basis for recognition of good performance. With recognition usually comes some form of reward. Employees feel they deserve to share in productivity improvements. Therefore, various incentive plans such as one or more of the following should be considered:

- Individual wage incentive plan
- Group wage incentive plan

- Special merit increases
- One-shot bonus
- Tie in performance with merit rating
- Tie in performance with salary administration
- Variable hourly rates
- Top pay for top workers
- Profit sharing

Job Enrichment and Work Measurement

Young people in today's work force are demanding a sense of participation and responsibility in organizations. And there has been a growing interest on the part of management regarding the behavioral principles and techniques that can be used to increase productivity and profit in an organization.

The intent of job enrichment is to provide true work motivation by improving the work itself—that is, feeding into the task additional opportunity for personal achievement, responsibility, recognition, growth, and advancement. In this way employees are challenged to grow and develop just as far as their abilities will take them.

Job enrichment is a process of giving subordinates who have demonstrated ability the privilege of making more decisions on their own about how they will do their work. There is no question that management will always decide what is to be accomplished. However, this program allows employees to innovate and devise ways on how they can best get the job done.

The goal of a job-enrichment program is to create an atmosphere where labor and management share the factors that make jobs satisfying. It creates a climate in which management's goals and employee's needs are met. Both feel equally accountable for the quantity and quality of work produced, and for the resulting corporate excellence.

But job enrichment does not work without work measurement. As Robert Ford said in his book, *Motivation through the Work Itself,* "It is not a good attitude that brings about a good performance, but rather the experience of performing well that brings about a good attitude among workers."

BENEFITS

The benefits to be derived from a well-conceived and carefully planned work-management program are:

Cost Reduction

This type of program usually results in savings of from 20 to 40 percent of measured payroll costs. In other words, for every 100 positions that are studied and brought under control, the same amount of work can be done by 60 to 80 people.

Improved Service

Since this type of study involves finding how errors are caused, detected, and corrected, and measures taken to eliminate them completely and to eliminate bottlenecks in the processing cycle, we find that service to customers improves.

Better Supervisors

When supervisors are given special training in modern management techniques and better tools to work with, the result is improved office supervision.

Improved Morale

When people have a better-designed job and a balanced work load and are recognized and rewarded for how well they perform their jobs, morale will naturally be high.

Better Management Information

The objective of all our efforts is to provide management with information that pinpoints problem areas and provides a basis for remedial action.

Communication and participation at all levels of the organization are the key to a successful productivity improvement/work management program. Whether you are at the stage of considering such a program or have a less than satisfactory existing program you want to revitalize, you will find employees, supervisors, and managers quite receptive and cooperative if they understand the objectives and their role in the program.

NOTES

[1] Delmar W. Karger and Franklin H. Bayha, *Engineered Work Measurement,* 3d ed., p. 208, Industrial Press, New York, 1977.

[2] Harold B. Maynard, *Industrial Engineering Handbook,* part 5, p. 108, McGraw-Hill, New York, 1963.

[3] Ibid., part 5, p. 110.

[4] Karger and Bayha, op. cit., p. 203.

[5] Harold B. Maynard, Gustave J. Stegemerten, and John L. Schwab, *Methods-Time Measurement,* pp. 14–15, McGraw-Hill, New York, 1948.

[6] Delmar W. Karger and Franklin H. Bayha, *Engineered Work Measurement,* 3d ed., p. 690, Industrial Press, New York, 1977. By permission.

[7] Ibid.

[8] *Master Standard Data,* pp. 145–164, McGraw-Hill, New York, 1962.

[9] Bruce Payne and David D. Swett, *Office Operations Improvement,* AMACOM, New York, 1967.

[10] Serge A. Birn, Richard M. Crossan, and Ralph Eastwood, *Measurement and Control of Office Costs,* McGraw-Hill, New York, 1961.

[11] H. B. Maynard, William M. Aiken, and J. F. Lewis, *Practical Control of Office Costs,* Management Publishing Corporation, Greenwich, Conn., 1960.

CHAPTER EIGHT

Multiple Linear Regression Analysis

DOUGLAS C. CROCKER

Technical Advisor, Management Services Division, Eastman Kodak Company

Managers want to know how many indirect workers they need to run the modern enterprise. How many chemists, physicists, physiologists, engineers, etc., are needed in basic research? How many in product design or service planning? How many in process development? How many in production? How many in distribution and marketing? How many in support functions (safety, medical, plant services, industrial relations, legal, etc.)? How big should those other staff groups be: purchasing, scheduling, quality control, etc.? How about payroll and the computer programmers? And how many clerical people are needed to support all these?

These are difficult questions. They are becoming more important questions as our enterprises gradually shift to employ more automation and to design products of greater complexity; to provide more services; and to assume greater responsibility for the safety of the worker and the consumer, and the protection of the environment. All these trends are accompanied by a gradual increase in the ratio of indirect to direct labor. Hence the skillful management of indirect labor costs continues to grow in importance.

As noted in Chapter 2, multiple linear regression (MLR) analysis is one method which managers can use to *help* them answer these questions, to help assess their needs for indirect workers. MLR analysis, used with care, understanding, and thorough diagnosis by a competent analyst (who can resist the pressures to abuse the technique), is a powerful and indispensable member of the quantitative methods team.

In concept, the procedure is quite simple and appealing. Variation in conditions causes variation in the labor power required to complete a task. When those many factors which contribute to variation have been measured or counted, their contributions can be simultaneously estimated by MLR analysis. The resulting equation becomes a model—an analogy—of the system and can serve a variety of purposes. This is an extremely versatile analytic process which has great utility—especially for dealing with historical (nonexperimental) data sets.

The reverse side, however, shows a technique which is subject to more misuse and misrepresentation than perhaps any other analytic process. (For a more extensive development of these concerns, see references [1], [6], and [7]). With respect to modeling indirect labor, there is a need to expose the dangers and the opportunities for misinterpretation which accompany the use of this technique.

The aims for this chapter, then, are to:

1. Characterize the MLR process
2. Establish relationships between analytic goals and types of indirect jobs
3. Provide guidelines for the construction and use of regression models
4. Provide precautions and warnings relevant to MLR, and establish what the technique should *not* be expected to do
5. Illustrate the use of MLR with examples of indirect labor modeling
6. Provide appropriate references to supplementary material

CHARACTERIZING THE MLR PROCESS

In a mathematical sense, regression analysis is just an extension of the familiar process of averaging. Where variability exists—for instance, in the time to perform some task—the arithmetic mean is commonly used to represent central tendency, or the typical experience. Where variability is small relative to the mean, the mean may be used for predicting future individual experiences. Of course, as is well known, the variability of sample averages grows smaller with increasing sample size. Thus, daily or weekly averages are expected to be more predictable than individual values or shorter-time-span averages—to be closer to some overall average. The arithmetic mean represents a choice of a central value about which the sum of squares of the distances to each of the individuals is minimized—a "least-squares" process.

Where *variability* of individual events is greater, the mean may not serve as a very good predictor of individual events—even though large-sample averages may still cluster closely about the grand mean. Also, individual events may no longer vary *randomly* but may vary in accordance with changes in *conditions*. Even large-sample averages may shift dramatically according to a shift in conditions. In such cases, what is needed is a *conditional average*—the value that can be expected (typically) for some *specified set of conditions*. Prediction then depends on specifying those conditions. Regression analysis provides the mechanism.

Regression Seen as Conditional Averaging

Regression analysis is simply a process for *conditional averaging*, a process for estimating the rate of change of the expected value relative to changing conditions.

In the indirect labor context, the labor power needed to accomplish a task is represented as the *response variable* Y_i, where the subscript denotes which task. In some cases, the historic value of the arithmetic mean $\overline{Y}$ will be an adequate predictor of the labor power needed for future occurrences of the task—say, for example, the number of labor hours to complete an industrial engineering assignment. This would be true if the individual times clustered closely around the average. The standard deviation of the response s_Y would be used to judge this.

However, if the assignments in question are all to develop floor layouts, the time might be directly related to the areas of those floors (among other things). Floor area then represents the *variable condition* and is called the *predictor variable* or simply the *predictor*.

The conditional average $\hat{Y}_i$ ("*Y* hat") then becomes an estimate of the expected time given the *i*th set of conditions, the area for the *i*th layout. This relationship can be represented as a straight line, as shown in Fig. 8-1, where 10 hypothetical past experiences are plotted. The general equation for the *simple* (one-predictor) model is

$$\hat{Y}_i = b_0 + b_1 X_{i1} \tag{1}$$

where b_0 is the *intercept* (in units of Y), b_1 is the *regression slope* (in units of Y per unit of X_1), and X_1 is the predictor—in this case floor area.

The intercept b_0 should be interpreted as representing the *average effect* (on the response) of *all the things* (potential predictors) *which have been left out of the model*.[1] (It has the same meaning with respect to omitted predictors as $\overline{Y}$ had with respect to the whole system before X_1 was isolated and accounted for.) The intercept will, of course, include time for those events which happen only once per task, regarded as "setup" time.

The regression analysis process chooses values for b_0 and b_1 which provide minimum *residual error variance* for the model given by (1). This residual variance $s_{Y \cdot X}^2$ is computed from the sum of squared deviations of the individual points about the regression line. That is, regression analy-

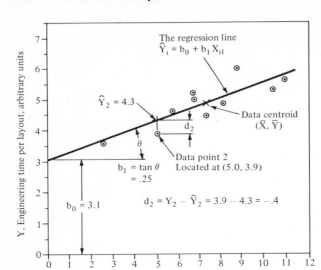

FIG. 8-1. Representation of a simple regression model.

sis, as developed here, is also a "least-squares" estimator—just as the arithmetic mean is, as discussed earlier. In Fig. 8-1, a representative residual deviation is shown by $d_2 = Y_2 - \hat{Y}_2$, a negative quantity indicating that the actual observation is below the line. The (sample) residual variance is given by (2).

$$s^2_{Y \cdot X} = \sum_{i=1}^{n} \frac{d_i^2}{n-2} \tag{2}$$

The square root of this variance $s_{Y \cdot X}$ is the residual standard error for this model. It is represented generically this way for whatever the model contains at that moment. It is literally the standard deviation of individuals around the model—"given X" or "given the model."

Judging Model Adequacy

Depending on goals (more about this later), *one way* to judge the adequacy of the model is to check the size of $s_{Y \cdot X}$: Is it as small as desired for the intended use of the model? Is the reduction from s_Y to $s_{Y \cdot X}$ (corresponding to the shift in model from $\overline{Y}$ to $\hat{Y}_i$) adequate? Later, some quantification of this question will be offered, along with some other criteria of model adequacy.

Now suppose that the *simple* model is judged to be inadequate because $s_{Y \cdot X}$ is too large. One possible course of action is to include additional predictor variables in the model—to create a *multiple* linear regression model.

Dealing with Two or More Predictors

The general form for the multiple linear regression model is just an extension of (1) to include P predictors as shown by (3).

$$\hat{Y}_i = b_0 + \sum_{j=1}^{P} b_j X_{ij} \tag{3}$$

It is regarded as multiple if $P \geq 2$. It is *linear* because the unknown constants, the b's, appear in linear form. (This permits the direct determination of the b's as weighted averages of the Y_i's, whereas nonlinear forms require recursive processes to find best solutions for the unknown b's.)

In developing MLR models, analysts make choices. They select potential predictors for the model based on knowledge of the system. They examine the set of potential predictor variables to see which ones make important contributions to reducing residual variability. The system can be thought of as a large set of true predictors which, as they vary, create variation in the response. It is virtually impossible to sort them all out and to account for all the variation in any real system. So the process is one of choosing the most important variables to include in the model while leaving behind as residual error the large number of small contributors. This process is depicted schematically in Fig. 8-2.

The shaded areas represent contributions to variation in the response variable. They accumulate here from very small at the right to the largest contributor at the left. Including the largest contributor as X_1 reduces the variance by $1/3$, the next by $1/4$, the next $1/6$, etc. The choice of a cutoff point depends on goals, on availability and cost of data, and especially on the interrelationships among the predictors. In this idealized representation, the first four largest contributing predictors were chosen to be included in the model, the rest (possibly all unknown or unmeasured) being left in the residual error.

Perhaps one broad generality can be offered to provide some sense of magnitude in association with this question of predictor subset selection. In adequately modeling *direct* labor tasks, it is often necessary to use three or four or even a dozen predictors. *Indirect* jobs are—pretty much by definition—more complex and more highly variable. That is precisely why their measurement has been so long neglected. It is rare in the author's experience for the more repetitive, most easily measured indirect jobs to be adequately modeled with less than four or five predictors. The guiding principle is that model *adequacy* rather than *simplicity* must be the goal. (Of course, this question is interrelated with *analytic* goals,

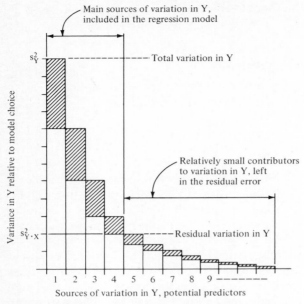

FIG. 8-2. Relative importance of sources of variation.

types of indirect jobs involved, and degree of job aggregation—topics covered below.)

The difficulty of the modeling process should not be underestimated. There are many interrelated factors—statistical measures and diagnostics, modeling techniques, as well as practical issues—which must be simultaneously considered in developing regression models. Thorough treatment of all the relevant topics is far beyond the scope of this work. Several textbooks provide adequate coverage of the theoretical/mathematical aspects of regression analysis (see [2], [3], and [9]). For a more philosophical and practical guide to the process of regression *modeling*, see [5]. Additional elaboration on several topics, important in the indirect labor modeling setting, can be found in the series of articles being prepared [6]:

Topic	*Article Number*
1. Common Fallacies in MLR	II
2. The True Nature of Residual Error	III, IV
3. Statistical Fundamentals for the Simple Model	III
4. Effects of Intercorrelation	IV
5. Interactions in Regression Modeling	V

GOALS AND THE ANALYTICAL PROCESS

MLR is often of assistance in the pursuit of a wide variety of goals. It is not difficult to list a dozen. Yet MLR is not a single procedure which can be explicitly written as a unique set of instructions. It is, in fact, a wide variety of processes, diagnostic tools, decision points, questions, insights, and results. These must be creatively strung together by analysts as they seek their particular goals. The chain, the sequence, the emphasis will be different for different goals. Therefore, it is extremely important to specify the project goal(s) clearly.

It is also critically important for an analyst to know who the client is, and for that client to be enlisted in the process. This will help to assure that: (1) the specified goals are in fact those of the clients and reflect their needs; (2) the client's knowledge of the system becomes a project resource; and (3) the client acquires understanding of the model. This third item might be called "faith and ownership." Without this involvement, the client will not develop faith in the model. Absence of faith often means that the model will not be effectively used.

There is another excellent reason for client involvement: clients will learn a great deal about their system—in direct proportion to their participation.

Categorizing Goals

Some useful mapping of the territory can be achieved by categorizing goals. The author's categorization scheme, developed in [5], consists of five broad goal classes which comprise four natural steps in the evolution of a model. The five classes are:

1. Exploration—learning about the system
2. Specification—picking a model form
3. Estimation—establishing the b's with adequate precision
4a. Prediction—use of the model for anticipating future events
4b. Control—use of the model to direct policy or to alter system performance

In a variety of situations and statistical environments, any one of these goals may serve as an end point in the evolution. Not all projects evolve to step 4. However, in modeling indirect labor systems, most projects will proceed at least to step 3. Exploration and specification will rarely be end goals in such studies. Typically, indirect labor models will have goals which fall into the last three categories as follows:

Estimation: cost accounting, economic evaluation/planning
Prediction: planning (for recruiting, training, providing facilities), scheduling, allocating, bidding
Control: detection of trends, changes, and deviant performance[2]

Of course, it is somewhat artificial to "force" goals into these categories which are not operationally mutually exclusive. For instance, *control* may be enhanced by detecting a trend, but *estimation* of that trend might then be an important aspect of the study. Also, many projects have multiple goals which overlap these categories. The intent is only to help clarify the process by providing an underlying structure, and abstraction to hang ideas on.

Notice, too, that most of these example goals are directed at increasing the *effectiveness of the organization* in quite indirect ways. That is where the major opportunities for improvement lie. Only in the last case, and there only in the most restricted sense (see under Some Precautions and Warnings), can regression modeling be involved with performance appraisal.

Indirect Effectiveness

The author feels compelled to state his personal conviction regarding the motivation of indirect personnel. The discussion under the next heading will offer some clarification of the relationships between types of indirect jobs and associated types of models. The discussion here pertains to people who are employed in the nonrepetitive jobs where specification of job content, duties, and functions is very broad and nonoperational, mostly "professional" people.

Managers hire people with talents which they hope will contribute to the goals of the enterprise. They cannot very well specify or measure those talents beyond the labels derived from college courses which have been taken. What people do is only roughly guided by specifications that can be crisply stated. These people are generally *highly* motivated. They *enjoy* their work. They *want* to be effective.

Now, it is easier to prescribe a solution than to effect one. It may not be easy to know specifically what to do, what action to take. But, idealistically, to achieve maximum effectiveness from professional workers,[3] managers need to:

1. Hire the right talents in the right numbers
2. Establish goals that are mutually understood
3. Provide the facilities required for the task
4. Provide an environment conducive to the performance of the task
5. Establish remuneration policies designed to keep creative talent creating

If managers will concentrate on these aims—will direct their modeling and other efforts at resolving these questions—they will have no need for schemes which offer artificial and superficial measures of effectiveness, which may have disruptive and dysfunctional side effects.

The Ambiguity Continuity

The indirect job family lies on a continuum (perhaps more precisely characterized as a *multidimensional space*) where "ambiguity" is the operative word. *Ambiguity,* with respect to job description or function specification, lies at the polar extreme from *structure* or *programmability.* Because of the ambiguous nature of most indirect jobs, it is difficult to know how many of "those folks" are needed. What they are needed *for*—hired to do—among other things is to cope with ambiguity, to absorb uncertainty. They can be especially successful in applying their other technical skills if they have a talent for *knowing and doing* what is needed without being *told* what is needed. These are self-directing people. But how many does it take?

Before discussing how regression analysis can help in answering that question, it may be useful first to examine in more detail the nature of this job space and how goals and assessment processes relate to it. Figure 8-3 illustrates these relationships. At the top, the job-type continuum slides across from the direct jobs at the extreme left (where jobs are extreme in their characteristics) to indirect jobs at the extreme right. Several closely related and overlapping scales of job characteristics are shown below that in relation to the direct-indirect scale. A direct job at the extreme left would be characterized as being highly structured, relatively uncomplicated, comprised entirely of predetermined steps, and having therefore low variability in content and time per cycle. At this extreme, this refined short-cycle task tends to be repeated with few interruptions from the performance of auxiliary tasks. The results are immediate, obvious, and countable. Examples are small-parts assembly, press feeding, packaging, keypunch operation, assembly-line stations, and garment stitching.

At the other extreme, jobs are complex and unstructured, and tend to require self-starting, creative behavior to solve problems. Each task or assignment may be unique in its requirements, but even where a basic pattern may be repeated, it will contain great variation in content and time per cycle. Typically, there will be simultaneous or overlapping attention to several projects—each of which may be months or years in duration. The quality and even the appropriateness of this activity is difficult to judge. Consequences of such efforts will be remote, dispersed in time and place, and extremely difficult to isolate or effectively quantify. Examples are the activities of research chemists, medical doctors, lawyers, architects, engineers, mathematicians, statistical analysts, product designers, process designers, plant and equipment designers, project coordinators, and teachers.

Job Type	Direct _____ (Continuum) _____ Indirect		
Job Characteristics			
Ambiguity	Highly structured		Generally unstructured
Complexity	Low		High
Creativity	Predetermined steps		Self-determined steps
Variability	Low		High when repeated
Repetition	Normal		Tend not to repeat
Task duration	Short		Long
Input-output association	Close, immediately assessable results		Remote, results difficult to assess
Assessment process	Direct assessment of individual tasks	Indirect assessment of individual tasks	Indirect assessment of aggregate tasks, functions
Regression role	Generalize results from direct assessment	Assess relationships of labor consumption to measures of production, task descriptions	Assess relationships of staff group-sizes to major task indices
Relevant Modeling Goals			
Estimation	Cost accounting, economic evaluation and planning, budgeting, wage determination	Cost accounting, economic evaluation, planning, budgeting	Economic evaluation and planning, budgeting, assessment of impact of societal changes
Prediction	Planning Scheduling Sequencing Expediting	Planning Scheduling Sequencing Expediting Bidding	Planning Allocating
Control	Detection of: Trends Changes Deviant performance (above and below expectation)	Detection of: Trends Changes Deviant performance (above and below expectation)	Detection of: Trends Changes

FIG. 8-3. Regression goals related to the job continuum.

There is a vast middle ground of jobs which fill in the continuum and tend to have intermediate positions on these job characteristics. Examples of these are the activities of some technicians, computer programmers, sales personnel, nurses, and some jobs related to warehousing, marketing, maintenance, and office functions.

The Role of Regression in Job Assessment

Referring again to Fig. 8-3 for relational characterization, we need next to tie in the job-assessment process. This process relates naturally and directly to the spectrum of job types shown above it. With *direct jobs, direct assessment of individual tasks is possible and economically practical.* Time study, use of predetermined time standards, and a variety of other techniques provide for assessment of these jobs.

As jobs ascend the scales of complexity, variability, and cycle duration, it becomes gradually less economical and physically less possible to use such means of direct assessment. Here, *indirect assessment of individual tasks* is possible. Farther up the scale, individual tasks become indistinct and overlapping to the extent that they can no longer be sensibly defined for direct assessment purposes. Here, *indirect assessment of aggregate tasks and functions* is the most that can be achieved.

Regression analysis techniques play a role in all three of these spectral subdivisions. In relationship to *direct* jobs, regression analysis is commonly used to *generalize results* that are obtained by more direct observation or study. In the *middle ground,* MLR can be used to *assess the relationships* of the amounts of time (needed to perform a task) to various measures of production or task descriptors. (For dealing with questions of performance effectiveness, the reader is referred to Chapter 2 under An In-Between Approach. The emphasis there is that determining acceptable performance is a matter of judgment and is not part of the regression analysis.)

As the *extreme indirect* end of the scale is approached, regression analysis can still be used to *quantify the labor content of aggregate tasks and functions* by finding the historical relationships of staff group sizes to major task indexes. For example, the size of the plant and equipment development engineering staff may be directly related to capital expenditures. Past research and development expenses might be expected to relate closely to product and process development staffs. (The particular nature of such relationships will be examined in more detail later.)

Goals and Reality

The bottom section of Fig. 8-3 relates various modeling goals to job type. This is done for the three broad classes of relevant goals discussed earlier. Obviously, relating goals to job type in this way implies that not all conceivable goals are appropriate in relation to all job classes. That is the case. For instance, as shown under the goal class "estimation," wage determination is often an appropriate modeling goal for direct jobs but would normally not be appropriate for indirect jobs. Notice particularly the absence of performance appraisal functions from the list of modeling goals in the lower right-hand box of Fig. 8-3.

In general, detection of trends or changes can be classed in this last row under Control. One somewhat subtle interpretation of "detection of change" would be the use of MLR techniques to evaluate experimental change or comparison of alternative methods. The specific technique for dealing with such cases is presented below under An Example to Demonstrate Some Technical Points.

At this indirect extreme, month-to-month, project-to-project assessment of performance and specific personnel needs can best be performed by local supervisors and managers who have familiarity with the project and its goals, the technology represented, and the individual capabilities of the people involved. No matter how strongly company executives feel the need to find a mechanism for supplanting this process, for gaining closer control, or for reducing the ambiguity they perceive regarding this process, no indirect assessment scheme can adequately serve this purpose. There simply is no magic formula—or mechanism for finding one—that can evaluate the simultaneous effects of hundreds, perhaps thousands, of contributing sources of variation.

This situation represents the extreme of the concept illustrated in Fig. 8-2. In these cases—the extreme indirect—the sources of variation are not only great in number but indistinct and qualitative rather than quantitative. The vertical predictor boundaries of Fig. 8-2 disappear, and the whole figure flattens out to a long, low, flat curve.

The situation is not at all as desperate as it may seem. The problem is its own solution. At the extreme indirect end of the scale where job content is least definable, the people are best able to *independently* achieve efficiency and effectiveness—to be productive. They will *find* ways to be productive, to *create* useful roles. Their natural behavior will be to induce growth. Management's task is then to make *aggregate* judgments about *validity:* How rapidly shall growth be permitted in response to these growth pressures? What level of indirect employment provides an optimal balance considering several conflicting factors which typically arise? Some of these factors are:

1. Smooth assimilation of new people including concern for recruitment, training and orientation, and provision of facilities

2. Avoidance of overreaction to growth pressures which can create instability and inefficiency, and induce expensive oscillation

3. Selection of projects which are cost-effective while avoiding submarginal projects which may be stimulating, interesting, and fun, but of low yield (validity, too, lies on a continuum)

In short, management must strive to be neither understaffed, missing fruitful opportunities, nor overstaffed, engaging in submarginal activity.

Regression modeling can be of enormous assistance in finding that middle ground and in planning the consequent future.

GUIDELINES FOR
REGRESSION MODELING

No attempt will be made here to offer a complete discussion of all the relevant statistical procedures which form the basis for regression analysis. Most of the technical issues are adequately treated in references already cited. However, a couple of technical questions are fundamentally involved in the evolutionary decision processes that comprise regression modeling. These need to be understood by the involved client, manager, or project leader who may not be entirely familiar with the general statistical procedures. The following example is intended to serve this purpose, to illustrate these particular concepts.

An Example to Demonstrate Some Technical Points

Real examples—actual collected data sets—have a way of providing too rich a feast. They contain too many diversions and lead to too many side issues. Contextual interpretations or judgments or policies might be questioned and become the focus of the reader's attention rather than the intended technical message. The following hypothetical data set (Fig. 8-4) was created in order to present several abstract concepts.

The two predictor variables X_1 and X_2 are intended to represent countable job characteristics. The third predictor, X_3, represents a job attribute, the presence or absence of some condition.

Attribute coding An attribute coding such as this (zero-one) can be used to introduce into a regression model any question whatsoever that can be logically conceived. It might represent a question about the influence of weather (with or without air conditioning). It could be used to estimate or represent the difference between two different methods, machines, or processes. *Two* such predictors could be used to account for differences in performance among *three* classes of machines—say, with respect to maintenance requirements. A code could be included to represent a shift in performance where a new training procedure was instituted. This concept of coding represents a very powerful and extremely versatile modeling device. Modelers should avoid restricting themselves to quantitative descriptions of conditions.

Interactions "Interaction" means that the *effect* of one predictor (its slope or regression coefficient) *changes* with respect to changing *values* of another predictor. An interaction is represented in a model by the *product* of two (or more) predictors. (The time to type a report might depend on the number of pages, the number of different Selectric-type ele-

i	X_1	X_2	X_3	X_4	X_5	Y
01	0.0	62.	0.0	0.0	0.0	109.1
02	7.0	37.	0.0	0.0	0.0	130.4
03	15.	19.	1.	15.	19.	310.7
04	2.0	45.	0.0	0.0	0.0	107.0
05	8.0	31.	1.	8.0	31.	271.8
06	5.0	73.	1.	5.0	73.	325.1
07	0.0	60.	1.	0.0	60.	253.6
08	0.0	47.	1.	0.0	47.	209.7
09	0.0	81.	1.	0.0	81.	294.9
10	12.	29.	0.0	0.0	0.0	135.6
11	10.	48.	0.0	0.0	0.0	151.9
12	3.0	59.	0.0	0.0	0.0	130.6
13	4.0	63.	1.	4.0	63.	291.4
14	9.0	71.	0.0	0.0	0.0	171.2
15	9.0	35.	0.0	0.0	0.0	134.0
16	17.	51.	0.0	0.0	0.0	173.9
17	4.0	70.	0.0	0.0	0.0	144.1
18	18.	17.	1.	18.	17.	334.0
19	12.	44.	1.	12.	44.	329.1
20	1.0	86.	1.	1.0	86.	317.8

FIG. 8-4. Data for demonstration example.

ments used, and the interaction of these two. That is, the time per page would increase with increasing numbers of element changes.) In the present data set, X_4 and X_5 are created as the products, respectively, of X_1 and X_2 with the attribute X_3. These represent a special case of interaction where the effect of X_1 and X_2 changes according to the condition represented by X_3. The two interaction terms then provide for the corresponding change (increase or decrease in slope of X_1 and X_2).

Intercorrelation Typically, in working with nonexperimental (collected) data, the various predictors will be found to correlate with each other. Correlation between predictors is usually called intercorrelation. Usually, the presence of intercorrelation makes it more difficult to discriminate the separate effects or relationships of the several predictors with the response variable. This is the case where the predictors are "confounded" with one another—where they tend to contain the same information by varying nearly in parallel.

Rather frequently, an opposite effect of intercorrelation will be experienced. That is, the relationship between two (or more) predictors will

SSReg 1 alone	3174
SSReg 2 alone	368
Sum	3542
SSReg 1 and 2 together	9041
Increase from resolving	5499
Percent increase	155

FIG. 8-5. Resolving effect illustrated.

serve to mask their separate effects unless they are simultaneously included in the regression model. The author has named this condition "resolving." A more detailed examination of this phenomenon is presented in [6], Article IV.

In the present example, X_1 and X_2 enjoy such a resolving relationship. This effect can best be appreciated by obtaining the regression sum of squares (SSReg) associated with each predictor introduced alone and then comparing the sum of these two quantities with the total SSReg for the two-predictor model including both X_1 and X_2. This comparison is shown in Fig. 8-5. The joint effect of the two predictors is 155 percent greater than the sum of their separate effects.

Examining the model   Figure 8-6 gives several summary statistics for the five-predictor model fitted to the data of Fig. 8-4. This brief summary does not provide all the diagnostic aids the analyst would normally examine during model development. It does provide the essentials for evaluating the model and the adequacy of the data set.

From the information contained in Fig. 8-6, the analyst will address several questions—in the context of the particular problem and with respect to the particular goals. Some of these are:

1. Do the mean values $(\overline{X}_1, \overline{X}_2)$ seem representative?
2. Is variation in X_1 and X_2 (represented here by s_X) adequate in this sample to permit predictor influence to be seen and estimated?

j	$\overline{X}_j$	s_X	r_{XY}	R_{jX}	b_j	s_b	t_j	$n = 20$
0	1.00	0	—	—	58.2	8.87	6.56	$\overline{Y} = 216$
1	6.80	5.84	0.151	0.823	4.37	0.401	10.90	$s_Y = 87.4$
2	51.4	19.7	0.052	0.880	0.960	0.142	6.78	$R_{YX} = 0.998$
3	0.500	0.513	0.931	0.981	56.9	13.4	4.25	$s_{Y \cdot X} = 5.79$
4	3.15	5.62	0.688	0.930	5.75	0.642	8.95	$s_{Y \cdot X}/\overline{Y} = 0.027$
5	26.1	31.7	0.782	0.977	1.25	0.186	6.35	% s_Y removed = 93.2

FIG. 8-6. Regression model summary values.

3. Are the multiple correlations of each of the predictors as related to the other predictors excessively high? (This might indicate any of a number of problems associated with intercorrelations.)

4. Do the b_j's make sense (sign and magnitude)?

5. Do the t-ratios (b/s_b) indicate that sufficient precision has been achieved in estimating the b_j's? If not, is it because the X's did not vary enough, because the sample size is too small, or because of intercorrelation effects? Or is it simply that the predictor in question does not have the expected association with the response?

6. Is $s_{Y·x}$ small enough? Is it as small as might be expected? Does examination of residual deviations suggest the omission of important predictors or the presence of data errors?

7. Considering project goals, is the model adequate?

Notice that the multiple correlation by itself is not a very useful statistic. It is a handy *index for comparing models* but does not relate directly to the question of *model adequacy*. This can be seen from the relationship given by (4).

$$\text{Percent } s_Y \text{ removed} = 100 \left\{ 1 - \left[\frac{(1 - R)(n - 1)}{n - P - 1} \right]^{1/2} \right\}$$

$$= \frac{100(s_Y - s_{Y·X})}{s_Y} \tag{4}$$

Here, R is the R_{YX} of Fig. 8-6. The first form of this expression measuring the reduction in variation in Y (going from the model $\overline{Y}$ to the model $\hat{Y}_i$) shows this *reduction* being a function of R. [The multiplication by the ratio $(n - I)/(n - P - 1)$ is just a correction for lost degrees of freedom.] But this (percent s_Y removed) can take on *any* value within its permissible range (and hence so can R) for a *fixed value of* $s_{Y·x}$, depending on what value of s_Y was obtained in the sample. This is shown by the second (equivalent) form in (4), where it is seen that the ratio can be completely controlled by choice of s_Y. In practice, where prediction and/or control are the goals, $s_{Y·x}$ is the essential measure of model adequacy. (A control model will generally be effective where $s_{Y·x}$ is less than 10 percent of $\overline{Y}$.) In estimation, the t-ratios will be the final measure of the adequacy of the analytic process. The absolute size of R simply is not of any use. (Further discussion of the interpretation of R can be found in [4].)

Notice in Fig. 8-6 that b_0 is approximately 27 percent of $\overline{Y}$. That is, the *fixed* part of Y together with the *average (uncorrelated) contribution of omitted contributors to variation in Y* account for about 27 percent of the average response. If, in this example, any of the five predictors had been omitted, this percentage would be correspondingly higher. This intercept value, b_0, rarely drops to insignificance and sometimes exceeds 50 percent of $\overline{Y}$, even with reasonably well fitting models.

Interpreting t-ratios The t-ratios may be the most important measure if estimation is the goal. In prediction and control, estimation is an important supporting process or intermediate goal and again requires proper interpretation of the t-ratios.

Essentially, the t-ratio for a predictor is a measure of its *unique* contribution of Y-related information (represented by predictor variation). Thus, in the example, it can be used to answer the question: "Do the interaction terms show evidence that they are real? (Does the structure represented by them really contribute to variation in Y?)" Here, t-ratios greater than about 2 in absolute value would be strong evidence of the reality of the interactions. So the conclusion here would be that they are *real* (as are all "main effects" including b_3, the coefficient for attribute code X_3).

But are the interactions of any *practical importance* in the model? This, again, depends on specific goals. It is possible for them to be real but still have their inclusion in the model not be of any practical importance with respect to the model's intended use. In this case, the conclusion would probably be that they do contribute substantially. For a more detailed examination of this question, see [8].

In the process of using the b's as estimates of the long-term relationships of Y with the X's in the model, the t-ratio has a direct interpretation given by (5).

$$E = \frac{200}{t} \tag{5}$$

Here E is the maximum probable percent error that might be expected in using b as an estimate of the "true" value. Thus a t-ratio of 20 would suggest that the estimate is within about 10 percent of the truth. With $t = 40$, the error might be no larger than 5 percent. This relationship is developed in [5].

Another feature of Fig. 8-6 deserves mention, the column of coefficients of correlation (r_{XY}) of each predictor with the response. In view of the overall ability of the model to reproduce the response variable, and the relatively large t-ratios associated with the first two predictors, one might expect to find fairly large individual correlations for these two. This measure is depressed in this case for the X_1, X_2 pair because of pairwise resolving. Confounding would act in a reverse manner; some predictor variables might be useless and have very small t-ratios even though their correlations with Y are very high.

Some Guiding Principles

With the foregoing discussion of some technical questions serving as a supporting platform, we can now examine some principles which are more practical in nature and will serve to guide the modeling process.

1. Establish reasonably specific goals for the modeling project at the outset.

2. Know which job-type spectral domain the target job belongs in and choose modeling goals that are appropriate to that domain.

3. Establish a project team that includes the client, other system experts as needed, and a competent analyst.

4. Use a computer program that provides adequate diagnostics.

5. Proceed with a cyclical, diagnostic, evolutionary approach to modeling through interaction of the system experts and analyst.

6. Start with a preliminary data sample. Extend the sample as needed to obtain precision.

7. Be alert to the effects of intercorrelation—both confounding and resolving.

8. Build models with complexity sufficient to represent the complexity of the system. Let adequacy, not simplicity, be the goal.

9. Recognize the probable need of an intercept term, the possibility of interactions, and the utility of attribute coding.

10. Ask meaningful questions regarding model adequacy. Use appropriate statistics to answer them.

11. There is no quarantee of success, but expect to learn a great deal about the system even though no useful model is derived.

12. Remember that change in the system should be expected. This implies a need for model maintenance.

13. Learning about and using MLR is like weaving a web of interconnected concepts. Do not expect it to be a ritualized connecting of links in a chain.

SOME PRECAUTIONS AND WARNINGS

Most of the principles are embodied in the foregoing list. But there are still some traps that the unwary might stumble upon. Some of these are listed below.

1. Watch out for estimation precision. It can easily happen that $s_{Y \cdot X}$ is nicely small, that the *model* is adequate in every sense, but that the coefficients have been very poorly estimated (small t-ratios) because of confounding among the predictors. It is likely that such a model will become unstable when used for prediction.

2. Be careful not to reject a promising predictor which does not relate to Y simply because, in the development data set, that predictor experienced insufficient variation. This could occur, for example, because that predictor was prevented from varying and had no opportunity (in *that* data set) to influence Y.

3. Be cautious in choosing predictors which are very difficult or expensive to obtain routinely. Some special operational procedures may be needed.

4. Be sure that predictors chosen for a prediction model can be themselves predicted or predetermined by plan, or their close association to the response will be of little value.

5. Be extremely careful in using regression models (any models, for that matter) in performance appraisal situations to see that the use of certain predictors does not in effect establish motivation to neglect (other) important functions. This danger is especially great where such a model is superficial and inadequate to represent the complexity of the system modeled.

6. In establishing control models and in some cases prediction models, it is important that known causal relationships operate in the proper direction. If A is a controlled variable (say the number of engineers devoted to process automation), and B is caused by A (say the output from the factory per direct labor hour), then it would be foolish to use B as a *predictor* of A even though it *correlates* strongly with A. A is directly controlled through (caused by) the budgeting/planning process. If, by some process, an increase in B is "predicted," that will not cause A to increase, whereas a deliberate increase in A is (statistically) expected to cause an associated increase in B.

7. No matter how strong the physical relationships may be, no analyst can sort out the relationships if there is no variation in the response. If data are collected in terms of so many this and so many that *per week* and a week *always* has 40 hours (or 17 people times 40 hours), there is nothing to learn from these data by regression analysis. The model $\hat{Y}_i = \overline{Y}$ will fit perfectly.

8. Probably no data set containing more than a few dozen entries has ever been collected free of errors. *Assume* that there are errors. Institute methods for finding errors (such as univariate preexamination of data, pairwise plotting of Y with each predictor, and close examination of back-substitution plots).

9. In the author's mind, this ninth and last precaution is the most important of all. It has to do with the interpretation of those residual "errors" or residual differences, $Y - \hat{Y}$. Using the most elaborate and complicated model imaginable—that is, accounting for "everything"—there will still be unexplained, residual variation measured by $Y - \hat{Y}$, the individual deviations above and below the model. These differences are composed of the large number of small, *unmeasured, unknown,* or *unknowable* contributions to variation in Y. It is reasonable and proper to account for any and all factors which can be suggested, even to speculatively *obtain* and include information to see if it associates with the response.

Further, it is essentially mandatory to examine those residual differences (associated with the members of the development data set) which are statistically *extreme*. The analyst would be alert to several possibilities:

(1) identifiable mistakes in the data, (2) existence of identifiable conditions which have not been included in the model but which should be, or (3) existence of identifiable conditions which the model is not intended to encompass—in which case data elimination would be appropriate. If, after careful examination, the cause of deviation cannot be found, it is certainly permissible and desirable to exclude such deviant points from the development set.

At this point, all knowledge about deviations has been exploited, incorporated, used, and/or accounted for. What is left in the residual errors is of *unknown origin*. There is absolutely no justification for a modeler to claim at this point that the residual deviations reflect *differences in performance. No such claim can be made.* The origins of the differences are *unknown*.

Further, in using such a model for predicting *future* results, suppose an individual point were to deviate quite widely from expectation. In a "control chart" sense, there is reason then to suspect an "assignable cause." That is, it is likely that some new condition or unrecognized change has occurred. It is proper to use this "trigger device" or "red flag" to prompt an investigation into the cause—to look for change or aberrant conditions. It is totally improper to arbitrarily attribute such a deviation to "performance."

Establishing appropriate control limits around a regression surface requires slightly complicated calculations {(see [6], Article IX)}. The limits widen as the combination of X values moves away from the center of the development data set. As a general rule for specifying these limits, it would be well to adopt a "3-sigma" (3-standard-deviation) strategy in order to avoid the expense of investigating deviations which are really part of the normal pattern of variation. Also, it is generally true that temporarily missing some real "assignable cause" will not have very serious consequences.

Suppose the model is intended to account for sales per territory where, for each territory, various relevant indexes have been introduced to try to account for variation in results—such as number of certain kinds of business or customer density (reflecting differences in travel time). Now a territory that falls below the model does so for *unknown* reasons. To suggest that it is due to poor performance is grossly unfair. The sales personnel in that territory may be making up for extraordinary difficulty by giving superperformance while those in a territory falling *above* the model may in fact be missing a great potential which could be realized by application of the diligent effort employed (unknown to us) by the former group.

The use of regression *residuals* as indicators of performance is totally improper—even though the models used to obtain such residuals may be the closest analogy to reality that is possible to obtain. The same follows a fortiori for less complete models.

EXAMPLES OF INDIRECT
LABOR MODELING

As indirect labor costs continue to climb, methods for increasing the productivity of white collar workers must be sought. Regression modeling is such a method. Its use can help to assess needs, plan for stable growth, allocate scarce indirect worker power resources, and in many other ways contribute to the increased effectiveness of the enterprise.

The following examples are some applications the author has experienced:

1. Programming time for numerically controlled machining operations as functions of machining specifications
2. Prediction of number of people needed in regional distribution offices and warehouses as functions of various countable activities
3. Punch press setup times as a function of die characteristics
4. Maintenance labor as a function of product characteristics and unscheduled downtime
5. Relationship of warehouse labor to various measures of activities such as order filling and packing
6. Sales volume by dealer as a function of market characteristics
7. Sales volume as a function of sales personnel strategies, including some which were experimental
8. Many instances of relating the number within a family of professionals to aggregate measures or indexes of related functions

A serious obstacle to modeling efforts of this last kind is the shortage of aggregate data. Typically, such things as research or capital budgets might be useful as indexes. But they are normally annual features of the system. History may provide only 15 or 20 years of data to relate family populations to functions. Indexes of these functions tend to be confounded, further complicating the task. Also, these relationships are expected to be dispersed over time, some members being involved in planning, some in execution, some in later staffing or associated with consequent sales.

Such relationships are expected, also, to *change* over time. For instance, we might expect a gradual *decrease* in effectiveness of some professionals in relation to their *primary* tasks because of increasing attention to *secondary* tasks arising out of legal, social, and environmental requirements.

Considering these several intermingled perturbations and the limitations imposed by a severe data shortage, the author was recently able to find an essentially perfect relationship ($r = 0.997$) between the average annual size of a large and rapidly growing staff group and an aggregate index of company activity. The raw correlation of group size to the index was around 0.18. But by exponentially smoothing the index (to approximate the way its effect would be expected to be dispersed in time) and by applying to it an exponent which grows linearly over time (to account for growth in secondary tasks), this very strong relationship was established. The model is sensible and can help management a great deal in anticipating future relationships and expected personnel requirements for this group of people.

NOTES

[1] That is, to the extent that the effects of such omitted factors have not already been picked up by their association—correlation—with the included predictor. See the discussion under Examining the Model.

[2] This last use regarding deviant performance must be carefully qualified. Please refer to the discussion under Some Precautions and Warnings.

[3] None of this should be taken to suggest that direct workers will not be responsive to the same treatment. That simply is not the issue here.

REFERENCES

[1] Box, G. E. P.: "The Use and Abuse of Regression," *Technometrics*, vol. 8, no. 4, November 1966, pp. 625–629.
[2] Chatterjee, Samprit, and Bertram Price: *Regression Analysis by Example*, Wiley, New York, 1977.
[3] Cohen, Jacob, and Patricia Cohen: *Applied Multiple Regression/Correlation for the Behavioral Sciences*, Lawrence Erlbaum Associates, Publishers, Hillsdale, N.J., 1975.
[4] Crocker, Douglas C.: "Some Interpretations of the Multiple Correlation Coefficient," *The American Statistician*, vol. 26, no. 2, 1972, pp. 31–33.
[5] ———: "Regression and Correlation," chap. XIII-6, *Industrial Engineering Handbook*, Gavriel Salvendy (ed.), Wiley, New York, 1981.
[6] ———: "Regression Analysis: Toward a Theory of Practice," *AIIE Transactions*, A tutorial series of 10 articles, in preparation.
[7] Hahn, G. J., and S. S. Shapiro: "The Use and Misuse of Multiple Regression," *Industrial Quality Control*, October 1966, pp. 184–189.
[8] Salem, M. D., Jr.: "Multiple Linear Regression Analysis for Work Measurement of Indirect Labor," *Journal of Industrial Engineering*, vol. 18, no. 5, 1967, pp. 314–319.
[9] Younger, Mary Sue: *A Handbook for Linear Regression*, Duxbury Press, North Scituate, Mass., 1979.

CHAPTER NINE

Common Staffing System

DAVID L. CONWAY
Consultant Industrial Engineer, International Business Machines Corporation

Common Staffing System (CSS) is an approach to indirect labor measurement developed by IBM. It is intended to be an *approximate* measurement of *groupings* of indirect labor using various productivity-type measures which relate the amount of worker power input associated with measurable work causes or outputs of the groupings.

Perhaps this chapter should be prefaced by pointing out that the rather unique styles/philosophies represented by this approach are quite different from the rigorous scientific or statistical treatment often followed by industrial engineers and discussed elsewhere in this book.

Several statistical models had previously been designed by the author and others in the company that had provided indirect measurements having a high degree of demonstrable validity; these, however, were understood and used by only a few industrial engineering people.

The approach described here is built on an underlying premise that, if it is to *achieve results* (i.e., improve productivity), a measurement system must be designed for the people who are in a position to make change—the first-level managers in all the locations.

The concept, then, is one that involves the active participation of virtually all indirect managers in the design of the measurements, gathering of data, and most importantly, following through on the measurement results to actually achieve the productivity improvements. It was decided that the technique to be employed for such a system must, of necessity, be simple and straightforward. It is therefore an effective *management system* but makes no claim to statistical sophistication or precision.

CSS has been used by IBM to make comparative analyses on a period-to-period basis, to obtain an index of individual location performance relative to other locations for both specific indirect labor activity as well as the total of all measured indirect activities.

While the originators and users of the CSS technique are careful to point out that it should not be regarded as an absolute measurement of indirect labor requirements or a precise assessment of performance, they do regard it as a *reasonable* management tool to assess *relative* indirect productivity levels, and as a method for identifying, in some detail, potential areas for improvement. It is also viewed as a valuable device to be used along with other inputs and judgments in planning future indirect requirements based on reasonable productivity assumptions.

CONCEPT

Basically, the program, which is variously called the Common Staffing Study, the Common Staffing System (CSS), or the Functional Performance System (FPS), depending on the business area, compares productivity over time and between different business units.

The CSS technique is based on identification of discrete activities or tasks performed as part of a particular job function. The activities are associated with the "equivalent head count" performing them. Each of the activities is also related to a quantifiable work cause or reason for its existence. The activity head count and quantifiable cause are the data base from which performance indexes are calculated and are the basis for comparative analysis.

The following examples are taken from the manufacturing CSS installation, but the same concepts apply for other business areas as well.

1. Various "functions" are identified and subdivided into "activities." For example:

Under the purchasing function, we may define such activities as *estimating, buying,* and *expediting*.

Under the accounting function, we may define such activities as *accounts receivable, accounts payable, bookkeeping,* and *asset management*.

2. Each activity takes place for some reason (or work cause). For example:

The reason (or work cause) for the accounts payable activity can be related to the number of receipts processed.

The reason (or work cause) for secretarial services is to support plant indirect personnel in performance of their jobs.

3. The amount of activity which takes place (or should take place) is related to (or dependent upon) the extent or amount of the associated

reason (or work cause). Some examples of activities and their corresponding work cause are:

Activity (Is a Function of)	Work Cause (Reason)
Production buying	Purchase dollars and/or volume of orders/items
Vendor billing	Number of invoices
Production scheduling	Shipped dollars
Facility maintenance	Plant floor space
Secretarial services	Indirect labor
Salary administration	Total labor

4. For each activity a work load is determined, which is the total equivalent people performing the activity during the period of evaluation (full and part time, regulars and nonregulars, overtime and purchased services). The work cause is also quantified for the period involved in terms of units or items related to the specific activity(ies) performed.

5. Data gathering and calculations:[1] The equivalent head count for each activity during the period of evaluation is separated along with the appropriate and relevant numerical work cause for this period. This information provides the basis for the following calculations:

   a. Calculate a *productivity ratio,* which relates equivalent head count for

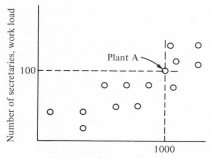

FIG. 9-1. Productivity ratios for each location are plotted.

the activity to the work cause for each location. For plant A,[2] the productivity ratio is

$$\frac{100 \text{ (secretaries)}}{1000 \text{ (indirect population)}} = 0.1$$

   b. Establish the *mean productivity ratio* (average), which is the total weighted ratio for all plants. It is calculated by dividing the sum of all the activity work loads (for all plants in the survey) by the sum of all the work-cause quantities (for all plants). For purposes of this example, let us assume that the mean productivity ratio for the secretarial activity was 0.09:

$$\frac{\text{Sum of secretaries for all plants}}{\text{Sum of indirect population for all plants}} = 0.09$$

c. For each location, calculate the *index work load,* which is the amount of work load the plant would have performing the activity if its productivity ratio was equal to the mean productivity ratio for all plants. It is derived by multiplying the plant's work-cause quantity by the mean productivity ratio. For plant A, the index work load is

1000(indirect population) × 0.09 (mean productivity ratio) = 90

d. Determine the *norm deviation* for each plant, which is an indication of theoretical potential improvement. For plant A, the norm deviation is

100(actual work load) − 90(index work load) = +10

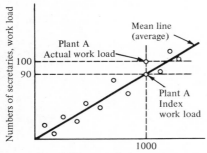

FIG. 9-2. The relationship for all locations between work cause and work load is indicated by the mean line.

e. Calculate a *norm index* for each location, which compares individual location "performance" with the average for all locations, adjusted for differences in work-cause values. For plant A, the norm index is

$$\frac{100 \text{ (actual work load)}}{90 \text{ (index work load)}} = 1.11$$

f. Calculate a *productivity index* for each location, which compares changes of location performance over time. For illustration, say that plant A had 100 secretaries in the current year and had the same number in the preceding year. During the current year the total plant indirect population had increased to 1000 from 800 in the preceding year. The productivity index for plant A would be

Productivity ratio for current year
─────────────────────────────────
Productivity ratio for preceding year

$$= \frac{\dfrac{100 \text{ (secretaries in current year)}}{1000 \text{ (indirect plant population in current year)}}}{\dfrac{100 \text{ (secretaries in preceding year)}}{800 \text{ (indirect plant population in preceding year)}}} = \frac{0.1}{0.125} = 0.8$$

6. *Analysis:* The norm index and the productivity index for individual locations are used to search for improvement opportunities associated with the activity involved.[3]

A norm index greater than 1.0 *tends* to indicate plant performance below the average for all plants. An index less than 1.0 *tends* to indicate performance better than average.

A productivity index greater than 1.0 *tends* to indicate a deterioration in plant performance over the time period considered, while an index less than 1.0 *tends* to indicate an improved performance.

The indexes indicate *apparent* efficiency or inefficiency for the involved activity from location to location and from time to time for each location. Further analysis of causes for index differences is needed in order to determine if they are due to inadequacies of the model (justifiable variations in local requirements, imprecise indicators being used, etc.) or are due to actual differences in productivity (by virtue of superior or deficient performance, innovations, etc.).

DEFINITIONS

Functions and Activities

As stated earlier, each indirect labor function within the organization is subdivided into activities. For example, Fig. 9-3 illustrates a partial subdivision of the Administration and Personnel functions into activities.

All indirect labor within an IBM manufacturing or service facility is associated with one or more of 115 defined activities. In most cases each activity is associated with one specific function. However, in some selected cases activities are associated with many functions and are treated in a gross fashion. For example, secretarial services are associated with so many specific functions that it is more useful to treat this set of activities as being associated with general management support.

Functions and activities should be defined in keeping with the intent for use of CSS, and the nature of the organization, reflecting judgment of those who will be involved and allowing for unique local conditions

COMMON STAFFING SYSTEM
SAMPLE ACTIVITIES GROUPED BY MODEL FUNCTION
ADMINISTRATION

Code	Title
101	Order entry
102	Administrative marketing support
103	Backlog management
104	Customer calls
105	Accounts receivable
110	Sales administration
111	DP administration programs
112	Scheduling
113	Inventory control
114	Field administration support
121	Telecommunications
122	Reprographics, office equipment, and supplies
123	General administration services
124	Security and safety
125	Cafeteria services
126	Mail collection and distribution

PERSONNEL

Code	Title
201	Personnel planning
202	Employment and placement
203	Personnel systems and records
204	Management development
205	Personnel and employee programs
206	Compensation
207	International assignments program
208	Benefits, reimbursements, and welfare programs
209	Suggestions, awards
210	Employee development and education
211	Personnel operations and administration programs
212	Health, hygiene, and safety program
213	Industrial relations

FIG. 9-3. Division of the administration and personnel functions into "functional" activities.

which create unique staffing requirements. These unique requirements should be allowed for and considered in subsequent location-to-location comparisons.

Each activity is defined in detail, for example, as illustrated by Fig. 9-4.

In summary, an activity is:

1. Generally, a logical entity of homogeneous effort performed by similar locations or units

---

CSS—COMMON STAFFING SYSTEM
ACTIVITY DESCRIPTION

MODEL FUNCTION: 1 Administration
SUBFUNCTION: 10 Field administration
ACTIVITY: Order entry   Code: 101
DESCRIPTION:

 Entering via teleprocessing, or preparation of data entry document to input the
 following transactions:

  Orders to install, orders to remove, replacements, displacements, alterations,
  cancellations, reschedules, installations, removals, software orders, installation
  confirmation, term plan data, literature, cable orders

 Customer master record maintenance at branch office level
 Up-dating and maintenance
 Filing and distribution of output documents

OBJECTIVE:

 The capture of data entry type work performed by specialist administrative staff,
 such as account administrators or order entry specialists, to up-date files via
 administrative systems

WORK CAUSE:

 Gross number of orders to install and to remove   Code: 051

                                                              Date: 29 April 19xx

---

FIG. 9-4.   Definition of a "functional" activity.

2. Sometimes a discrete identification of *valid differences* between organizations or units (e.g., differences in job content due to legal requirements in a location or country)

3. Effort in support of the specific mission of the operating unit (e.g., salary administration, customer billing)

4. A means to "normalize" differing organization structures into common "standard functions"

5. The "lowest common denominator" across similar organization units

6. Selected such that it can be related to a logical work cause (quantifiable)

7. A complete and thorough definition of effort that can be understood and interpreted consistently by all locations or units (i.e., where it starts, where it ends, list of things it includes, what it does not include, various key words and terminology)

8. A statement of work effort that, when added to all other activity

work efforts, equals the total effort for the unit (i.e., all indirect work load must be accounted for)

Work Causes

A measurable "work cause" or indicator is identified for each activity. These attempt to help explain why the activity is required. For example, the number of invoices is a measurable work cause for order entry. For simplicity, only one work cause is generally identified for each activity. Conversely, the same work cause may be shared with several activities. Work causes can be changed with time or as business conditions dictate. Number of items per invoice rather than number of invoices may in time become the work cause for order entry. A work cause is:

1. A definition of what *causes* indirect effort to be different between locations or through time.

2. A means of compensating for differences in size, complexity, etc.

3. A quantity that is generally readily available and forecastable

4. A value that has a relationshp with an activity that is either:

a. *Cause and effect,* such as number of receipts versus accounts payable, or

b. *General,* such as total labor power versus salary administration

5. Related to an activity in a way that is *logical and understandable*

6. Described over a given time span (period, month, quarter, year) such that it smooths out short cyclical trends but is also reasonably current

7. Sometimes phased to reflect different timing (e.g., activity equivalent head count today may be related to next year's work cause)

8. Divided by some multiple of 10 to reduce it to a value generally greater than 1 and less than 100 at a location or unit level (e.g., $68,000,000 would have a divisor of 1 million; so the indicator value in the CSS system would be 68)

9. Sometimes comprised of more than one cause (e.g., the indicator for buying activity might be number of purchase documents, plus number of purchase dollars)

10. Sometimes used for more than one activity

The tacit assumptions underlying the work causes is that they are gross indicators of the amount of indirect labor resource required to accomplish the activity. In most cases a single indicator or work cause cannot entirely explain work required to accomplish the activity. However, for simplicity, IBM elected to use a single indicator or work cause for most activities, recognizing that some sacrifice in precision would result. They use 60 different types of indicators for the 115 activities in manufacturing plant application of CSS.

In some cases it is difficult to identify single work causes or indicators which adequately "measure" activities and which are economical to record and report from normally available data sources. Resolution of how elaborate the measurement of work causes should be, and whether single or multiple indicators are appropriate, should be on the basis of the economics of the situation—the final test, in addition to the predictive value of the indicator and its measurability, being affordability.

Equivalent Head Count

The "work load" or equivalent head count (EHC), is determined for each activity and its work-cause quantity. The EHC is reported periodically through a survey form prepared by first-line supervisors. This includes regular plus nonregular and contract or purchased services expressed as regular equivalents; for example, a part-time employee working a 20-hour work week would be counted as 0.5 equivalent regular labor power. A person's time may be split between activities in $^1/_{10}$ increments. An order entry clerk may spend 0.7 of his or her time on order entry and 0.3 on another activity such as pricing verification.

Data Calculation

Each location activity ratio of equivalent head count to work cause is established. This is then compared with the average ratio of all locations, its own prior ratio, and its own projected ratio.

Reports

In order to provide meaningful reports for various management levels, the results are summarized for each activity, function, location, and geographical area. Also, many of the reports are designed to provide two distinctly different types of management focus:

1. The "standard function" (or "model function") reports are summaries in which the activities have been grouped into the same hypothetical organizational structure for all locations. That is, all the different location organizations have been "normalized" so that their functional identities, such as Personnel or Finance, encompass the same activity sets or work scopes. These formats provide headquarters people with consistent measurement perspectives across their different locations in spite of widely varying structures. We sometimes call this providing organizational transparency.

2. The "local function" reports are aimed at giving each location's management team a "real-life" set of performance summaries that are tailored to their unique organization. In these summaries each function (e.g., Personnel, Finance) has a "true" identity with a manager who is accountable for that portion of the resource and expense. Obviously these reports are provided to assist the location management teams in their efforts to follow up with action plans to achieve productivity improvements. Sample reports are presented as follows:

Figure 9-5—activity comparison by country for order entry

Figure 9-6—a computer printout of work cause versus work load for order entry showing relative performance by location

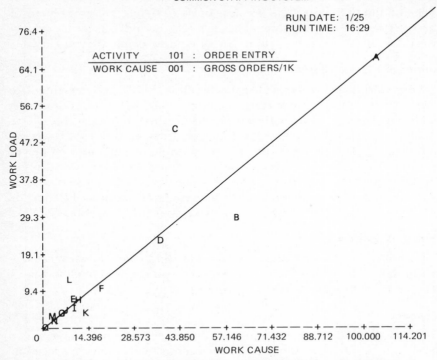

FIG. 9-5. **A computer printout order entry activity comparison by location.**

COMMON STAFFING SYSTEM

ACTIVITY WORK CAUSE   101   001   ORDER ENTRY   GROSS ORDERS/1K

Country	Work load input	Work load noncompared	Work load compared	Work cause	Production ratio	Index work load	Norm index	Norm deviation
A	68.7	0.0	68.7	103.901	0.661	70.1	0.98	-1.4
B	27.9	0.0	27.9	60.408	0.462	40.8	0.69	-12.9
C	50.6	0.0	50.6	41.520	1.219	28.0	1.81	22.6
D	22.3	0.0	22.3	36.683	0.608	24.7	0.90	-2.4
E	6.9	0.0	6.9	9.374	0.736	6.3	1.10	0.6
F	10.0	0.0	10.0	18.116	0.552	12.2	0.82	-2.2
G	3.8	0.0	3.8	6.159	0.617	4.2	0.90	-.4
H	6.0	0.0	6.0	10.821	0.554	7.3	0.82	-1.3
I	4.0	0.0	4.0	9.615	0.416	6.5	0.62	-2.5
J	4.2	0.0	4.2	7.707	0.545	5.2	0.81	-1.0
K	3.8	0.0	3.8	13.869	0.274	9.4	0.40	-5.6
L	12.3	0.0	12.3	8.674	1.418	5.9	2.08	6.4
M	2.5	0.0	2.5	3.100	0.806	2.1	1.19	0.4
N	2.0	0.0	2.0	3.559	0.562	2.4	0.83	-.4
O*	0.0	0.0	0.0	0.000	—	—	—	
P*	0.0	0.0	0.0	0.000	—	—	—	
Q	0.3	0.0	0.3	0.448	0.670	0.3	1.00	0.0
Total	225.3	0.0	225.3	333.954	0.675	225.3	1.00	0.0

Index work load calculation: 0.675 × work cause
Correlation coefficient: 0.931 acceptable

*This country was excluded due to incomplete input.

FIG. 9-6. A computer printout, reproduced in tabular form, of work cause versus work load for order entry, showing relative performance by location. Country names would appear on the actual reports.

```
                        COMMON STAFFING SYSTEM
               COUNTRY ACTIVITIES BY STANDARD FUNCTION
                        COUNTRY: COUNTRY A
                  STANDARD FUNCTION: ADMINISTRATION

                              Equivalent                    Equivalent
                                 H/C            Norm           H/C
             Activity          compared        index        deviation

  101 Order entry                68.7           0.98           -1.4
  102 Administrative marketing support
                                 95.2           1.02           -1.9
  103 Backlog management         59.6           0.87           -8.6
  104 Accounts receivable        16.9           0.50          -16.6
  105 Sales administration       25.3           1.04            1.0
  106 Scheduling                 31.4           1.34            7.9
  107 Inventory control          31.7           1.13            3.6
                  ↓                 ↓              ↓              ↓

  Standard function totals       794.0          0.87          -115.4
```

FIG. 9-7.   A computer printout, reproduced in tabular form, for activity performance in a standard function for one location.

Figure 9-7—activity performance in a standard function for one location

Figure 9-8—standard function comparison by location for one function

Figure 9-9—summary of standard function comparisons for one location

Figure 9-10—total of all functions comparison by location

Figure 9-11—comparison of activity totals in a local function for a location

Figure 9-12—summary by local functions for a location

Other presentations of the basic CSS data are easily obtained and may be used in directing attention to unusual situations for further and more detailed analysis.

```
                        COMMON STAFFING SYSTEM
                     STANDARD FUNCTION COMPARISON
                  STANDARD FUNCTION 1: ADMINISTRATION

                    Equivalent                       Equivalent
                       H/C              Norm             H/C
    Country          compared          index          deviation

       A              794.0            0.87            -115.4
       B              642.6            0.99              -3.7
       C              572.9            1.35             150.0
       D              471.0            1.17              69.4
       ↓                ↓                ↓                ↓

     Total           3364.2            1.00              0.0
```

FIG. 9-8.   A computer printout, reproduced in tabular form, for comparison of performance in a standard function by location.

```
                    COMMON STAFFING SYSTEM
             COUNTRY SUMMARY STANDARD FUNCTION
                    COUNTRY: COUNTRY A
```

Standard function	Equivalent H/C compared	Norm index	Equivalent H/C deviation
1 Administration	794.0	0.87	−115.4
2 Personnel	138.4	1.02	3.3
3 Finance	487.4	0.99	−7.2
4 Distribution	207.2	0.87	−31.4
5 Information systems	593.5	1.10	52.0
↓	↓	↓	↓
Country totals	4553.7	0.92	−375.1

FIG. 9-9. A computer printout, reproduced in tabular form, summarizing standard function performance at one location.

```
                    COMMON STAFFING SYSTEM
                  TOTAL COUNTRY COMPARISON
                       ALL FUNCTIONS
```

Country	Equivalent H/C	Non-compared	Equivalent H/C compared	Norm index	Equivalent H/C deviation
A	5171.1	617.4	4553.7	0.92	−375.1
B	5076.1	1125.4	3950.7	1.09	314.8
C	2827.1	315.9	2511.2	1.07	167.1
D	3037.0	344.5	2692.5	1.06	158.7
E	941.6	102.8	838.8	0.95	−45.2
↓	↓	↓	↓	↓	↓
Total	XXX	XXX	XXX	XXX	XXX

FIG. 9-10. A computer printout, reproduced in tabular form, presenting performance for a total of all functions by location.

```
                    COMMON STAFFING SYSTEM
             COUNTRY ACTIVITIES BY LOCAL FUNCTION
                    COUNTRY: COUNTRY A
             LOCAL FUNCTION: 23 ADMINISTRATION
```

Activity	Equivalent H/C compared	Norm index	South equivalent H/C deviation
01 Managers	21.0	0.77	−6.3
03 Secretary	112.6	0.90	−13.2
010 Order entry	23.3	0.93	−0.5
102 Administrative marketing support	31.2	1.02	0.6
321 Cashier/banking	9.1	1.10	0.8
902 Procedure management records	2.5	1.39	0.7
↓	↓	↓	↓
Totals	325.0	0.90	−36.3

FIG. 9-11. A computer printout, reproduced in tabular form, of activity performance for one function, at one location.

```
                    COMMON STAFF SYSTEM
             COUNTRY SUMMARY BY LOCAL FUNCTION
                  COUNTRY: COUNTRY A

                               Equivalent              Equivalent
                                  H/C          Norm       H/C
            Local function      compared       index   deviation

01 General management              7.0         0.75       -2.3
02 IS and administrative management 28.2        0.74      -10.0
03 Personnel                     221.8         0.94      -13.8
04 External affairs               80.0         0.73      -29.6
05 Treasurer                     226.6         1.02        4.3
              ↓                     ↓            ↓          ↓

Country totals                  4553.7         0.92     -375.1
```

FIG. 9-12. A computer printout, reproduced in tabular form, showing performance of local functions at one location.

BACKGROUND OF
TECHNIQUE DEVELOPMENT

IBM's operations, with very minor exceptions, are in the field of information-handling systems, equipment, and services to solve the increasingly complex problems of business, government, science, space exploration, defense, education, medicine, and many other areas of human activity. IBM's products include data-processing machines and systems, information processors, office systems, electric and electronic typewriters, copiers, dictation equipment, educational and testing materials, and related supplies and services. Most products are both leased and sold through IBM's worldwide marketing organizations.

IBM is organized into six primary operating units—Data Processing Marketing Group, Data Processing Product Group, General Business Group, General Business Group/International, IBM World Trade Europe/Middle East/Africa Corporation, and IBM World Trade Americas/Far East Corporation (see Fig. 9-13). The two major product

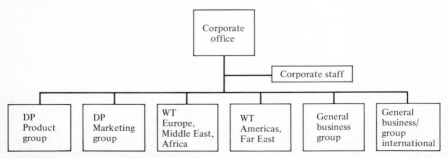

FIG. 9-13. IBM organization chart.

lines (office products and data-processing products) are developed, manufactured, marketed, and serviced out of these groups. Manufacturing is done in 42 equipment plants distributed throughout the world. One plant may manufacture typewriters, another tape drives, a third processors. At a number of locations, particularly in the United States, the development laboratories are situated on the same site as the plant. At such sites, general services for the plant and the laboratory are generally combined. A typical site organization can be depicted as follows:

TYPICAL SITE ORGANIZATION

Plant Manager	*Site General Manager* *Site Service Manager*	*Lab Manager*
Manufacturing	Personnel	Product manager
Manufacturing engineering	Controller	
Quality engineering	Information systems	
Industrial engineering	Legal	
Production control	Facilities engineering and services	
Purchasing	Community relations	
Distribution		
New products		

Of all the categories listed above, only one, "Manufacturing," contains what IBM terms "direct" labor, i.e., employees who "have their hands on" and physically alter the product being manufactured. The rest of the employees are considered indirect.

For many years IBM has employed several general indicators of manufacturing productivity. A couple of the primary indicators, for example, are the announcement product cost commitments (APCC) and product cost targets. The principal difference between these two types is the time span involved. APCC is developed only once, at the time a new product is announced to the market. It covers the entire life of a product. Product cost targets are developed during each planning cycle (twice per year) and cover the 2-year operating plan time frame. A plant manager who establishes cost targets does so keeping in mind the APCCs for the products which will be produced in the plant over the next year. Therefore, the cost targets are used to measure actual costs against the original estimates of cost as well as to measure the plant manager's performance in producing all products from year to year.

Other indicators used by IBM manufacturing are the burden rate (the manufacturing overhead costs divided by the number of direct manufacturing hours), the indirect-to-direct ratio (number of indirect people for each direct person) and output per person (manufacturing output dollars for each person).

In the direct manufacturing category, the more conventional area for productivity measurement systems, IBM has used a predetermined time system for a number of years. This system is used not only to assess the productivity of the direct manufacturing departments but also to serve as a basis for cost estimating, scheduling, planning, and layout.

The value of measuring productivity in the direct category led the managers of the manufacturing function within IBM to test the notion of measuring productivity of indirect labor at the plant site, a cost component that was gaining an increasing share of the total costs incurred. Such costs had long been viewed as complex and immeasurable. Past attempts, such as staffing tables, work accountability, and sampling techniques, had fallen short of what was needed to understand how to measure, plan, and improve productivity in most of the indirect manufacturing functions.

New Technique — Common Staffing Study

In 1968, IBM began to develop a technique for measuring relative indirect productivity known as the Common Staffing Study (CSS). Since its initial test in one of the manufacturing divisions, CSS has been employed in an increasing number of plants so that it now provides a measure of relative indirect productivity among 36 plants located in 13 countries.

The major purposes of CSS are:
1. To highlight areas of potential improvement
2. To provide a measure of a location's indirect productivity improvement from year to year
3. To provide a relative productivity measurement among various plants

An important qualification to the purpose of CSS is that it is not designed to be used as a precise measure of performance. Even though CSS has been modified and refined over the years to make it more accurate, it is a management tool to be used only as an indicator. CSS is designed to foster a spirit of friendly cooperation among plants.

Extension — Common Staffing System

In 1977, IBM elected to extend the CSS approach to cover nonmanufacturing locations in Europe, Africa, and the Middle East. Indirect labor activities associated with field support such as general services, information systems, distribution, finance, marketing support, purchasing, and personnel are now covered by CSS for the majority of the 25,000 plus nonmanufacturing, nondevelopment employees in 17 European countries. Direct sales and field servicing are considered "direct" in these environments and are not yet included in the CSS.

One motivation for this extended development of CSS was to attempt to significantly decrease the growth rate of indirect labor, compared with that which had been experienced during the 1970–1977 period. Actual results demonstrate that dramatic progress was in fact achieved, and the CSS was a key contributor to that work.

The European, Middle East, Africa (EMEA) part of IBM covers 78 countries, of which 17 represent the majority of their business there. Within these 17 countries, business volume varies greatly, with a range of 50 to 1 from largest to smallest. Organizational and work practice differences from country to country are expected, owing not only to size differences but also to varying legal and cultural differences, with resulting wide variations in productivity levels of individual groups and countries. It was hoped that CSS would be a useful tool for measuring and isolating the effects of these differences and would serve as the basis for determining what actions would assist in improving overall productivity levels, e.g., striving for minimum requirement levels for a given business volume; the unique staffing requirements due to specific local cultural or legal requirements.

The CSS approach or technique was intended to provide a comparison of indirect labor productivity between countries as well as within countries over time. It was designed to achieve an equitable basis for comparison of indirect labor input for agreed-upon common activity descriptions scaled for the magnitude of demand, and thus to achieve organizational transparency not achievable through other operating systems. The EMEA CSS has achieved these objectives; it is incorporated into the planning process, both strategic and operational, and supports the planning process by allowing comparison among various functional/business areas.

The initial development of the extended Common Staffing System late in 1977 was achieved in approximately 3 months by a 16-person task force, with membership from five countries representing all major functions of the business. Two members were from headquarters, one from planning and one the program director.

Activities and work causes were identified and defined and tested during a 6-week period, with the task force interacting extensively with those individuals involved with the actual operations.

The next phase in developing the system was accomplished by a project office of seven professionals and one secretary working with a designated CSS coordinator for each location. It involved complete development of the system and obtaining approval from senior-level management. Implementation of CSS was initiated in January 1978.

Briefing sessions and discussions concerning the system and its design and use were conducted through February, followed by user input data surveys and analyses during March, April, and May on a test basis. Refinement and expansion of the system took place from May through August. A second survey for input data was done during September and August. Usable CSS results were available from June forward.

As an example of the effort involved, the labor required to accomplish development and implementation of this CSS in the nonmanufacturing areas of Europe was:

5 labor years from the task force and project office
9 labor years from individual field functions
1 labor year from systems and data processing

This CSS installation was made operational in 17 countries, and required 21 labor years annually for operation, of which 14 labor years represented a net addition of labor power. Functional administration was assigned to IBM Europe headquarters in Paris.

CSS offers the following potential uses for *line management:*

- Resource balancing
- Productivity enhancements
- Eliminating duplicative efforts
- Organizational studies
- Target setting
- Indicating who is doing better
- Strategic planning

Used by *staff* for:

- Target setting
  By function
  By plant or location
  By country
- Assessing/approving operation unit plans

Strategic planners

- Volume/population studies
- Work-load projections
- Consistent communications
- Information system payback tracking

COMMENTS ABOUT USE

The very names *common staffing study* and *common staffing system* indicate the primary intended use by the originators of the CSS technique: comparative analysis of indirect labor measures for common activities from location to location (within a large multiplant, multi-installation organization).

However, the underlying concept upon which the technique is developed, partial measures of productivity for indirect labor activities, is probably applicable to other organizations also. IBM has demonstrated that most indirect labor functions can be defined in terms of constituent activities and reasons or causes for these activities. Associated work load for indirect labor resource inputs can be determined, and from these data an assortment of meaningful partial productivity measures for most of the indirect labor within an organization can be developed. Analysis of these partial productivity measures can be done on the basis of variation from location to location and/or from period to period. IBM does both. In a smaller organization comparative analysis may be possible only on a period-to-period basis (or with other similar small organizations); however, it is quite likely that within even a modest-sized organization some common activities (such as secretarial services) may be performed in more than one function and that these can be analyzed in a comparative manner.

In addition to using CSS for period-to-period comparative analysis, evaluation of resources required for performance of various activities and functions, in terms of cost versus benefits, can be a useful approach to improving indirect labor productivity within any organization. The CSS technique concept can probably be adapted and adopted by many organizations to fit their needs, and can serve as an effective productivity improvement tool. In implementing a CSS system, the following points should be kept in mind:

1. CSS does not provide qualitative assessments.
2. A simple ratio (plots always go through the origin) is used for the productivity "benchmark."
3. Head count by functional area is prepared by first-level supervision through a survey.
4. The results of the measurement must be viewed somewhat subjectively and caution must be stressed to avoid misusing this measurement tool as a stick, "big or little."
5. Initial mailing of the survey forms to feedback of results plus data correction cycles takes 2 months.
6. It is recommended that two surveys per year be done until the credibility of the system has been established.

The principal ingredients which have made this an effective tool are probably:

1. *Simplicity:* The norm index is calculated as a simple ratio of equivalent head count to work cause and does not involve multiple regression or other sophisticated analysis. The data may be plotted on an x/y axis graph or tabulated on a chart.
2. *Acceptance and participation:* Every effort is made to involve the entire management team in the CSS process—from the initial design, through the implementation phase, annual data surveys, and most importantly, follow-through with appropriate action plans where potential productivity improvements may be indicated.
3. *Organizational effectiveness:* The system enhances organizational transparency, permitting management to better understand the complexities and inter/intra relationships within the business, and it frequently leads to methods improvements, through cross fertilization of concepts and ideas on work simplification.

In summary, the system is not a total factor productivity measurement of any activity or location. It must be viewed in the proper perspective by all levels of management. It is not a precise or absolute measure and it is not a qualitative assessment of performance. However, it is simple and rugged and it provides managers at all levels with a valuable yardstick for assessing the relative productivity of indirect labor, a segment of the organization that has traditionally defied analysis.

NOTES

[1] Productivity is defined in the true sense as output/input. In the development of the following indexes this definition is inverted to be input/output. However, the relationship of an independent variable "causing" the behavior of a dependent variable is preserved.

[2] Data used are not actual, but only for illustration.

[3] As mentioned in Footnote 1, the usual definition of productivity has been reversed to develop these indexes as relationshps of input/output.

PART FOUR

Service Interchange Structure

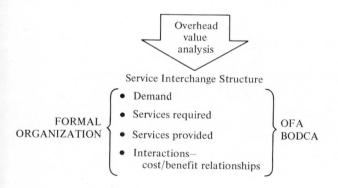

The service interchange *structure is conceptually an elaboration of the formal organization, to profile and evaluate the services provided by and furnished to each organizational unit. Improvement of white collar productivity by analysis within this structure is based on the concept that each organizational unit provides services to help achieve organization mission. By identifying the demand for these services, and by evaluating the cost/benefit relationships for each, one is in a position to evaluate the contribution and alternative ways in which services can be eliminated, enhanced, or made less costly. This can be done in a variety of ways.*

The overhead value analysis (OVA) approach developed by McKinsey & Company, Inc., is perhaps unique in its comprehensive treatment of white collar overhead activities. OVA, offered as a consulting service by McKinsey, is described in general terms by its originator, John L. Neuman, in Chapter 10, which is reprinted from the Harvard Business Review. *Mr. Neuman and his associate Thomas G. Hardy have described the procedure in more detail in "Gaining a Competitive Edge through Participative Management of Overhead," which is included in* The Handbook of Planning and Budgeting, *to be published by Van Nostrand Reinhold Company about the same time as this volume is published.*

Original planning for this volume anticipated a contribution by Neuman and Hardy with substantial procedural detail about using OVA, but policy decisions prevented its inclusion. Chapter 10 contains sufficient advice and description to allow the potential user to make "first-cut" decisions concerning usability of OVA within his or her organization. Reference to the handbook material will provide additional detail to develop a definitive course of action—using either internal resources or consulting services, either following established procedure or adapting to local needs.

OVA addresses analysis of all, or substantially all, services provided and services required by organizational units or entities within the organization being considered. Each service provided is "costed" by the furnishing group; benefits of services provided are determined by the users; alternatives for modifying user needs or for satisfying them better are explored; a range of options for reducing costs and improving benefits/cost relationships are identified; risks and impacts of the options are evaluated and priority recommendations are prepared; and decisions are made at upper levels to ensure compatibility with organization strategies, objectives, and contribution to mission. Service interchange is evaluated in terms of what "is" relative to what might be the maximum value of contribution to organization mission via the functional organization, objectives, and strategies.

The approach has been used in a number of organizations, mainly large ones, with dramatic results. The individual improvements tend to be modest, averaging only about $10,000 savings each. However, overall cost savings from all options implemented over all services aggregate to impressive sums. A 15 to 30 percent reduction in total *white collar costs is a typical result. About two-thirds of savings are due to modification of needs, and about one-third to improvement of internal processes used to provide services. The focus is on evaluation of the cost-benefit relationship of all services required, with a systematic and forced search to identify options for improving productivity and reducing costs by modifying need specifications or improving the ways in which services are produced. Each service is evaluated, and each option for improvement or cost reduction is treated as an element in a potential productivity budget. Concentration on the service interchange structure fosters improvement in effectiveness and internal efficiencies of overhead white collar activities* and *also encourages final decisions for changes which are related to* *improving the validity of efforts as they contribute to organizational mission and objectives.*

OVA, based conceptually on zero-based budgeting and value engineering, is a unique approach to white collar productivity enhancement. It focuses on validity of white collar efforts in a macroscopic way, and also directs attention to reasoned consideration of ways to improve the effectiveness and efficiency of these activities.

Many modifications to the philosophy incorporated in OVA can be visualized. The thoughts presented in Chapter 2 regarding autonomy and enterprise economy, and formal use of transfer pricing among white collar units may have utility in certain settings. Selected services or activities, which are perhaps highly significant in regard to impact on business strategies or are high-cost elements, could be singled out for analysis. Rather than approach analysis by organizational units, one could visualize analysis which is focused on interactions which cut across (or through) a number of units and which is related to one or more business objectives or strategies. One could also visualize approaches directed toward the decision-making chain involved in execution of a specific endeavor.

As far as I can determine, OVA and the McKinsey approach is unique. Many other consulting organizations claim that they have their own approaches, which include and go beyond OVA. But available information, in my opinion, does not support these claims. Several of the alternative, supposedly competitive approaches, do have unique, attractive, and potentially useful features for the reader. Most of these approaches are proprietary, available only through consulting assignments, and have limited information describing concepts and procedures publicly available. However, a brief description of the concepts may be useful as the basis for borrowing elements of the approaches or for considering the possible engagement of consultants.

One interesting approach is operation function analysis (OFA) developed by Bruce Bumbarger of the Bumbarger Group, Atlanta, Ga.[1,2] Reprints are available through his office, public seminars are conducted in various locations, and a book is currently in preparation which thoroughly presents OFA procedures.

OFA concentrates on analysis of the demands which require work within organizational units, and the interactive interorganizational work flows associated with these demands. The primary aim is to identify how demands placed on each unit can be changed to reduce and eliminate unnecessary work, and to facilitate the work accomplishment associated with demands placed on other units. The approach is a participative one. The consultant provides training and guidance to a group of middle-level managers representing the organizational elements which have interaction in their work flows, and the internal team of managers then systematically analyze unit demands to which they respond, and the impact of these demands on unit work loading. Work loading is related to the characteristics of the imposed demand, and alternatives for improvement are developed. Since the employees themselves conduct the OFA program, they view it as theirs, not that of outsiders. As a result, necessary changes are easier and benefits are more lasting.

The OFA approach has proved useful for a number of organizations and is an easy one to use, directing attention to functional interaction and improvement of white collar work within and between organizational units.

Peat, Marwick, Mitchell & Co., in collaboration with Robert R. Bramhall & Associates, Inc., offer a comprehensive approach to reducing and controlling overhead costs, designated BODCA (Bramhall overhead decision-cost analysis). The conceptual basis for this approach is one of benefit/cost evaluation for individual decisions, recognizing that a large share of overhead costs are caused cumulatively by individual decisions creating imposed demand or work load within various functions across the organization. Their approach identifies work activities throughout the organization which are caused by individual decisions, and develops a decision-cost matrix which is used as the basis for modifying decision patterns for more cost-effective operations. They claim impressive results—savings opportunities identified and expressed as a percentage of a client's sales ranging between 5 and 20 percent. They also caution that: "Our fees to provide this service are substantial." The approach is an intriguing one.

NOTES

[1] W. B. Bumbarger, "O.F.A.: Key to Lasting Overhead Productivity Improvements," *Financial Executive,* September 1977.

[2] Bruce Bumbarger, "Operation Function Analysis: The Next Step beyond Quality Circles," *Proceedings of the World Productivity and 1981 Spring Annual Conference,* Institute of Industrial Engineers, Norcross, Georgia.

CHAPTER TEN

Make Overhead Cuts That Last*

JOHN L. NEUMAN
Senior Associate
McKinsey & Company, Inc.

*Substantial and permanent reductions in
overhead costs are possible if users and
suppliers of services work together in weighing
costs and benefits and identifying options and
risks.*

Deepening recession and continuing inflation have caught many companies in a cruel cash and profit squeeze. A growing number are fighting for survival and trying to cut costs to the bone. Thus inventory slashing and all-out attacks on material and direct labor costs are very much the order of the day in many companies.

Usually, however, even in real crises, one major area of cost—overhead—escapes successful application of the cost-cutting ax. In most cases there is a simple explanation for this: past efforts to chop overhead expenses have yielded only a meager, short-lived trickle of savings. And that is not surprising. In the average company, thousands of small, frequently unrelated activities make up the bulk of overhead costs. Rather than evaluate each of these activities by itself and in relation to others, as a thoroughgoing attack on overhead would require, top management typically chooses an easier way. So the edicts go out: "Cut overhead costs

* Reprinted by permission of the *Harvard Business Review*. John L. Neuman, "Making Overhead Cuts That Last," *Harvard Business Review*, May–June 1975. Copyright 1975 by the President and Fellows of Harvard College; all rights reserved.

by 10 percent across the board!" or "Hold this year's budget down to the level of last year's actual costs."

Employees understandably perceive such actions as unfair and arbitrary, as indeed they are. Sometimes only a few recently hired employees are laid off in each department. Sometimes substantial cuts, based on quick employee assessments, are made at every level. In either case the jobs these employees held still have to be done. Since the "survivors" thus become overburdened, frustrated, and demoralized, the cuts are not effective.

When management does specify activities that it wants cut, it usually sticks to a few highly discretionary, "big-figure" areas like training programs, advertising, or overtime pay, ignoring sizable opportunities elsewhere. And because the cuts are almost always restored after the heat has died down, the savings turn out to be ephemeral. Small wonder that most knowledgeable managers tend to look elsewhere for ways of improving the "bottom line"!

Recently, however, there have been some notable exceptions to the pattern of ineffectual dealing with overhead costs. With a technique called overhead value analysis, a score of corporations in the United States and Europe, threatened by potentially dangerous cost situations, have in the past 3 years successfully cut their overhead costs (defined very broadly) by roughly 15 to 30 percent. The dollar savings of these corporations, which include insurance companies and banks, have ranged from under $1 million to about $100 million a year. And these cuts are structural. The savings will stay.

In concept there is nothing very complicated about an overhead value analysis. In traditional value analysis, a study team first determines what performance criteria a selected product or item must meet and then either develops a better, lower-cost design or devises an engineering method to accomplish the same results more economically without sacrificing the required level of quality. Companies have adapted this same technique to overhead functions and their costs. In an organized way, the analysis provides an efficient discipline for scrutinizing all the many thousands of activities that make up overhead, identifying all the areas where cuts can safely be made, and where high quality is a factor, providing a framework for balancing costs and estimated benefits.

But overhead value analysis differs from traditional value analysis by making both the managers who incur the costs (suppliers) and those who benefit from them (receivers or demanders) responsible for identifying which costs to cut. Top management and the CEO make the final decisions, but they are guided by the combined judgment of the entire management team.

Moreover, overhead value analysis can work quickly. In a company with 2000 "overhead" employees, such an effort can and should be completed in 4 months without disrupting day-to-day operations. Usually, the implementation that follows the analysis can be completed within a month if the need is great enough. But the process, though swift, is not painless. Since overhead expenses are typically 70 to 85 percent people-related and most savings come from work-force reductions, cutting overhead does demand some wrenching decisions.

Nevertheless, unless pressures on profits unexpectedly ease off in the months ahead, many companies may find themselves faced with the question not of whether to cut their payrolls, but of how. Overhead value analysis may well provide the most acceptable answers.

In this article I shall describe how the approach works, offer some suggestions for its application, and propose some diagnostic questions a company should consider before deciding to launch a full-scale overhead value analysis. First, however, it will be helpful to examine briefly the processes by which overhead costs grow.

WHY OVERHEAD AREAS GROW

Many businessmen recognize that their overhead has grown prodigiously in recent years. Between 1950 and 1970 the number of nonproduction workers in manufacturing industry, for example, increased six times as fast as that of production workers. They now account for no less than 40 percent of all payroll costs.

These people are engaged in an immense variety of activities. In a typical industrial or consumer goods company those that can fairly be called overhead make up such functions as corporate accounting, personnel, R&D, and planning, plus a good many subfunctions of so-called line organizations, such as plant engineering, sales administration, brand management, and so on. In the typical company, moreover, one can confidently assume that every one of these activities is costing more than it ought. This is a safe assumption for two reasons: first, because the activities themselves are inherently resistant to analysis and control; second, because the normal functioning of the organization positively encourages them to grow. Let us look at each of these reasons in turn.

They Are Scattered and Hard to Evaluate

Given the enormous diversity of overhead activities, it is easy to see why they are so hard to cut. Each of the many types of activity performed in support of a company's line functions may include a variety of distinct skills or areas of expertise. Even subdisciplines within a single functional area may embrace diverse specialties; accounting, for example, can include cost accounting, capital budgeting, tax accounting, and so on.

Generally, this diversity almost guarantees that some overhead activities will be inadequately reviewed by even the most cost-conscious managements. Top executives are quick to see that there is no leverage in assigning someone to study different overhead activities if the results of the work cannot be extended to cover many positions in many departments. Overhead areas in which a number of employees perform similar repetitive tasks, such as typing pools and keypunching, are clearly suited to quantitative analysis. Yet in most organizations activities like these account for a small portion of total overhead costs. Most of the potential savings are elsewhere, scattered throughout the whole organization.

At the same time, it is hard to assign tangible benefits to most overhead activities. Partly this is because accounting data tend to hide the real costs of a service; for example, most department budgets show totals for salaries, overtime, telephone, and so on, without breaking these down by individual services. In any case, who is to say precisely what the services of an additional public relations executive or a corporate lawyer are really worth? Or who can really quantify the benefits from the company's investment in advertising, R&D, or the company newspaper?

Finally, the prospect of reducing staff puts any manager in a painful position. It is hard to contemplate eliminating the job of a friend or acquaintance, and harder still when one has very little objective justification. In all likelihood, the termination interview will be an emotionally bruising experience for everyone concerned. Unlike line managers, who are obliged by volume and productivity measures to get used to making hard personnel decisions, most staff managers shy away from such confrontations. Some will even invent elaborate projects just to keep their people occupied.

Organizations Foster Them

Over and above the inherent difficulties of controlling overhead activities, almost every company in its day-by-day functioning does three things that tend progressively to inflate its overhead costs.

1. Organizations establish clear boundaries between areas. The necessary division of activities into manageable units separates the suppliers of overhead services from the users. A manager who requests a service, unless he knows the costs of creating it (and he rarely does), cannot judge the ultimate value to the company of providing him with it. Conversely, the supplier of services usually does not know their value in use.

Because of this ignorance on the part of suppliers and users, many services are supplied for purposes that do not justify their cost. Others are provided after the need for them has diminished or disappeared. In a food processing company, for example, the accounting department annually produced a substantial report for the government. In examining his overhead costs during this process, the manager made an interesting discovery: the directive requiring the report had been withdrawn 5 years earlier.

2. Organizations hire professionals to run and staff their service-performing departments. Typically, these people march to a different

drummer. They measure themselves against their professional colleagues in other organizations, and they tend to get so absorbed in the technical aspects of their jobs that they lose sight of the overall value of their work to their employers.

More often than not, they perform their services at a quality level out of proportion to actual need, and they tend to encourage requesters of these services to demand more of the same. For example, in a package goods company, the head of a market research group was periodically devising new approaches to allocating advertising and promotion funds. The manager was, of course, responding to his perception of the need. Unfortunately, his innovations were concentrated in a period when most of the company's products were in decline. Furthermore, the marketing managers did not believe or use his data.

3. Organizations reward responsive behavior. Managers tend to be rewarded more for pleasing their superiors than for running a tight ship. Indeed, most managers are sure to be criticized if they don't come up quickly with the professional answer to a question, or if they fall behind schedule in providing some service. Rather than risk being caught short, most managers would naturally prefer to overspend.

The headquarters of one conglomerate, for example, had a telephone system that was elaborately configured to include an impressive array of switching, transferring, multiple-line, and push-button options, with unlimited WATS access. Instead of determining what the communications cost/benefit balance for the company was, the manager was making sure that no one was unhappy with the telephone service—but at a high cost.

The managerial instinct for self-protection also encourages overstaffing. It does so in two ways. First, since a manager's compensation and status are often directly related to the size of his department, he is naturally inclined to build up his area as much as possible. Second, since a manager who finds major opportunities to reduce costs is open to the charge of bad management in the past, most managers are reluctant to take a really critical look at their own staffing levels.

In short, overhead costs are a nuisance to control both because of the diversity of the activities they reflect and because they are inherently hard to evaluate. And in most organizations they also have a natural tendency to grow out of control. If a company is to gain effective control of its overhead areas, therefore, it must find a way not only to deal with their troublesome diversity and ambiguity but also, to some extent, to thwart the natural dynamics of the organization itself.

HOW THE PROCESS WORKS

If, in the face of these difficulties, the enormous task of reducing overhead costs is delegated (in a special way) to every manager in the company, overhead can be successfully cut. All managers either request or supply overhead services, and so together they can recommend in detail which services can be pared back without damaging the organization. By formally placing the burden of the task on all managers at once (usually the lowest-level managers included in the process are those who have roughly 20 to 40 subordinates), overhead value analysis brings requesters and suppliers together to work on what they can see is a common, companywide task. In this way, managers feel freer to recommend changes.

To ensure that the recommendations are soundly based and to guide, even challenge, managers as they go through the process, stage by stage, the chief executive officer will need to appoint a small, high-level task force.[1] Three to five task force members working full time for as many months are normally sufficient for a company with up to $75 million in overhead. For larger organizations, more team members, even multiple teams, may be required.

Before actually embarking on an overhead value analysis, it is difficult for a company to determine what the optimum low-risk/cost-reduction level is in each organizational unit or function. Inter- or intracompany comparisons or trend analyses seldom shed much light on this question, and in any case they are always open to challenge. Accordingly, to ensure that no reasonable option for cutting costs escapes examination, top management should set an initial cost-reduction target, uniform for all functions, that overshoots whatever the true potential may be.

The target that has worked best is 40 percent. This is a jolting figure when first announced, and admittedly arbitrary; a case can be made for varying it by as much as 10 percentage points either way. But it is not too high to be credible. True, in most functional areas attractive cost-reduction opportunities will most often fall in the 15 to 30 percent range. Nevertheless, savings opportunities totaling 40 percent or more are not unusual.

Only a really challenging target will (a) foster an exhaustive search for savings options, (b) permit a proper balancing of cost-reduction decisions across the organization, and (c) support, if necessary, a fundamental rethinking of basic services. An additional benefit of the intentional overshoot is that—since no area has been singled out beforehand to achieve a higher target than others—managers down the line usually perceive the target as fair, though rough.

Once the target has been set, the overhead cutting program proceeds in four stages:

1. Estimate the cost of overhead end products and services flowing between organizational units.

2. Create an extensive list of options for eliminating or reducing the demand for most of these.

3. Recommend all those options whose cost savings outweigh their likely adverse consequences.

4. Decide the actual cuts to be made. This step is reserved for top management.

Let us now consider each of these steps in detail.

Estimate the Costs

In the course of supplying end products or services to another unit of the organization, the average manager incurs overhead costs. Ordinarily, he provides these services with reasonable efficiency, and the best way of substantially cutting their costs is to reduce the demand, or requirements, that led to their creation in the first place. Accordingly, each manager responsible for a cost center will be required to: (a) identify the various services his department receives from other cost centers in support of its own activities: (b) list each of the end products or services he supplies (for example, reports, completed forms, analyses, advice, decisions), and state to whom they go; and (c) estimate how much total effort and expense go into each of these services (the results are often eye-opening).

Thus a service should be broken down into its various components and their costs. For instance, the end product of one company's market research unit, which was sent to all branch managers, was a bimonthly analysis of the Nielsen report on each product category. The unit's effort was supported in turn by processing in the EDP department. Annual costs for the analysis in each product category, then, were made up of the cost of the Nielsen reports, $40,000; the processing in EDP, $5000; and the market research effort, $2600—a total of $47,600.

It would, of course, take months to trace the flow of every single end product or service and get an accurate fix on its cost. In practice, the task force will need to guide managers in deciding between speed and detail and in estimating, roughly, how much of their subordinates' time is spent on each of the various services. Because later judgments on the value of these services will be understandably rough, only an order-of-magnitude cost for each service is required.

Certain functions, such as EDP and engineering, typically engage in nonrecurrent, and in some respects unique, projects or assignments. Each project, whether currently under way or in a backlog, should be costed as if it were a service. The subsequent search for cost-reduction options will consider not only the impact of paring down the existing projects but also the potential of reducing total in-house staff capacity to handle such projects over the uncertain longer term.

One side benefit of this costing step is that it enables managers to compare their list of end products and services with the basic mission or charter of their cost center and with that of major supportive functions. Inconsistencies or mismatches are often clues to services that can readily be reduced or dropped.

In one company, for example, the accounting group was responsible for "providing management information for controlling expenses." Its supporting functions were "preparing budget" and "analyzing and reporting on progress against budget." The principal supportive tasks for each function and the specific end products were also defined. Before questioning the end products of the supporting functions in detail, however, the manager examined the basic content of the accounting overhead budget, which included such features as elaborate allocation, and even reallocation, of corporate overhead to the operating divisions. Because the basic mission of "controlling expenses" was only marginally satisfied by some of these budget features, dramatic reductions were immediately seen to be possible.

Another side benefit of pinpointing costs is that elements of the resulting data base, along with certain other features of this approach, can later on be built into the ongoing budgeting process, providing top management with a better basis for challenging budget submissions.

Identify the Options

Given the demanding target and the cost estimates, each supplier of services assembles, with task force assistance, a series of "challenge groups," made up of suppliers and receivers of a related set of services, to analyze the services and suggest options. The assessment of the options occurs at the next stage. Most services have one primary receiver; so the receiver representatives in each challenge group will be drawn from just one area. For services with many receivers—market performance reports or in-house newspapers—a few representative users should be selected to participate in the challenge groups.

Occasionally, managers who do not actually receive a particular service or end product should be included in the relevant challenge groups because they are concerned with some aspect of the service. For instance, an insurance company lawyer who sets overall specifications for policyholder contracts would be needed when the specifics of these contracts are questioned.

In some companies, the number of meetings required is held to a minimum by: (a) holding meetings for only the highest cost or risk services, and (b) using a "turnaround" form that goes back to the supplier from the receiver; in this way reactions of receivers (with their new ideas) can be documented.

Once assembled, the challenge group should take each end product and service in turn and, with the guidance of the task force, should (a) examine feasible ways of reducing requirements for it and (b) suggest a series of possible incremental reductions, short of eliminating the service entirely. Fig. 10-1 shows a framework that has proved useful for thinking through ways of reducing demand. It forces managers to consider every combination of service and cost-reduction options to meet the stretching target. In some overhead areas, it is worth making some effort to find

Options for reducing overhead

End products or services	Eliminate	Defer	Reduce quality	Reduce amount	Reduce frequency	Substitute
Reports			●		●	
	●					
Forms			●			
				●		
Analysis					●	●
	●		●			
Advice		●		●		
			●			
Decisions		●				
	●					●

FIG. 10-1. **Identifying the options.**

options for streamlining (where a specific service is unchanged, but the costs to produce it are decreased), but in most areas this added effort produces only marginal improvement on the basic approach.

As a rule, most of the options that might be listed are already known to the supplier of the services. Thus, rather than go through a long analysis of the obvious, the task force should start by asking the manager to produce a tentative list of feasible options. Subsequently, the challenge group will seek to modify and build on this list.

Consider the example of a textile manufacturer who was looking for ways to reduce his sales payroll from a total budget of $4 million. One option—closing marginal offices—would have been worth $100,000. Another, worth $500,000, was to get rid of salesmen who sold less than $1 million a year and redistribute their accounts. A third possibility, worth $50,000, was to reassign regional management responsibilities to the office managers of the largest offices, eliminating the regional positions.

The challenge group should attempt only to list the best feasible ways (and associated pros and cons) to make substantial cuts in the costs of and demands for a particular service. The group should list all options, no matter how risky, as long as they are technically possible and legal, until it has identified enough of them to meet the initial overall target. After reviewing all the options, top management decides which cuts will actually be made.

Effective self-searching by the challenge groups is vital for two reasons:

- Suppliers know the costs and technical details of producing services for other organizations, but not the specific benefits. Receivers know the benefits but not the costs.
- A reduction in service is almost never in the receivers' interests, particularly if they are not charged for the services. Nor will

suppliers normally be happy to see demand for their services reduced.

Each member of the challenge group, therefore, whether supplier or receiver, should assume the individual responsibility to search out all the options and try on his own to identify the best possible ways to achieve the target. The best way to make sure that this happens will differ considerably from company to company and from function to function. In every case, however, it is essential that top management clearly assign the burden beforehand. To reinforce that assignment, companies have used a variety of tactics:

- Arranging for senior executives to attend several selected challenge-group meetings to make sure that the search for feasible options is thorough and overlooks no sacred cows. Although some managers are inhibited by the presence of their bosses, the value of the senior executive's broader perspective can prove decisive.
- Requiring each receiver, as well as each supplier, to approve and sign the final list of options to indicate that he knows of no other possibilities.
- Demanding separate lists of all end products and services for which no feasible options have been identified. Since no manager wants to admit he lacks ideas, this demand often yields a surprisingly short list.

Weigh the Savings versus the Risks

The amount the company saves from implementing an option identified by a challenge group is usually quite small—a few thousand dollars on average, or less than a full year of work for one person. Consequently, managers are not justified in spending a great deal of time gathering data on each option and deliberating its attractiveness. Rather, they must try to use only the available facts and judgments in deciding between savings and risks. The procedure is as follows.

For each of its options, each challenge group states the work-load reduction and cost decrease it expects the change would make. The group also explicitly states the possible adverse consequences of each option, their severity, and the likelihood of their occurrence. If, as often happens, receivers and suppliers disagree sharply on these points, both points of view are recorded for consideration by higher management.

Finally, the group ranks its choices among the options in descending order of attractiveness. This step forces lower-level managers to weigh and choose among many diverse alternatives. Whether or not they believe any of the various options should be implemented, they are obliged to indicate a priority list should top management decide that some of the options should be acted on. The challenge groups' rankings then move up through the chain of command as illustrated in Fig. 10-2.

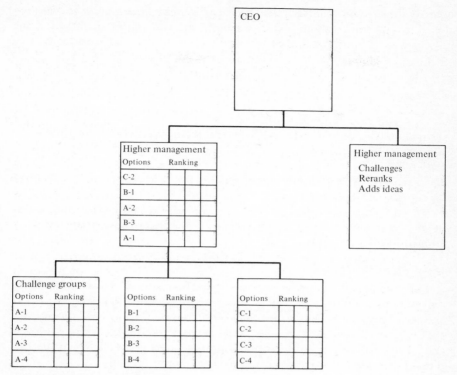

FIG. 10-2. The review process.

Each higher-level manager critically reviews the resulting options and rankings, challenge any judgments that appear questionable, possibly introduces his own ideas (for example, increasing spans of control, or cutting out a layer of management), and reranks the options according to his own perspective. He may also convene a new challenge group in order to develop additional options or improve judgments. The final ranking decisions are made at whatever level the chief executive officer deems appropriate. In any case, he carefully reviews all options, paying particular attention to the marginal ones where the pros and cons appear to balance.

For example, a fairly large bank was weighing the option of getting out of the stock transfer business (which was a manual operation running at a loss) and transferring it to a competitor with efficient, computer-based systems. This would have saved $90,000 a year on payroll costs, but it would have been at the risk of antagonizing one or two key customers. The challenge group ranked this option very low on its list.

In the course of the review process, however, top management challenged that option and asked for an intensive search for other feasible options in the same area. The group eventually developed a safer alternative: improving the service and restructuring the prices to achieve break-even. This option both protected jobs and plugged a continuing cost drain without the risk of jeopardizing customer relationships.

Three aspects of the challenge and review process are worth noting:

1. Top executives, with their broad, companywide perspective, have a chance to see a spectrum of detailed options that are normally known only to lower-level managers.

2. Top management, suppliers, and receivers all agree to all decisions that are made to pare back on the frequency, extent, or quality of services. The responsibility for decisions is thus shared. This is essential, for unless all three parties participate in the decision, the supplier could be "burned" for inadequate performance, the original service level could be reinstated, or both.

3. Top management can use the detailed, ranked lists to tailor overhead reductions in each department or function to appropriate and roughly uniform levels of risk.

Make Final Decisions

The final decisions are a series of rough trade-offs between possible cost savings and possible adverse consequences. A decision matrix is shown in Fig. 10-3. As a rule, management should approve all options that can be realized at little or no risk, regardless of the savings involved (Fig. 10-3, column 1), and drop all options where risks clearly appear to outweigh potential savings (lower parts of columns 2 and 3).

| | Adverse consequences | | |
	None or low	Medium	Severe
High	Certain approval	Likely	Not likely
		?	?
Medium	Certain approval		Certain rejection
		?	
Low	Certain approval	Certain rejection	Certain rejection

(Cost Savings)

FIG. 10-3. The trade-off decisions.

With options where the possible penalties and savings appear about equal (upper parts of columns 2 and 3 in Fig. 10-3), management's decision will depend on the company's strategic need for savings, its management style, and its overall capabilities. And it should be made only after a thorough review. Options left after this review can form a valuable ranked contingency plan to be put into effect should worsening economic conditions make deeper reductions necessary.

As most options chosen fall into the low-risk, small-savings category, many managers may wonder how really large overall savings can be achieved. The answer is simple: because so many options are identified and all the decisions are approved at the same time, a company can eliminate a large number of employee positions. Thus with 20 options that represent 12.5 man-years of work spread across 30 employees, management should be able to rearrange work and jobs to eliminate at least 9 or 10 positions.

How rapidly the company should implement the options will depend on its circumstances. If the need for cost savings is acute and attrition rates are relatively low, then a certain number of terminations may be required (mitigated as far as possible by generous severance arrangements, job-search assistance, and so forth). Otherwise, the company can wait for attrition to eliminate the jobs and achieve the dollar benefits.

Although the associated risks are rarely greater than they appear, the management team may underestimate the adverse consequences of a given option. Most options identified by the challenge groups are reversible, however; the end product or service can be reinstated at a later date if necessary.

So far I have been considering only reductions within departments in the company. Where there are companywide services and expenditures, such as copying, telephones, entertainment, travel, management perquisites, and secretaries, that are often centrally controlled by policy, the task force, rather than interdepartmental challenge groups, should be responsible for evaluating the services and analyzing available options. Most of this work can be completed at the same time as the interdepartmental cutting program, though occasionally more time will be needed to develop a sufficient number of feasible options.

IS AN OVERHEAD VALUE ANALYSIS FOR YOU?

A process of this kind can not only cut a company's overhead costs by one-fourth or more but also yield a number of intangible benefits. First, managers throughout the company often become more sensitive to cost-benefit trade-offs. Second, communications between departments often improve. Third, the program encourages systematic and innovative thinking. Often, managers bring up ideas that are truly creative.

Sometimes they are unrelated to overhead costs—for example, modifications to products, changes in sales promotion, and shifts in strategic emphasis. In one company, for example, the program tipped the scales from adding new capacity to three existing plants to building a new plant in a different state.

Finally, although top management may be uneasy about the effects of the program on the company's image with the investment community and the press, investors and investment analysts are more likely to applaud than deride a company for any determined drive to trim excess costs.

Top management should, however, watch out for possible undesirable side effects. First, employee morale and motivation may suffer, since many jobs will have to be eliminated. However, when employees become aware that the company is encumbered with low-value or make-work activities and is in serious economic straits, the odds are that morale and motivation have nowhere to go but up. Second, since turnover rates are often highest in the job brackets where minority-group employees are typically concentrated, the company's minority representation may change, thus laying the company open to pressures from the Equal Employment Opportunity Commission.[2]

Because its effects are uncertain, management probably ought to consider a companywide attack on overhead costs in only two situations: (a) when short-term needs to improve profits are acute, and all other areas of cost reduction have been exhausted; or (b) when a badly needed competitive edge in the marketplace cannot be gained without a decisive improvement in the company's economic structure.

Granted either of these conditions, there is one other prerequisite, namely, a strong management structure. Forceful leadership by a tough, tenacious chief executive officer is absolutely essential to make this approach work. And the CEO, in turn, must have the support of a management that is both willing and able to follow his lead. The CEO's vigorous guidance and active involvement are indispensable throughout. In fact, he needs to make this program his chief priority until it is finished. Although this approach can be confined to particular divisions within a company, such as manufacturing or marketing, its full potential (even within a division) cannot be realized unless it is applied across an entire company.

In fairness to himself and his company, then, any CEO who proposes to embark on an overhead value analysis program should try to think through all its ramifications in advance. Specifically, he should ask himself, "Am I prepared to do what is necessary? Would I . . .

. . . *commit myself to achieving a truly demanding cost-reduction goal?"* Commitment to such a goal means more than making a public announcement. It requires readiness to make tough decisions about individuals and departments. Is the CEO prepared, for example, to fire the number-two executive in manufacturing if that is a sensible money-saving move? Would he actually drop a substantial part of the market research department for two years or more?

. . . *appoint my best managers to control the process?"* If an overhead review is to be the company's top priority for a short time (as it must be to work properly), the task force must be of the highest caliber. But despite the prospect of a large and early payoff, taking three to five of the best and most respected managers away from their regular duties for as long as 4 months is not easy, particularly if the company is in a shaky economic position.

. . . *refuse to accept less than the target already established?"* The purpose of a demanding 40 percent savings goal for every organizational unit is to make sure that almost all cost-cutting options are identified and fairly evaluated. The CEO needs to review in detail each challenge group's efforts. If he should discover that a particular group has been less than thorough, would he direct them to go back through the process and come up with better options? Would he insist that they keep at it no matter what?

. . . *draw sharp lines despite a lack of hard data?"* The final decision on each option will result from the systematic but imperfect process of weighing savings versus consequences. The CEO must be prepared to decide on particular options on the basis of data that may be inaccurate or incomplete. And he must be willing to trust the discipline of the process itself to ensure that the recommendations that ultimately reach him have been adequately challenged and considered as they come up the line. For him to insist on elaborate documentation or analysis would hopelessly blunt the thrust and impact of the program.

A chief executive who has thought these questions through may well feel a few qualms. There are risks in undertaking any sweeping program of change. But the possibility of cutting total overhead costs by one-fourth, with a consequent profit improvement of up to 100 percent or more, supplies a powerful incentive to take the required risk.

NOTES

[1] See Derek G. Rayner's Ideas for Action article, "A Battle Won in the War on the Paper Bureaucracy," *Harvard Business Review,* January–February 1975, p. 8, for discussion of an entirely different task-force approach that focuses on cutting unnecessary reports.

[2] See, for example, Theodore V. Purcell, "Case of the Borderline Black" (Problems in Review),*Harvard Business Review,* November–December 1971, p. 128; see also Antonia Handler Chayes, "Make Your Equal Opportunity Program Court-Proof," *Harvard Business Review,* September–October 1974, p. 81.

PART FIVE

Information Structure

Information is the lifeblood of an organization. It provides direction, instruction coordination, evaluation, and corrective action which should facilitate efficient, effective, and valid performance.

White collar productivity improvement within the information structure can be approached in many ways—by decision analysis, systems and procedures analysis, forms analysis, computerization, decision support systems, etc. We have elected to emphasize the participative approach to improvement in information systems by those individuals who are directly affected by these information systems in their daily work. This is an approach based upon participative work simplification, designated paperwork simplification *by its originator, Ben S. Graham, Sr.*

In Chapter 11, Ben S. Graham, Jr., who has carried on and extended the pioneering work of his father, presents an excellent summary of many lessons he and his clients have learned in years of working with paperwork simplifications. He stresses the process involved, and not the details of analytical technique. The process has received insufficient attention to this point in time, and the deficiency is well addressed by Dr. Graham.

CHAPTER ELEVEN

Paperwork Simplification

BEN S. GRAHAM, JR., Ph.D.

Industrial Engineer & Behavioral Scientist, President, The Ben Graham Corporation

Paperwork simplification is defined as the *organized* application of *common sense* to eliminate waste and improve the productivity and effectiveness of paperwork. The organization is achieved by using techniques which enable people to see the work in ways they have not seen it before. The common sense is provided by those who have been doing the work.

Since paperwork affects many people and involves the use of specialized equipment, many people are involved. Our skills in helping these people work together effectively are crucial to determining the success of the effort. The primary purpose of this chapter is to explain how to do this.

WHO IS INVOLVED

Paperwork simplification is primarily a bottom-up approach. This is because most paperwork is processed by people at the bottom levels of the organization, who because they are closest to the work are best able to see what is needed to make it more productive. However, senior managers and middle managers must be involved at the start and at certain key points during a project. Throughout this chapter, I will point out those events which call for management involvement and offer suggestions for handling them.

To help to understand the roles of the various levels of management in this process, it is useful to consider one unique but dominant characteristic of paperwork. The decisions involved in setting up paperwork procedures often seem trivial, but their effects are far-reaching. Decisions well within the abilities of the most junior clerks have effects far beyond the scope of their responsibilities and authorities. This tends to push decision making up in the organization to inappropriate levels, such as a corporate president making routine decisions on filing or mail delivery. Or the routine decisions may be ignored and in their place senior managers make decisions which seem appropriate to their level. Systems are totally overhauled with staggering expenditures for amazing new equipment, and in spite of the size of the investment and the impressiveness of the technology, the problems persist. What was needed was only a minor decision which still has not been made.

This process is dysfunctional in two ways. First, it denies a large number of employees (since 1971 the clerical segment of the U.S. labor force has been the largest in the United States) the opportunity to do things of which they are thoroughly capable, which are needed, and which obviously make sense. Second, it locates decision making at a distance from reality which guarantees that, at the operating level, much of it will not make sense.

Paperwork simplification is intended to deal with this dominant characteristic of paperwork. When it is done properly, management succeeds in organizing people at the grass roots level of the organization to work together to make those commonsense decisions.

THE REASON FOR GRASS ROOTS INVOLVEMENT

Consider a typical paperwork procedure such as order processing or procurement in manufacturing companies or patient records in a hospital or policy renewals in insurance, and capital acquisition in almost any organization. Two things are common to all these procedures. They involve many people and the people work in different units on different parts of the work. For instance, a procurement procedure involves purchasing, receiving, data processing, accounts payable, etc. Let us put some numbers on a procedure.

Imagine that we have a procedure that involves 50 people in 6 or 8 different groups. These people include managers, supervisors, professionals, technicians, and quite a few clerks. Some of them have been with the organization doing this work for a short time, and some have been doing it most of their lives, 20 or 30 years. For purposes of discussion let us imagine the average amount of experience with the procedure is 5 years. If 50 people have an average of 5 years of experience there are, distributed throughout the group, 250 years of firsthand experience with this work.

Analysts and consultants are often prone to downgrade the importance of this experience with comments such as "One day of experience and five years of repetition," a logic which seems to justify ignoring this experience and squandering the judgment of the largest segment of the world's most highly educated work force.

If this procedure is like most, there are parts of it that are not functioning well, causing dissatisfaction and frustration. Management has decided to do something about it. They decide to assign a consultant, from either inside or outside the company, to straighten it out. Their decision to use the consultant is arrived at partly because they associate the ineffectiveness of the procedure with incompetence among the performers. Or they may feel that they do not have time to involve the people or they may distrust the process, etc. Regardless of their rationale, they opt to use a consultant to get things squared away.

Now the consultant gets started. He or she may use one of a number of styles ranging from talking only to the most senior person and ignoring all the detailed experience, to talking to everyone—in this case 50 people. Let us assume that this consultant is enlightened about working with users and takes the time to talk to everyone. This amounts to a few minutes with some and hours with others. On average it is about ½ hour with each of the 50 people. That gives the consultant 25 hours of secondhand information.

Now let us consider the quality of this information. When a procedure is not operating well and management sends in an expert to correct it, that person is often perceived as threatening to the people on the job. Not everyone is threatened, however. Some are irritated because management has ignored them and brought in the consultant. Others may choose to be completely cooperative. Regardless of how the consultant is received, the fact remains that after the interviews he or she is limited to 25 hours of secondhand information, some of which is apt to be distorted, misleading, omitting important details, etc.

Next, using 25 hours of sometimes faulty, secondhand information, the consultant redesigns the procedure. The amazing thing about this process is that invariably, in spite of the paucity of the source data the consultant is able to come up with some obviously beneficial improvements which were overlooked by the users despite their 250 years of firsthand experience. This has led many consultants to make a serious mistake. They come to the conclusion that they are much better at figuring out how to do this work than the people who are doing it. Then they compound this mistake with a second one. Having made several obviously useful discoveries, they proceed to redesign the entire procedure, and the further into the detail they proceed, the more mistakes they make.

The reason that the consultant was able to discover some obvious improvements which had gone unnoticed by the users is not superior analytical skill. It is perspective. Consultants are the first to see the big picture. They got it by walking through all the different units involved in the procedure, and despite the limited amount of information gained and its dubious quality, they have a picture which was not available to any one of the users. This is a very easy thing to do. I have personally trained thousands of people to do it, and while it does not make them any smarter it enables them to see things which simply were not visible before. But it does not substitute for all the detailed user experience which consultants cannot pick up.

When the consultant uses this big picture to make detailed decisions, mistakes are bound to occur. The procedure is designed, written up, and issued, and the users read it. They see its obvious flaws, often shaking their heads in disbelief with comments such as, "The last time they redesigned this procedure I was sure they couldn't do it any worse but I was wrong."

Think for a moment about the perspective of the consultant. It is similar to that which we get from an airplane at commercial jet altitudes, 35,000 feet or so. The world looks clean and simple from up there, and you can see pattern. You see how things fit together in ways that you simply cannot see from the ground. However, there is a great deal that cannot be seen from 35,000 feet. You do not see the detail. You do not see what is under the trees and inside the buildings. You do not see what you do see at ground level, the details which make up the everyday experience of the users.

At 35,000 feet decisions are made which involve commitment to major investments. Then comes installation. Now it is time to make it work. The people who must do this are the same people whose experience and judgment we have been ignoring. And we hear from them. Here is a form design that will not work, after we have paid for 50,000 of them and they are on our shelves. Now we find that the forms do not fit the files or the equipment does not fit the room or will not work because information it needs is restricted by law or by union agreement. All kinds of real-world details come into play, such as weather, dust, humidity, union rules, commitments to special customers, obscure legal matters, and turnover, after binding decisions have been made.

Next the adjustments begin. The new system which looked so clean and simple at 35,000 feet is modified for reasons which may seem inconsequential from up there but are major issues on the ground. Patch by patch we adjust to reality until we finally have it working, and we find that we now have two systems, the new one, working very imperfectly, and a good deal of the old one, working very imperfectly, and perhaps we vow once again to leave well enough alone.

After going through this a few times managers begin to take on attitudes such as, "If it is working at all, leave it alone" and "Don't change anything which will affect anyone outside of our office." But then there are changes in management, new executives become aware that things are in a mess, and they too choose to ignore the bungling incompetents who have got them into this; so they decide to look for a topflight consultant.

Paperwork simplification is a skillful process which includes the users during the time of development rather than ignoring them until installation. In terms of the analogy concerning perspective, we take users up to 35,000 feet to work on the procedure while it is being designed rather than hearing from them after commitments have been made which are inconsistent with the detailed realities. The rest of this chapter explains how to do this.

To begin with, management must have confidence that their people can bring to their work the experience and judgment needed to improve it. Usually, this confidence is accompanied by visible pride in the organization and a desire to share that pride with as many members of the organization as possible.

SETTING OBJECTIVES

A procedure needs attention. Management and a paperwork simplification coordinator who will fill parts of the consultant role described previously discuss what is wrong. They define the objectives of a paperwork simplification project. If they cannot agree on objectives, they should continue their discussions until they can because participation simply will not work without objectives. If we do not know where we are going, people cannot help us to get there.

Naturally, the objective of "getting rid of as many employees as possible" will not inspire participation. So our goals must involve making a better organization, not simply doing what we have been doing with fewer people. This is fundamental. When we go to work on improving productivity, we work on improving productivity and not simply cutting expenses. To assure that this is understood, management should make it clear that no one will lose employment because of work improvement. Jobs will change and many will be completely eliminated, but people will not go. If we are not prepared to assure this, we simply cannot hope to have our people cooperate enthusiastically. Employees of strong character will refuse the assignment. The others will be at each other's throats or hiding, etc.

SETTING BOUNDARIES

Once objectives are set, commonsense decisions can be made about the boundaries of the project. If the goal is to speed up the processing of customer orders, we will want to chart those orders and likely some other documents generated from them, such as a bill of lading or an invoice, starting with the receipt of the order from the customer and ending with the goods and the bill being sent to the customer. Whatever the project objectives may be in a paperwork study, we determine our project boundaries by selecting the appropriate documents to study and deciding where to start following them and where to leave off.

Not only does this give us a pretty good idea of the scope of the project in terms of the paperwork to be studied, it also tells us what work-units will be involved—in this case the mail room, the order department, inventory, data processing, credit, shipping, billing, accounts receivable, etc. In the case of a procurement study we find purchasing, receiving, the warehouse, data processing, accounts payable, etc. This also enables us to proceed with the next step in establishing the project—selecting the participants.

SELECTING TEAM MEMBERS

Logically, if we intend to involve users in the study, they should come from the areas to be affected. A team is formed with at least one representative from each of the affected work-units. Choosing these people is also done by management, and the criteria for selection are important. If we are serious about user input, these choices should provide us with a team composed of people who are currently the most knowledgeable in their units concerning the paperwork processing. Management support is essential if this is to happen.

If management clearly establishes that the project is important and they intend that it be successful, they will insist that a highly knowledgeable employee from each work-unit be made available for a small amount of time. Naturally, this person is often the hardest to spare, and it is necessary that an agreement be negotiated concerning the amount of project time which will be required, usually 4 or 5 hours per week in meetings scheduled to avoid interfering with operations.

It is easy to see that if team formation is not gone into carefully and seriously, with visible management support, the criteria for selection will easily deteriorate into, "Whom can you spare?" If this happens, the representatives often turn out to be newly hired employees who are not yet performing important tasks in their units. While these people will usually be enthusiastic, they cannot bring with them the experience which is the essential user ingredient. Then, later, when the project is completed and the recommendations are submitted, they lack the credibility which they would have if they were presented by more knowledgeable veterans.

When work-units are poorly represented, it is usually because the supervision in those units does not feel that the effort is serious. This is an issue for senior management to resolve. It is vital to get it across that the project is important and that management genuinely intends to respect the judgments of the team. Things are going to change, and each of the units which will be affected by the changes must be properly represented.

A case can also be made for assuring that each of the participants be a volunteer. They should want to be involved in the project. However, this is not often a problem. If management gives strong visible evidence of the importance of the project, most of the more capable people in the organization will want to participate. It is a respected role. The most common reaction I have heard through the years from employees who are invited to help clean up their procedures has been, "It is about time they asked us."

Once the team members are chosen, they meet with senior management and the project is discussed. The objectives and the extent of the team members' participation in hours per week are made clear. A rough estimate is usually given of how many weeks the project is expected to take. In discussing project duration, it is important to get across that management does not expect the team to design a system which will be perfect for all time. They are simply expected to improve. This can usually be done rather quickly. After all, the world is not perfect now and it will not be perfect when we are through with it, but it will be better.

SOME COMMON SENSE ABOUT SYSTEMS CHANGE

On this note there is an item of systems philosophy which has caused grievous harm to many organizations and needs to be put aside. I am referring to the notion that in systems and procedures all things are integrally related and nothing can be changed without affecting everything else. Naturally, parts of a procedure affect one another. Together they add up to the mess in which we so often find ourselves. But that does not mean that we have to leave it that way until some distant future when the new electronics will erase all our problems. There is something irresponsible about an organization which tolerates ineffective performance for the time being. There is something seriously wrong when an organization refuses to allow its people to make things better, and there is something reprehensible about a systems or consulting group insisting that users not be allowed to play a role because they, the consulting or systems group, are the only ones who should be allowed to touch procedures.

Consider improvements such as these. We discover we have delays simply because documents sit waiting for a messenger. Customers are being lost. Discounts are being missed. Interest on deposits is being forgone. Patient health is deteriorating. Machines and their operators are idle. All these things and many more could be corrected at once by no more than carrying the documents immediately to where they are needed. Teams find things like unnecessary duplication of forms and in a few weeks they complete an analysis which consolidates seven forms into one. Another team discovers that through a simple change in sequence, checking a form before its parts are separated and distributed, they can save issuing over five hundred memorandums a day. Processing time drops from several weeks to one day, or from several days to several minutes, all through the simple expedient of allowing the people who do the work to see the big picture and figure out for themselves how to do it better. These people already know the ground-level detail. Once they have the big picture as well, they have all they need to make sense out of the procedure and to prepare recommendations.

It has been my experience that most teams discover some things which are so obvious that changes are made at once. Later, when their recommendations are presented to management, these are mentioned as already in effect. Then there are a larger number of recommendations which involve the redesign of a form, training, etc., which can be accomplished in a few weeks or months. Other changes, which usually involve the selection, purchasing, installing, and programming of equipment, may take many months or even years. To wait a year to do what we could do today, to put off today's results waiting for a promised tomorrow which may never materialize, does not make a great deal of sense. And it gets worse when we wait for that great day and find that the orders are not getting out any faster, the patients are still suffering under delays, the machines still sit idle, etc., because we are still posting unnecessary records, documents are still sitting in out baskets waiting for a messenger, etc., and because we were so preoccupied with the electronic portion of the solution we never actually dealt with these details.

It is useful to think of this type of improvement as preautomation work. We clean up the system as well as we can with common sense. Once we get it clean, there is a good chance that what will be automated will work. There is also a chance that we will discover that this is one of many procedures which can be accomplished more efficiently and effectively without automation, and when this is the case we have saved not only the headaches but also sometimes staggering losses and the attendant ruined careers.

ORGANIZING THE TEAM

This philosophy is imparted to the team members, and they are given a small amount of training in how to participate on an improvement team. They are introduced to procedure charting, the technique which will give them the big picture. They are given an opportunity to experience some creative problem solving with some classroom exercises, and perhaps they are shown a film or two describing paperwork simplification. This is accomplished in a training workshop of one or two days conducted by the improvement coordinator who will be preparing the charts and helping the team throughout the project.

At the close of the workshop the user team members usually select their team leader. This should be a user, not the coordinator, who is a staff person. If it is the coordinator, it will interfere with the users assuming ownership of the project. It is hard to get a group of users excited about helping a staff person to figure out how they should be doing their jobs, but it is not at all difficult to get a group of users excited about fixing the jobs themselves.

It usually works well for the team members to choose their leader. However, sometimes this choice is made for them by management. If this is the case, it is important that the person who makes the appointment be high enough in the organization that all the team members report to him or her. During the project the team members must be responsible to the team leader. This rules out having that person chosen by a manager or a staff person to whom the team members are not responsible.

The team also selects a recorder who will be responsible for keeping track of ideas as they surface and keeping a list of assignments.

PROJECT ANNOUNCEMENT

As you can see, the role of senior management in initiating a project is significant. And it is not yet over. The next thing is for the project to be announced to all the people in the areas to be affected. This is best done in one large but short meeting conducted in an auditorium or the cafeteria or a lounge area or even a hallway. This meeting is led by the lowest-level senior manager whose authority spans the scope of the project. Because of the nature of paperwork, described at the beginning of this chapter, this is usually well up in the organization. This manager announces the project by describing what is to be studied and the reason or reasons for the study. The team members are introduced and the team leader and recorder are identified. The paperwork simplification coordinator is also introduced, with an explanation that the coordinator will be coming around shortly to observe how the documents are processed in order to prepare a procedure chart.

The manager assures everyone that the team members only represent their departments, that they are not the only ones allowed to think, and that anyone with ideas can discuss them with the team member. The manager also makes it clear that when the chart or charts are prepared everyone who wishes will have a chance to see them. The manager finishes with a few enthusiastic words about the ability of people to improve their own work, indicates that the project is important, asks for everyone's support, and finally asks for questions.

The most common questions express concern about loss of employment. Unless the senior manager is prepared to guarantee that there will be no loss of employment as a result of work improvement, the project will quickly head for the rocks. However, if the manager is ready to state that jobs will change and some may be completely eliminated but there will be no loss of employment, the meeting is apt to end with employees feeling enthusiastic. Here is a key example of the need for top management support. Obviously it does little good for a manager of limited authority to make these assurances and it does no good at all for a staff person to do so.

This public meeting is a quick way to establish visible management support for the effort. If it cannot be done, the next best alternative is a memo signed by the same senior manager and posted in all affected areas. This memo should cover the same major subjects as described for the meeting—objectives, scope, participants' names, a statement of the project's importance, and a request for everyone's help. Even when the public meeting has been held, it is a good idea to back it up with the memo, and putting the participants' names on the memo is important. One of the names should have the words "team leader" behind it. This does some amazing things to user commitment.

USER COMMITMENT

Think for a moment about the effect of such a public statement on the person singled out. Senior management, often the team leader's boss's boss's boss, has publicly announced that this is one of the most important things going on in the organization and this person is heading it up. A mixture of pride and anxiety is generated. The team leader knows that if this project is a failure he or she will look bad. The leader also knows that if it is a rousing success his or her name will ride with it. We do not have to explain this to the leaders; they feel it. In response, they do exactly what is best for themselves and for the organization. They do anything they can to make the project a complete success.

Occasionally the anxieties outweigh the perceived opportunity and the leader finds excuses to beg off. When this happens, the best thing to do is let it happen. However, the more confidence we are able to instill through the support of management and effective training the more the pluses will outweigh the fears. Usually the amount of anxiety is just about what is needed to assure mature, responsible performance.

Management often observes this performance and is surprised. They find employees who have never done so before coming in early, staying late, taking work home with them, and indicating genuine enthusiasm for the organization.

"How did you do it?" I have often been asked. I did not. They did it. They did what people naturally do when they are publicly committed to an assignment which combines substantial opportunity for benefit or loss. Inadvertently many organizations reserve these situations for management and then wonder why it does not seem that their employees care. Conversely, many individuals spend a lifetime avoiding these situations for fear of the attendant risk and wonder why they never seem to get the breaks. Inadvertently they denied themselves the opportunities.

MANAGEMENT STEPS BACK

Now the project is underway and it is important that management step back and let the team get to work. Managers may drop in on a team meeting, briefly, from time to time to provide visible evidence of their interest and support for the project, but they must not get involved in the actual solution of the problem.

It should be made thoroughly clear to the team members that their judgment is being sought. They are not expected to present ideas which they think management will support. They are to present ideas which they think are the best for the organization. If managers stay too close during the awkward stages of creative improvement, they are apt to interfere with this process. And if a manager puts pressure on a team member in order to influence the recommendations, the results can be disastrous.

CHART PREPARATION
AND FAMILIARIZATION

Meanwhile, the team members go back to their usual work, while the coordinator is gathering the facts and preparing the procedure chart. Sometimes team members may assist in this effort, but more and more often organizations are finding that this role is best filled by a staff person skilled in the process and able to devote full time to the effort.

In two or three days or two or three weeks, depending on the amount of time needed for the charting, the team meets again. At this point the coordinator, if not properly coached, is apt to make a couple of mistakes which seriously interfere with user involvement. Because of extreme familiarity with the chart (having just drawn every line and symbol on it) the coordinator assumes that it is just as clear to the other team members. This is not so, and when we stop to think about it, it could not be, but this is one of those times when people often do not stop and think.

Engineers and analysts have been making this mistake for years. Then they wonder why participation does not seem to work. They say things like, "We invited users to participate but they really didn't come up with much." The fact is that they were not given much opportunity. They were left at ground level working without the big picture. To get them up to 35,000 feet, they must become familiar with the chart.

The coordinator is the logical person to explain the chart, but there is little hope and no guarantee that simply by walking through the chart with the team members they will understand it well enough to work with it effectively. So, more time is put into familiarization than simply one walk-through. It is made clear to the team members that before the procedure can be improved everyone on the team must be familiar with it. This is done by having each team member in turn explain the charted procedure. Usually the team leader goes first after the coordinator and then the other members follow. A little appropriate symbolism is involved here. The team leader leads, and because of the commitment of the team leader described earlier, he or she is usually eager to do so, perhaps having developed a little familiarity with the chart ahead of time by dropping in on the coordinator while it was being prepared.

It is important during this familiarization effort that each team member explain the entire chart. Occasionally teams decide to have members explain only that portion of the chart which involves their area. Unfortunately this achieves just the opposite of what we are after. The team members already know far more about their areas than the chart can show and the tendency is for them to start elaborating. This not only keeps them at ground level; it also uses up valuable time trying to do something which cannot be done—tell everybody on the team all the details of all the different departments.

HELPING USERS TO
DISCOVER IMPROVEMENTS

The other error which coordinators often make which interferes with the team's getting going is to grab off all the easy, obvious ideas for themselves before the team members have a chance to find them. Some improvements are so obvious that they cannot be missed. Information is being prepared and sent out and never used. Urgently needed information is traveling by an extremely circuitous route, and delays are exaggerated even further because the people in the places where the documents are traveling have no idea of their importance. Discoveries like these lead to instant improvements. Do not send the documents where they are not needed. Do send the urgent information directly to where it is needed.

Who is the first person to discover these obvious improvements? Naturally, the staff coordinator who drew the chart. Coordinators who are eager to grab the credit for these discoveries may appear to run away from the group, and the group may let it happen. They have taken all the easy ones, leaving the more difficult ones for the team, which may not find any soon enough. The team loses its confidence and quits, leaving it for the coordinators, who have demonstrated they can do it. If coordinators get going, by themselves, too fast, the team members may actually turn negative on the whole project and use their ingenuity to prove that the coordinators are not really as smart as they think.

And why should a group of users try to help a staff person demonstrate that he or she knows better how to do their work than they do? Of course, the coordinator is always on their turf, and if they decide to use their ingenuity to shoot down ideas they usually succeed. Next the coordinator will be saying, "All users ever do is resist change." Naturally they will if you steal from them the opportunity to be involved and excited about change. Let them find the easy ones. As they do, their confidence grows, and with it comes the excitement which is needed to carry them through the more difficult parts of the study.

RESISTANCE TO CHANGE

A few words on resistance to change are appropriate here. You rarely see a staff person who is assigned to bring about change resisting his or her own efforts. In fact most staff people tend to get very enthusiastic about what they are doing. Unfortunately, few others in the organization share their enthusiasm.

Often the resistance experienced by the staff is little more than perceptual. The users may be heading the same way, but with less excitement, and they seem to be resisting. To get rid of this form of resistance all that is needed is to slow down and give the users the opportunity to share in the excitement. Once they get started, things tend to take off rapidly and it is all that the coordinator can do to keep up.

CHECKING THE CHART

During the familiarization session two important things are accomplished. First, the team members get the picture. Second, they gain confidence in the chart. They discover that it does in fact give them an accurate representation of the flow of documents. While they have been learning the chart, they have also been checking it out. Minor errors may be discovered, but they should be few.

Errors in charting can be kept to a minimum if the coordinators make it a point to put onto the chart what they have actually observed and avoid charting what they have only heard. This is a reality-oriented approach to improvement, and demonstration is far closer to reality than words can ever be. (Many an improvement effort has foundered on the rocks of faulty fact gathering. When I hear coordinators tell me that every time they return to the workplace they get a different story, I encourage them not to chart stories. Get them to show you.)

Also, while the chart is being reviewed, a comment often emerges such as, "Yes, but it doesn't always happen that way." Usually this need not be a matter of concern. In charting procedures we have techniques which enable us to chart alternative ways of processing. Some are processed in one way, others in another. Major alternatives are charted out, but it is not necessary to chart every minor deviation. This becomes an unending task and is not needed because the user team members already know these variations better than any chart could display them. When charting gets into too much detail, it tends to defeat its main purpose, which is to provide the big picture. The chart need only show how most of the work is processed. The team members bring with them the ground-level detail, including knowledge of these minor exceptions.

Analysts who are constantly frustrated over not having enough facts are usually the ones who are overeager to do it all themselves. They never get enough facts to do that. If they would just be willing to take advantage of the experience of the users, they could save themselves a lot of time and occasionally avoid some rather embarrassing, silly assumptions. So, when concern is expressed that the chart does not show all the variations, the users should be assured that it is not intended to. That is why they are there. Meanwhile the chart provides the big picture for the bulk of the work.

EXPLAINING THE CHART TO OTHERS

After the team has become familiar with the chart and is confident that it is representative, it is made available to everyone in the affected areas who wants to see it and hear it explained. Meetings are set up and the coordinator often explains the chart many times to different groups of people. Sometimes several hundred people will take advantage of this opportunity, and the more people who do, the more there are who have a good idea of what the team is doing. Obviously, several hundred people could not possibly participate on a team. However, all can get a chance to see what is going on, and many may take the initiative to make suggestions to the team member from their area.

Managers are cautioned against doing this because, as discussed earlier, this is apt to put pressure on the team member and undermine the team effort. However, if the team members are properly chosen they are people who are respected by the others in their areas. They are the best people to represent their coworkers. While they may be helped, they will not be pressured by the ideas of their coworkers. If, however, the department is represented by an extremely junior employee, this will not be the case and there will be problems.

Familiarization sessions are also conducted for management. After all, there is no great harm in managers finding out what their employees are doing. However, when managers are going over the charts they too begin to see possibilities, and there is a tendency for them to want to jump into the solving of the problem. This should be discouraged, for if it is allowed to proceed not only will the managers begin to influence the thinking of the group, but inadvertently they will also cut themselves off from the ground-level detail which is available only when ground-level people are involved in working things out for themselves.

USER OWNERSHIP

Now the team is on its way. They have visible management support. They have a chart which gives them the big picture which they understand. And perhaps their confidence has been bolstered with the discovery of several obvious improvement opportunities. They are ready to begin the step-by-step analysis to generate ideas for improvement.

At this point it is important that the users assume ownership of the project. To an extent this is formalized by having the user team leader head up the meetings. At the outset the project belonged to management. During the data gathering and chart preparation and during the familiarization sessions the coordinator has led. Now the coordinator sits back and it is the users' turn. This is hard for some coordinators to do because they are eager for the project to be successful, and willing and desirous of playing a key role in the solution.

Coordinators have got things going, have had a chance to demonstrate technical skill, and probably feel good about the respect gained. It is natural for the team members to continue to turn to them for help and it is natural for them to enjoy being turned to and to want to help. But if the coordinator continues to play a leading role it is likely that the quality of the user participation will be poor.

To help to transfer leadership from the coordinator to the team leader, the team leader formally takes over the meeting and the coordinator takes on the role of backup recorder. The coordinator can actually sit back, listen quietly with head down looking at a note pad, and write down the ideas as they come forth. As long as the coordinator remains silent, the voices in the room will be those of the users. Slowly they begin the unfamiliar process of group problem solving. Soon they pick up speed and are in control, and when the coordinators get the idea that they are not needed at all, the chances are the coordinators have done their job very well.

GENERATING IDEAS

As the team leader formally opens the improvement session, it is useful to restate the project objectives. Some teams have found it useful to have the objectives printed in large letters and prominently displayed. The team leader also sets ground rules for the session, such as, "We want all the ideas we can get, large or small, and don't think anything is too small to be worth considering." Often ideas which appear on the surface to be trivial turn out to provide the greatest benefit. This may be because they are details which have been unattended for years, since they have always appeared to be so trivial.

The team leader also encourages the team to work on the procedure one step at a time. Do not rush ahead and do not worry about ideas for revising steps at the start of the procedure which will affect steps later on. We will get there. Before we are through we will analyze all the steps. Furthermore, the ideas which we are writing down are tentative. We will adjust them as needed.

The team leader should emphasize that they are not looking for grand sweeping solutions. Often a team member will interrupt a discussion with a comment such as "We really don't have to get into all that detail. After all we are going to automate it anyway." Or, "We don't have to get into all that. It is obvious. We are not getting the job done so we need more people." These comments are dysfunctional, and it is disappointing to see a team intimidated by such logic, perhaps because it sounds so managerial. Once we understand the participative process, it is clear that this attitude will result in another 35,000-foot solution without ground-level input. It is nothing more than a plea to ignore ground-level input.

But, if we will stick to the chart, step by step, we will find that the sweeping logic just does not hold up. Automate? Automate what, things we should not be doing in the first place or things which could be done far more efficiently and effectively manually? More people? If we have not figured out how to do our work well, it is not likely that more people will help us to get it done any faster. In fact, more people may add more delays and confusion.

As the meeting progresses, it usually picks up speed because the team is working on very familiar ground, talking about what they do every day at their jobs. Armed with the comprehensive picture provided by the chart and working directly with the people from the other departments, simple, natural conversation turns up one possibility after another.

"It would really help us if they were sent to us in date sequence." "Well, as a matter of fact we work on them in date sequence but we thought you needed them by customer name. Resorting them has always been a headache for us."

"I really don't know why we keep that log. Nobody ever looks at it." "I think we used to need that back when we moved into the new building ten years ago but we certainly don't need it now."

Implicit in both these discussions are ideas. But notice that the people were just talking. They did not start their sentences with "Say, I have an idea. . . ." They simply talked. If we are not careful, the ideas slide by and are lost. The role of the recorder is all we have to assure us that they will not be missed or forgotten. For that reason, having a backup recorder is worthwhile. It is more than just a device to help the coordinator draw back from leadership. It is a vital function, and the coordinator will usually develop genuinely professional skill at doing it. Unfortunately, improvement is often so exciting that people do not stop to write things down.

At the end of each improvement session the two team recorders compare their notes. Each usually picks up something the other missed.

Let us return to the second of the two conversations above, the one about records which may have been needed ten years ago. That conversation might have continued with, "Does anyone know if that log is being used?" "Not me." "Not me." "I'm not sure." "Can we find out?" "Sure, I can check into it."

At this point one of the team members has agreed to check into something. An assignment has been agreed upon and it is also recorded. The two major tasks of the recorders are to write down all the ideas which emerge during the meeting and to list all the assignments which are agreed upon. Before the next meeting these will be cross-checked by the two recorders, written or typed out carefully, and copied so that as the team members enter the next meeting they will have the information which they will need to pick up where they left off. Failure to attend to details such as this will guarantee that the team will get bogged down, repeating itself, not following through on ideas, and probably losing interest.

Another conversation: "If we were to do that it would be difficult for our department to handle it, but I can see how it would be better for the company."

Implicit in that statement is a powerful accomplishment. The sentence starts at ground level and is completed at 35,000 feet, exactly what we need to clean up paperwork. When we achieve this we hear people saying things such as, "This is the first time we have ever got together to solve our problems rather than simply fighting over them." Later, after the project results have been presented to management for approval, some senior executive may say, "This is the first time I have really seen my people working together to try to solve my problems instead of just everyone fighting over their own." The chances are both those statements are true because heretofore we have not done the things needed to enable these people to work together effectively.

ENTHUSIASM

As the study proceeds, it becomes increasingly obvious that 4 or 5 hours a week of the users' time is enough to get a great deal accomplished. The users tend to operate at an enthusiastic pace during the meetings, a pace they could not be expected to maintain on a full-time basis. But, do not be surprised if their enthusiasm leads them to squeeze in an extra meeting from time to time, coming in early, getting together after hours, etc. This is natural and should be encouraged. Conversely, there is something basically wrong about organizations where people are denied this opportunity to become excited about their work.

I recall visiting an insurance company a few years ago for meetings with a project team. I arrived at the airport at nine-thirty on a Sunday evening, and one of the team members was at the airport to pick me up and drive me to the office where the rest of the team was waiting. We worked on the project until about a half hour after midnight. That was unusual behavior for the clerks, underwriters, first-line supervisors, etc., of this insurance company. It is a one-shift company, closed on weekends. But when we add the fact that these people wanted to review with me their proposal which was to be presented to the corporate president and the senior managers of the company at nine o'clock the following morning, this behavior was natural. By noon the next day they were celebrating the enthusiastic acceptance of 14 or their 17 recommendations.

TECHNICAL SUPPORT

As the team progresses, enthusiasm mounts. They may expand their vision and do something unexpected. They now talk about computerizing or bringing in a specialist in word processing or micrographics or communications equipment. We expect this to happen with managers who regularly go outside to try to solve inside problems, but we do not expect this from the people on the job. Usually they resent these intrusions. Now they are inviting them.

When this happens, it should be encouraged but with a word of caution. We want to use anything that will help us to do the best job possible. We pull up another chair for the specialist who now joins the team, bringing specialized experience which is no more valuable or less valuable than the experience of the users who are already on the team. The specialist lives in the field of word processing; they live in the purchasing department, the receiving department, accounts payable, etc. Together they make a beautiful procedure which they could not have made separately. Whenever it appears that changes will involve specialized technology, a specialist should join the team. This is no more than a further extension of participation by the people who know the work.

The word of caution, however, is important. Historically, many specialists have been expected to do the job by themselves, and some believe this is the only way it can be done. If they join the team with comments like, "You don't have to worry about all that detail, we can do the whole thing for you," the team must not quietly follow them up to 35,000 feet and let them try to do it alone. If the specialist gives indications of wanting to take over the project completely, he or she should either be straightened out or replaced by another specialist who is willing to work as an equal, on a team.

The most tempting part of this situation is that team members may encourage the efforts of the specialist to take over the project. Perhaps their anxieties about the project are getting the best of them and they are looking for more than help. They are looking to get off the hook. We have placed them in a managerial role with attendant opportunities and risks. They are now thinking like managers, and we should not be surprised if they make some of the mistakes that managers have been making through the years. But we can avoid this mistake and keep the team involved.

LOSS OF MOMENTUM

Sometimes a study begins to drag. The enthusiasm runs down. People drift into dispute. They do not seem to be willing to work on the detail. They feel that they are at an impasse because much of what they are working on hinges on the willingness of management to go along with one major innovation or a significant interpretation of policy or shift of responsibilities. Whatever the cause, this is where team leadership and the supporting efforts of the coordinator will be critical. They push the work along, hurrying toward conclusion while reassuring the team that they have no obligation to present to management something that management will like or be comfortable with or, for that matter, will approve. They do, however, have an obligation to present to management what they genuinely believe is best for the company.

To keep the team moving the team leader keeps bringing them back to the chart, working on it step by step while the coordinator, between meetings, prepares new charts reflecting the team's ideas. Recharting the procedure is important. It enables the team to test its ideas on paper. Just because an idea sounds good is no reason to believe it will work. If we are unable to chart it, that means we do not know how to accomplish it. Once it has been recharted, however, we know that we have it figured out.

Regardless of how well the team is led, we can expect their anxieties to mount as the time for presentation approaches. They are facing an important moment of truth, and while it is easy to say they have no obligation to present ideas which will be accepted, it is important to them that their ideas be accepted. A lot can be done to improve those chances by the way we go about preparing the proposal and presenting it.

PROPOSAL PREPARATION

First the team should have an idea of what a proposal should look like. It should be a summary of what their ideas will add up to in terms of costs and benefits, followed by a list of the specific changes they are recommending. This is usually done on two or three pages.

Care should be taken to avoid putting justification statements into the proposal. These tend to become argumentative and distracting. List only the conclusions, and by no means let the proposal become a massive assemblage of backup data which seems to say, "Look how busy we have been." Management cannot read and assimilate all that, nor do they have the firsthand experience to evaluate it properly. If management wanted to figure it out for themselves, they should not have bothered with the project team in the first place. These people were not brought together simply to gather facts for managers to think about. They were brought together to think the problem through to conclusion, and conclusions are what they should give to management.

Once the team has a clear idea of what a proposal should look like, preparing it is not difficult, but it must be done carefully. The key to getting started is the chart. If we have a chart which clearly shows the present procedure, and another chart which just as clearly displays the proposed procedure, we can compare those two charts step by step and list all the differences. Those are the things which we intend to change, our specific recommendations. The more carefully we work with the charts the clearer our proposal becomes.

Next we list the recommendations and determine the benefits and costs associated with each. This involves phone calls to determine prices of forms eliminated, equipment to be purchased, etc. People take work counts, daily volumes, annual volumes, etc. Time measurements are made, with one of the team members performing a task and being timed a few times. The coordinator may provide additional training in cost and benefit analysis, introducing the team to work sheets designed to lead them through these calculations and coaching them in how to use them. During this training it is useful to point out that their figures do not have to be minutely accurate but they must be honest, which means that when questioned they can explain how they were arrived at. While this sort of analysis is unfamiliar to most team members, it does not usually turn out to be difficult because the subject matter is the work they do every day.

Anyone can write up the proposal, even the coordinator. However, before it will be ready to present it will go through several stages of rewriting. Eventually it must be in words which are completely acceptable to the people who will present them. The team leader reads the summary statements, and each of the detailed recommendations will be read by the team member from the department most strongly affected by the recommendation.

When the proposal draft is ready, the team meets and reads it through aloud. As they are reading they stop for discussion and changes are made. The team does this several times and then separates, with each team member taking a portion. Having heard all the comments of the other team members, team members now work alone to get their parts worded the way they think they should be. They should be cautioned at this point not to justify or get defensive. They should simply state what they want to change.

The group meets and reads the proposal through again. There are additional changes, but by this time they are usually few. Before this meeting ends, the group should read it through once without interruptions just as they intend to do at the presentation. It is a good idea to time it. This not only provides useful information but also assures that the reading will not be stopped for discussion. It is also a good idea once again to reinforce the notion that these recommendations are in fact what we believe should be done. If they are not, we should not be recommending them. If they are, we should read them as though we believe in them. This leads to discussion of the staging of the presentation. We do several things to indicate our confidence, hoping to share that confidence with management. If we succeed, we leave with their acceptance.

PROPOSAL PRESENTATION

The proposal is presented to the same managers who helped to set up the project. This includes the executive whose authority spans the full scope of the project as well as those managers intervening between that executive and the team members. Other key professionals may attend, and there may be people from staff groups which would be involved in implementation and occasionally one of two people who are just interested. The latter should be kept to a minimum. The main purpose of the meeting is to enable the team to talk with the managers who are to decide.

The proposal is to be presented by reading it aloud. It should not be distributed ahead of time. If it is, we run the risk of unnecessarily losing the benefits of all the work which has gone before. Since the proposal is only a few pages long, and since it should be something which is vital to the managers involved, the chances are that they will read it. If they do, it is almost certain that they will begin to evaluate it and they will be doing this at about 80,000 feet without the chart available and with no ground-level input. If the managers then begin to discuss their evaluations with one another, the risk is very high that they will become committed to decisions based on considerable misunderstanding. When this happens, we find managers rejecting portions or even all of the proposal for no apparent reason. It may be simply that they have indicated to other managers ahead of time that they were going to do this and they would lose face if they did not. What a shame to go through all the work to obtain detailed grass roots input and then ignore it when it comes to the final decisions.

To avoid this, we do not distribute the written proposal except in a setting where the people who figured it out are available to answer questions and defend it. This style of proposal presentation is not appropriate for all types of management meetings, but when it comes to paperwork improvement it is vital. The people who live with the paperwork and figured out the improvements must be on hand to help management as they decide.

It is important that the team members get to the meeting room early. One of the reasons is mundane, and that is to tidy up and make sure that the room presents a clean, orderly appearance. A second reason is to control the seating. The table or tables are arranged so that all the people sit around the outside looking at each other. The team members distribute themselves around the table so that the managers will be sitting between them. There is some symbolism involved here, and it is functional. We are serious when we say that we want the team members and management to work together. This seating gives visible evidence of this and helps to set the tone.

At the head of the table are two chairs, one for the team leader and one for the senior executive. The executive has had a chance to discuss this meeting in advance, usually with the coordinator. Of course, the coordinator does not tell the senior executive what he or she is to do, nor for that matter does an outside consultant like myself, but we talk to the executive about what we hope to get out of the meeting and how we hope to achieve it. Invariably we find that the executives have high hopes for the project and want to do what they can to make it succeed. Once they understand the rationale of the meeting, they fill their role with enthusiasm, which includes sharing the head table with the team leader (again symbolism of cooperation) and wrapping up the meeting, which will be explained shortly.

At the start of the meeting there may be a comment or two from the senior official such as "I have been looking forward to this, etc." Then comes the formal reading of the proposal, without interruptions for discussion. The team members are usually nervous about this part of the meeting, but it does not take long and if their nervousness shows it is honest and natural.

After the reading (5 or 10 minutes), the proposal is up for discussion. This is the part of the meeting where the team members shine and the proposal is usually sold. While they may have been nervous during the formal reading, now things are different. They are being asked questions about the work they do every day, questions about changes that they have been working on very carefully for several weeks, questions which they are better prepared to answer than anyone else in the world. It took a lot of preparation to get here, but in the next few minutes all that went before is justified. It becomes apparent that the team members really know what they are talking about. They sound intelligent. They are obviously conscientious. They are telling management how they want to do their work to do the best job for the company, and before long decisions are being made. All recommendations are not accepted, but most are. Many are obviously beneficial and need no discussion, but there are those which will take more time. Here is where skill in wrapping up the meeting becomes important.

When the discussion runs down or when the allotted time is about to run out, the meeting is turned over to the senior manager. This is a formal transfer of ownership. Now it is time for management to do their part, which is to decide.

The coaching which the senior executive has received has been somewhat as follows. These team members have put a lot of work into this project and much of what they will be presenting will be obviously beneficial as well as at a level of detail far below the executive's responsibilities. But these things are very important to the people who have figured them out. The worst thing that could happen to these people would be that they would go through all this effort and the meeting would end with a statement such as, "It is very interesting. We'll think about it." Some of the recommendations obviously do not require time to ponder. At the close of the meeting the recommendations should be reviewed one by one. Some get an obvious yes. Some get a no. Others need further work. Decide as follows. If you think it is great, say yes. If it worries you, do not. If you are indifferent, say yes because those people have worked hard on this and they will want to do everything they can to see that their ideas work out.

IMPLEMENTATION

Usually within a week or two of the meeting the final decisions are worked out and implementation begins. Here we get a return on our investment in participation because the people who worked it out are working every day in the departments where the changes must be made. There is, however, more to managing installation than simply depending on the dedication of the team members. It takes some strategy and technique. To prepare the team for this, they are given a little more training.

The principal strategies involved in implementation involve leadership and planning. The leadership role must be handled by one person. This is important because during implementation the amount of participation increases manyfold. Heretofore we have had one representative from each department. Now everyone in those departments is involved as well as other groups such as form design, forms suppliers, purchasing, equipment vendors, engineering, carpenters, electricians, painters, the telephone people, and computer programmers. Unless one person is clearly assigned to coordinate this, the delays will be exhausting. This person should be a user, often the same person who was the team leader.

The reasons for having the implementation coordinated by a user are as follows. First, they work right in the area and know the work and the people who do it very well. Second, they will continue to be in the area long after the implementation is over to see to details and problems.

The staff paperwork simplification coordinator can give this person a great deal of time and assistance but should not be officially in charge of the installation. A staff person who manages it may find it very difficult to finish it. There is always some little detail to be attended to. However, if the person in charge is a user, the time will come when the staff person can leave, with the responsibility for working out those details left to the people who do the work.

As for planning the implementation, this involves attention to maintaining the momentum of the effort. Following the presentation there will be some who are quite enthusiastic about the changes and others who frankly do not believe anything will actually happen. Too often we scuttle our efforts by concentrating on the wrong people. We waste a lot of time if we try to get such a perfect result that we can counter all the arguments of our detractors. And while we ignore our supporters their enthusiasm wanes.

This tendency is exaggerated by many staff analysts who enjoy detail work and because they are somewhat introverted prefer to postpone activities which are public. As a result the project disappears from view for several months while detailed preparation is going on. Every day that passes reinforces the views of those who were sure nothing would actually happen and reassures those who genuinely hope that nothing will happen. And every day it becomes more difficult for those who were enthusiastic to maintain their enthusiasm. When we finally get it put together and bring it out, our detractors are thoroughly entrenched and our supporters have lost their steam.

As an alternative, it is useful to arrange visible public activities at regular intervals throughout the installation period. New equipment is brought in and people are invited to an open house to see it. Go to work on the office layout as soon as possible and when the walls change it is difficult for detractors to insist that nothing is going to happen, just as it is reassuring to supporters who see things actually getting done. Call a meeting to test a roughly designed form or discuss a procedure write-up. The supporters will be there. Do not worry about the detractors. Keep on with the job and sooner or later it will be obvious to everyone that it is happening and the choice is simple, get on board or get left behind. In this way resistance to change is converted to momentum for change.

There are also techniques to help keep track of the installation. We start with a simple work sheet on which the approved recommendations are listed and check marks are placed in columns indicating the type of work which must be done to accomplish each of them. These check marks indicate forms needed, equipment needed, programming needed, policy write-up needed, training, workplace design, etc.

The work sheet enables us to locate all the activities which must be accomplished to complete the installation. Next these activities are assigned to the appropriate people who will carry them out. If the installation is complex, a network schedule is also prepared organizing these activities in logical sequence with estimates of how long they will take. This is usually prepared with the help of the staff coordinator, who should be well schooled in the technique. If it is done properly, it will enable the user who is coordinating the installation to keep track of the progress on all the activities while concentrating attention on those which are most critical to staying on schedule.

SEEING THAT IT WORKS

Soon the forms are ready, the equipment is in place, the training is completed, and now comes the final question, "How do we get them to do it the way it has been figured out?" That is a question which has driven consultants, both external and internal, wild for decades. But with participative improvement it is a relatively minor issue. How you get them to do it answers itself when you stop to think who figured it out. Naturally, all the users did not figure it out, but in each of the affected departments there is one, a respected coworker, who helped to figure it out and understands it thoroughly. Management can help by recognizing their accomplishments, calling attention to what they have done, and building their pride.

One useful way of reinforcing this pride is to stage open houses to show off the new setup. Invite whom you like, dignitaries, family, other departments, whatever. Things will somehow get polished up for the occasion. Issue commendations, acknowledge the success in the corporate newsletter, make a before and after video tape, send a personal letter from the senior executive, etc. All these things help to build the pride in the new ideas that is needed to get them working and keep them working.

Then comes the final return on participation. The team members have put 4 or 5 hours a week into the project for several weeks, a total of as few as 20, rarely more than 100 hours apiece. But from now on their jobs will never be the same again because every time they fill out that form they see a piece of themselves in it. Every time they deal with that procedure they get a little bit of the intrinsic reward that comes from having helped to create it. Meanwhile, the company has gained an employee who has less reason to blame the organization for its faults and more reason to care.

SUMMARY OF INVOLVEMENT

Throughout this process several levels of management have been involved as have people from the operating departments. Each has participated appropriately in accordance with his or her responsibilities. The time investment of the staff coordinator is several months. The time investment of the team leader/installation coordinator has been similar. The time investment of each of the team members has accumulated to add up to 20 to 50 hours. And that of the managers is a few hours. Meanwhile, problems which have plagued the company for years are gone, people are working together, and paperwork simplification has achieved its purpose.

PART SIX

Physical Resources /Technology Structure

- *Facilities*
- *Equipment*
- *Computers*
- *Information Technology*

Physical resources and technology provide the "assets" which make things possible. People make things happen. Technology and physical resources are fundamental to the improvement of productivity and have had a favorable impact on white collar productivity. However, the office is virtually an underdeveloped area in terms of what can potentially be done to enhance productivity compared with what has been done to date.

An indicator is the relatively low investment per office worker compared with that in production of manufactured and farm goods. One consequence, many experts claim, is the almost zero (or negative) increase in office worker productivity experienced by many organizations.

A wealth of technology is available to support improvement of white collar productivity, and more is available every day. Some of the basic issues associated with exploitation of office technology are presented in Chapter 12. The message applies to both small and large organizations. Both have need to address the role of office technology and to manage its adoption formally, on a selective and directed basis, for the benefit of their organizational productivity.

The following chapter is addressed to those organizations which have already installed sizable computer-based operational-support systems and are searching for ways to upgrade them.

Many organizations have large-scale real-time computer systems which are at the heart of their business operations. These systems have been designed with considerable care and effort to accomplish a variety of data-storage and manipulation operations, and they are usually interactive with many human operators. The intent of all these systems is to provide information and to support real-time (or almost real-time) decision making which directly affects operational performance of the organization.

Information and computer technology has developed rapidly in the past 25 years, and many systems have undergone a series of almost revolutionary changes. The driving force behind these changes has been almost exclusively focused on what the technology could be made to do, with very minor attention being given to its effect on the productivity of those humans who interact with the system. Within limits, this is logical. Basic changes in the systems and procedures which are involved have allocated to the machine so much of what were previously human activities that from a relative standpoint the remaining human component is almost insignificant. However, attention to facilitation of human performance is really critical, for the power of the system is not productively used unless the task of the intervening human operator is made productive and easy to perform.

Large-scale systems have pushed the state of the art which was available at their inception. However, as additional technology, both hardware and software, becomes available the full exploitation of these developments becomes more difficult. Some are incorporated, often by "patch-up" of the system and its software. But many other advances are not exploited because of the extensive reprogramming required and the uncertainties associated with systems performance which might be achieved by following various alternative paths of change.

Recognizing that many technological advances are available, that the cost for incorporation into an ongoing system operation is very high, that the benefit to be achieved from alternative changes is somewhat uncertain—and that continuing operation of present systems is essential—how can one best proceed to upgrade current large-scale, real-time, operation-based business computer systems? In addition, how can the philosophy of systems design be shifted to emphasize the ease and productivity of those humans whose job performance the computer system is intended to support? These are the key questions addressed in Chapter 13 by the RESCAP group at Eastern Airlines, under the direction of Paul Cowdin.

Eastern Airlines and IBM embarked on a joint project to determine how to best exploit new technology, both hardware and software, for Eastern's computer-based reservations system. The present system is a very complex and modern one. However, its basic design is about 12 years old and is oriented more toward the system and its internal efficiency than toward the effective performance of the humans which the system supports. Since the original system design, additional technology has become available, and some elements of newer technology have been incorporated into the system. However, much more change is possible. Determination of what elements of additional technology should be adopted to facilitate human performance is a principal focus of the joint study. It is directed toward an evaluation of what changes not only would most effectively support the human component of their system but would aid the human component in making a maximum contribution to achieving the basic objectives of the organization.

The procedures used by the RESCAP group demonstrate a generalizable methodology for upgrading large-scale systems, which has potential utility in many settings—for evolutionary incorporation of newer technology, and to establish the criteria for extensive system redesign.

Office Technology

ROBERT N. LEHRER
Consultant

Technology, with the exception of the computer, has had rather modest impact on the office. In many situations where computers are in use one would have reason to doubt that white collar productivity has been substantially improved, particularly in the area of the knowledge worker. However, there is mounting evidence that this situation will change and that a range of technology will find useful applications in the office, with a major impact on knowledge worker productivity.

Opportunity for enhancing the productivity of knowledge workers by more extensive use of available technology is identified in a recent study by Booz Allen & Hamilton.[1] "Our findings: sound cost-benefit justification can readily be made for saving approximately 15 percent of a typical knowledge worker's time by 1985. In monetary terms, the U.S. value of this saving alone is equivalent to more than $100 billion."

The annual cost in the United States associated with office-based white collar workers, ranging from chief executive officers to file clerks, is $800 billion. The cost is likely to increase, in particular because of increasing demands placed on managers and professionals (coupled with inflation), to almost $1½ trillion by 1990.

Managers and professionals account for about 73 percent of the total cost, clerical for about 27 percent. The use of technology as measured by purchased information resources amounts to about $71 billion, which is a modest 9 percent of total white collar costs. The bulk of this expenditure is directed at clerical work, about $30 billion, or 70 percent, with

	Managers	Professionals	Clerical	Total
Direct costs	$240 billion (72.73%)	$225 billion (88.24%)	$135 billion (62.79%)	$600 billion
Support	78 billion (23.64%)	21 billion (8.24%)	30 billion (13.95%)	129 billion
Technology	12 billion (3.64%)	9 billion (3.53%)	50 billion (23.26%)	71 billion
	$330 billion (100%)	$255 billion (100%)	$215 billion (100%)	$800 billion

	Direct costs	Support	Technology	Total
Managers	$240 billion (40.00%)	$ 78 billion (60.47%)	$ 12 billion (16.90%)	$330 billion
Professionals	225 billion (37.75%)	21 billion (16.29%)	9 billion (12.68%)	255 billion
Clerical	135 billion (22.25%)	30 billion (23.26%)	50 billion (70.42%)	215 billion
	$600 billion (100%)	$129 billion (100%)	$ 71 billion (100%)	$800 billion

FIG. 12-1. United States white collar expenditures. In the United States in 1979, $800 billion was spend for office-based white collar work. (SOURCE: *Booz Allen & Hamilton estimates based on published sources for 1979.*)

only $9 billion, or 13 percent directed toward professionals, and $12 billion, or 17 percent to managers (see Fig. 12-1).

One inference which can be drawn, without much risk of error, is that investment in office technology has short-changed the knowledge worker segment of the white collar group. This inference is further supported when one recognizes the sorts of technology which are currently available which could potentially be of benefit to knowledge workers. Further insight is provided by typical patterns of knowledge worker efforts, particularly time spent on various tasks which can be aided by technology.

The Booz Allen study showed that about 25 percent of knowledge worker time is typically devoted to activities which are basically unproductive time wasters, such as searching for information or people, copying, scheduling, and traveling to and from meetings. "Technological fixes" are presently available which substantially eliminate these activities, as shown in Fig. 12-2.

In addition to substantially eliminating many time-wasting activities, technology has the potential ability of allowing better decisions to be made, increasing knowledge worker contribution to organization mission, and improving the quality of working life. The potential economic benefits are substantial, but improved ability to contribute to organization mission and objectives is of even more potential value.

The Booz Allen study indicates that a 9 percent productivity improvement could be achieved within 18 to 24 months by selective application of available technology, with a rate of return on investment of well over 50 percent. A 15 percent productivity gain is easily achievable within 5 years. Substantial additional benefits can be achieved within 10 years, with potential annual savings approaching $300 billion.

TECHNOLOGY

The potential benefit to be derived from more extensive use of technology in the office is dramatic. We have emphasized the use of technol-

Time wasters	Available technological fix
Seeking information on sources of supply	On-line access to external supplier data bases and internal records of supplier performance
Reaching key colleagues on the phone	An easy-to-use desk-top keyboard or speech mail system
Traveling to periodic internal status meetings	Videoconferencing
Excessive "what-if" number-crunching iterations	Automated decision support system
Seeking the status of an order	Desk-top access to an information tracking system
Extensive corrections/revisions to documented reports and correspondence	Nearby access to a powerful word-and-graphics composition and revision processor
Scheduling meetings	Desk-top displays of executive calendars available to both executives and secretaries
Generating reminders to subordinates to meet agreed-upon schedules	Tickler system that generates automated reminders

FIG. 12-2. Typical knowledge workers spend 15 to 40 percent of their time in totally unproductive activities for which "technological fixes" are potentially available. (SOURCE: *Booz Allen & Hamilton study.*)

ogy to support the knowledge worker, because this is an undersupported sector of white collar work which badly needs to improve its productivity. The opportunity for substantial improvement is at hand for all white collar work, *particularly* for the knowledge worker. A variety of technology is available, and more is on the way. Rather than discuss specific technology, we now turn our attention to the basic process associated with exploitation of technology—how an organization can stay abreast of developments and selectively use what is available, in a proactive manner, to assure that technology is put to productive use for the benefit of the organization.

MANAGING TECHNOLOGY

Basic Policy and Strategy

The role of technology should be associated very intimately with the basic strategies of an organization. This is particularly true for product, process, and production technology but is also true for office technology. The strategy significance is generally recognized in the former, and is reflected in commitment to R&D, the monitoring of relevant technological developments external to the organization, a commitment to invest in appropriate technologies which fit with strategic plans and objectives, and internal mechanisms for incorporating selected technology into the products and processes of the organization in an effective manner. The techniques and methods for *managing* technology are well developed and effectively used by many organizations. Unfortunately, the management of technology typically is not extended to the office area within many organizations. The same concepts and procedures which have been used successfully in the product and process area can be adapted to manage office technology as well. Why this has not been done more extensively is largely a matter of failure of top management to recognize that it *can* be done and that it *should* be done within their organizations.

The exploitation of office technology is first of all a matter of strategic decision relative to organizational mission and objectives. Recognizing that white collar overhead costs, both in general and for a specific organization, are increasing much more rapidly than direct costs, what strategic approaches fit with overall business development plans? What increases or decrease in these costs are appropriate, and how can the desired cost patterns be achieved? What changes in validity of these activities are desirable? What is the potential for use of office technology? What funds are available or can be made available for investment in office technology? What is an appropriate rate of return for such investments? Is technology to be viewed as a way to decrease white collar labor costs, as a way to improve the quality of job performance, or some of both? What allocation of responsibility for exploitation of technology is desirable? Should it be centralized or decentralized? Where is responsibility now centered? Is this appropriate, or should it be modified? How is potential office technology now made available within the organization? How are decisions made to adopt new office technology? How will the use of office technology complement or conflict with other efforts to improve white collar productivity?

These questions, and many more, should be addressed by top management. The evidence in favor of commitment to selective and more extensive use of office technology is compelling and merits the formulation of a well-thought-out office technology strategy at the top level. This is so for large organizations in particular but is also appropriate for small organizations. Large organizations will develop more formalized approaches to pursue their policies and strategies than will small organizations, but the basic elements of pursuit will be much the same.

Understanding

Once basic commitment to office technology has been made, strategic direction defined, and a policy framework developed, the next step in managing technology is to develop an awareness of this commitment throughout the organization. This is then followed by efforts to develop an understanding of office technology and how it can usefully be incorporated into the ongoing operations of the organization.

Staying abreast of technology requires specific assignment of responsibility, and development of technological "savvy." Larger organizations can justify separate organizational units, with staff "experts" for the various bits and pieces of knowledge and skill. They can also justify additional responsibility assignments and resources to enable existing organizational units to perform the necessary functions. Many smaller organizations must rely on expanding the responsibilities of *an* individual to include the tracking of technology, and are likely to draw heavily on resources furnished by vendors, equipment shows, and trade publications.

Understanding available technology is not too difficult. However, disseminating this understanding throughout the white collar portion of an organization *and* developing an understanding of how it can be usefully adopted is a difficult matter.

The usual approach to understanding technology is to centralize the expertise and to centralize the authority to consider its use. This pattern has developed within many organizations as a mechanism to "control" the "misuse" of various data-processing equipment. It has some merit, but it also has severe disadvantages. It tends to give the "expert" ownership of technology and to deny it to the nonexpert individuals who should be the user-owners of the technology.

The policy of centralization may achieve control of misapplication and prevent duplication of equipment, but it usually also results in the blocking of many appropriate applications—and it discourages widespread understanding of potential applications of other technology.

Dissemination

Monitoring of office technology and disseminating information about it within an organization can be approached in many ways. Each organization is likely to want to approach these two things in its own unique way, which is appropriate. It should be done in a planned manner, with particular attention being paid, first of all, to the assembly of information about office technology in general and what it can do, without much regard to specific vendor items and to relative advantages and disadvantage of specific equipment.

Second, recognizing that many people are awed and intimidated by technology, the approach to dissemination should be educational and nonthreatening—intended to develop an appreciation on the part of potential users of how technology might possibly be usefully applied to work activities which both directly and indirectly affect and involve them. The objective of this planned dissemination is to sensitize the white collar work force to office technology and to the organization's commitment to use it effectively.

Focused Understanding

The next phase of dissemination should be focused, directed specifically to those individuals and elements of the organization which have the best potentials for productivity improvement via technology. The objective of this phase is to provide understanding about specific technology and either how it has been used successfully in similar settings or how it might be used by the targeted individuals and organization units. This effort might be viewed, cynically, as one of propagandizing, but the intent is educational.

Not only should the positive aspects of potential application be stressed, but limitations and difficulties should also be included—particularly the realities of necessary changes in work patterns, relationships, and habits. The objective is to achieve understanding and a sense of "ownership" of knowledge about technology on the part of those who will be affected by its use.

Co-opting

Office technology, while basically similar to product, process, and production technology, is also different in two significant ways. Its impact tends to cut across organizational lines more extensively, and it has a greater potential effect on people, both negatively and positively. The management of office technology should address these issues. One way of doing so is to *co-opt* the user. All individuals who will be affected, both directly and indirectly, by the application of technology are involved in the process of adopting the technology. This starts with involvement of various levels of management, and of workers, in planning for the use of office technology, progresses to direct involvement in the decision making associated with developing application systems, and goes on to similar involvement with installation.

This approach to co-opting the user is commonly used with an open style of management and reinforced by quality circles, paperwork simplification, joint problem-solving team efforts, and other programs of involvement and participation. It is a highly effective approach but has found limited use in dealing with office technology.

The "experts" often feel that getting the user involved as deeply as necessary to achieve co-opting is too cumbersome and not necessary. Upper levels of management frequently feel that the experts should be in charge and that individuals who are affected will accommodate to desirable change—or else.

The process of gaining understanding and commitment, and of developing sufficient skill to participate, is slow and cumbersome. The participative process is also slow and cumbersome. However, the benefits in terms of better using human potential for improved performance outweigh the disadvantages.

The role of the expert   The above materials tend to indicate that the technical expert is of use only to provide education to and to develop an understanding on the part of potential users of office technology. These are important roles for the expert, and they provide the basis for managing change by the change agent approach. The expert is the catalytic resource which makes possible the user-controlled adoption of office technology. The expert also has responsibility beyond this, particularly related to the overall plan for systematically infusing office technology throughout the organization, and for implementing the plan. A variety of skills and expertise are required, which may justify teams of experts being involved in the planning and execution of an office technology effort.

Some of the key elements which imply need for expertise in managing office technology are:

Developing the background for organizational commitment to office technology:
- Technology assessment and forecasting to understand what is available and what is likely to become available
- Economic, demographic, and social forecasting to understand what changes are likely and to assess how the organization will be affected by them
- Assessment of how the above two elements can be made to have a favorable impact upon the organization

Developing an organizational commitment to office technology:
- Delineating the role of office technology, defining its functional mission and objectives, organizational position, responsibilities, authorities, working relationships, and resources
- Development of strategic plans, based on assessment of application opportunities throughout the organization, development of benefit/cost relationships, determination of priorities for application, targeting specific applications and projects for execution, and development of action element plans to support strategic plans
- Development of tactical plans for developing applications identified in strategic planning, resources required, development required, time phasing, funding, and coordination

Execution of programmatic efforts:
- Co-opting the potential users, gaining understanding of office technology and commitment to its use
- Revision of strategic and tactical plans, with particular emphasis on project execution and implementation
- Project execution, providing needed technical and organization behavior support, continuing project management, and heavy user involvement

- Implementation and evolutionary development, assessment of performance

Continuing assessment of technology and opportunity for additional applications

Revision and updating of strategic and tactical plans

This listing is only of the highlights but is sufficient to imply many additional details and to determine how formalized an approach is desirable for a specific organization. A wealth of literature on technology management is available. A limited amount dealing specifically with office technology has been published, but the amount will increase.

DEALING WITH BARRIERS

The process for managing technology implicitly addresses various barriers to the effective use of office technology. However, it is useful to recognize these barriers explicitly, for they are real obstacles to achieving useful results and can cause great difficulties if they are not fully dealt with in a proactive manner.

Commitment

The first and foremost barrier is lack of organizational commitment. The use of technology, the exploitative use for the benefit of the organization, should be addressed in terms of basic strategies for achievement of organization mission, keyed to business strategies and the basic objectives which are main-line for the organization. A vision of what technology might contribute is essential, as is a commitment to provide appropriate organizational responsibility assignment, and resources to further develop visions of what might be done and to translate these into useful applications.

Understanding

Once basic policy in support of productivity improvement and the use of office technology has been made for the organization by top management and the board of directors, this commitment must be institutionalized throughout the organization. Conviction that white collar productivity can and will be improved, and that technology has a major, *constructive* role to play must permeate the entire white collar organization. Lack of such conviction and understanding is a major barrier.

Lack of understanding throughout the organization can block use of additional technology and can also prevent effective use of that which is already in place.

Changes Are Too Radical

Some uses of technology, particularly large-system applications, cause drastic change in work patterns for large sectors of an organization. These changes are drastic and present substantial problems of individual accommodation. However, many other applications are more limited in their impact, can be approached in a staged manner, using modular elements of technology, and provide opportunity for individual accommodation—particularly when change is undertaken by the individuals who are directly affected and is supported by the change agent approach.

Technology Degrades

Even when change is approached in a managed way, some technology imposes such drastic departures from past practice and custom that personal image and security are threatened. The use of computer terminals by managers is a case in point. Most executives think that the use of a keyboard is not in keeping with their status—and many do not have typing skills. Emotionally, they are ill equipped to acquire the understanding and skill necessary to use a cathode-ray-tube (CRT) unit as a working tool.

Speaking of the benefits and problems of introducing computer technology to a large legal firm, Francis H. Musselman cites major benefits and also mentions, "Some of the partners had to retire . . . and some executives had to be fired, but we did it."[2]

"James Ogorchuck, assistant vice president for office automation at Maine Midland Bank in Buffalo—which has placed 3000 CRTs among its 10,000 headquarters and branch employees—sees the executive ego as a genuine hurdle, but one that can be jumped. 'You can introduce the concept in a classroom setting,' he explains, 'but you can't train there; too much ego involved. It's better to train in private, with the trainer being someone of similar corporate stature'."[3]

Investment Is Premature

Office technology is changing rapidly. Many managers fear that the changes are so rapid that investment should be deferred, awaiting stabilization of developments. Such an attitude is self-defeating and results in potential benefit forgone, perhaps on a continuing basis. Much available office technology can be cost-justified on the basis of 50 to 100+ percent return on investment (ROI). Even if future developments make technology obsolete with such ROI rates, benefit can be obtained from using and discarding it when something better becomes available.

Modularity also is a significant consideration in guarding against rapid obsolescence of office technology. Newer technology can frequently be incorporated without disrupting the integrity of an entire system when modular applications are used.

Too Costly

Office technology usually requires capital investment. As with any capital expenditure, investments in office technology should be made within a structured policy framework. Capital budgets should reflect organizational policy and commitment to invest when candidate investment opportunities and proposals meet specified criteria. The total available investment pool and general areas for appropriate expenditures are normally determined by organizational policy, with procedures for approval of specific expenditures outlined. Office technology should be considered as an investment opportunity, with potentially available funding specified by top management and the board of directors. Candidate proposals for expenditures should be required to compete for funding, with a minimum ROI required for consideration and for approval.

Office technology is expensive but represents an area of investment with excellent potential returns, well above 50 percent for many projects. Such rates of return are attractive and justify reasoned investment planning to ensure that funds are available and expended where needed.

Organizational Prerogatives

Office technology extends well beyond one functional area and well beyond any one technical specialty. Organizational realities being what they are, conflict, power struggles, politics, preservation of prerogatives, guarding of territorial rights, and so forth, often have a deleterious effect on efforts to improve white collar productivity and to use technology. Some major barriers are frequently raised because of these realities. Information is not shared freely, and individuals (and also organizational entities) pursue their own ends rather than those things which would be of benefit to the organization as a whole. Overcoming these barriers requires that they be anticipated and recognized, and that they be removed.

Fear of Complexity

Even when an understanding of technology is diffused throughout an organization, much uncertainty and anxiety about how to cope with complex change is likely to persist. Such doubts are compounded when the introduction of technology is imposed by the "experts." Those who are affected have an intellectual and emotional need to feel that they are not being manipulated, that they are at least partially in control of what is being done to them by technology, and that they can cope with new situations. An additional measure of individual growth is needed, and change should be managed via the change agent approach.

Technology Is Not User-Sensitive

Technology is cold and impersonal, unless it is viewed by the user as a *desirable* aid to enable him or her to achieve what he or she desires. If this is the view, any real or imagined "hostility" of technology will be tolerated and allowed for in its use. Unfortunately, many individuals who are directly affected by office technology do not view it as a desirable aid to help them achieve their ends. We can either help the individual develop a conviction and understanding of how technology can assist in achieving what they desire (a very complex endeavor), or we can make technology more "user-friendly." *Both* should be attempted.

Most people have a deep-seated and potential resentment of being manipulated—particularly when the manipulation is done by an impersonal "thing," a machine or a system. This is well stated by Sharon S. Stromberg, director of the Office Systems Center, U.S. Office of Personnel Management.[4] "Machines are friendly all right—but to the system and not the person." She continues her comments, stating that she knows of instances where "employees have drawn lots to see who would sabotage the system so it would go down that day." What more compelling reality could there be to motivate those who are responsible for office automation to address the issues of how to devise situations where individuals view technology as a "friendly" means to help them achieve their ends—ends which are directly related to helping the organization achieve its ends?

Implementation

Any change intended to be an improvement is not successful unless improvement is actually achieved. An obvious and redundant statement? Yes. But many well-formulated changes for improvement do not live up to their billings. The potential benefits are not fully achieved. Implementation of technology in the office setting is a major barrier. Part of the barrier is caused by lack of thoroughness in planning the change. Systems interactions are neglected. An even larger portion of the barrier is caused by imposition of change. The obvious remedy is to be more thorough in analysis of interactions, particularly in regard to ultimate objectives (contribution to organization mission), and to manage the change process—by developing ownership of change on the part of those involved. Skill and vision in analysis of organizational interaction and human/organization behavior are required.

Lack of Organization–Wide Vision

Many elements of office technology are expensive, and many others which individually may not be very expensive are expensive to put into operation and to support in use. I recall the frustration of one of my associates when he could not "sell" a recommendation for use of a text editing application to improve the productivity of an engineering group. The text editing program cost was insignificant and the potential productivity improvement for the engineers was very attractive. However, the cost to adapt the communications and computer system to support the application was just a bit too high for the savings to justify. This he had no difficulty in accepting. His frustration was caused by his inability to get the "organization" to recognize that there were other potential productivity improvement opportunities which would be made possible by the "investment" required to support his proposed use of text editing in engineering. These other opportunities, if captured, would also be beneficial in improving productivity in other areas, and collectively would more than justify the investment which a single application would not. The organization did not have a mechanism for assessing potential applications of specific technology throughout the organization, and for systematically cultivating complementary applications. No one cared. No one had responsibility for the organizationwide exploitation of technology.

Starting from the Wrong Base

When evaluating proposed uses of technology, one should be extremely cautious concerning the basis for justification. The most favorable alternatives for improving productivity cannot be used if they are not considered. This is an obvious statement, but the wrong basis for justifying the use of specific office technology is not entirely uncommon. It arises in two principal ways: failure to consider how to modify the present situation without use of technology, and not considering a sufficiently broad range of technology. These barriers can be overcome by diligence, making certain that the situation being dealt with is assessed first in regard to the effectiveness of the output and then in terms of the efficiency and effectiveness of performance. Modifications to output requirements and to changes to improve internal efficiency and effectiveness without additional use of technology may well achieve sufficient improvement that additional technology is no longer needed. When this is done, available alternative technological applications need to consider a broad enough range to provide confidence that the "best bet" is included. The technology expert needs to provide guidance.

ORGANIZATIONAL IMPLICATIONS

Technology has been *the* driving force behind improvement in productivity. Capital investment to support office worker productivity lags well behind other areas, about $2000 per worker, compared with $25,000 per factory worker and $36,000 per farm worker. Increased investment in office technology is not likely to reach the levels of capital-intensive manufacturing but will represent major investments for many organizations.

Investment in office technology should be a reasoned *part* of an overall white collar productivity improvement program, one to which organizational commitment and resources are provided. The potential for enhancing productivity, particularly for knowledge workers but also for clerical workers, represents an attractive investment opportunity. In addition to top management commitment and involvement, which is an essential prerequisite, all sectors of the white collar organization should be involved.

The Booz Allen study concludes that knowledge work is eclectic, and the potential gains, while cumulatively large, will come in small pieces. If not planned and measured, the benefits could leak away. The planning of benefits should be keyed to business strategies, their critical success factors, and the managements by objectives (MBOs) they generate. The improvement program should be viewed in the larger context of an overall strong top management commitment to good people, attractive rewards and incentives, and sound organization structure.

The major obstacle to success is not, as some have asserted, end-user receptivity to technology but the magnitude of financial and people resources needed to achieve widespread use. The shortage of well-qualified people to assist the organization in understanding and adopting useful technology is the most critical obstacle.

Most organizations would be well advised to designate an organizational entity to guide and support such an effort and to ensure that the necessary human resource skills to complement technological expertise are available.

The study suggests the following organizational structure to complement the designation of an office technology entity:

- A top-level steering committee, to demonstrate commitment and support, to ensure that benefits to be achieved are driven by business strategy and that implementation will be from the top down
- Task forces, one level down, to cut organization lines, to furnish direct participation in program and project development and execution, to furnish needed business (user) expertise, and to ensure a range of needed expertise in human resource and technology disciplines

Early applications are likely to be based upon potential improvements which can be achieved by use of off-the-shelf modular units of office technology, against a background assessment of knowledge worker time spent in avoidable, unproductive activities. Subsequent applications can evolve to more elaborate use of available and new technology.

NOTES

[1] The Booz Allen & Hamilton study is drawn upon in materials that follow. For additional details, see Harvey L. Poppel, "Information Resource Management: An Overview," *Electronic Office: Management and Technology,* New York, Auerbauch Publishers, Inc., 1980; and Harvey L. Poppel, "Managerial/Professional Productivity," *Outlook,* fall–winter 1980 (published by Booz Allen & Hamilton).

[2] "Friend or Foe?: World of Computers Can Be Treacherous," *Industry Week,* June 15, 1981, pp. 100–102.

[3] Ibid.

[4] Ibid.

CHAPTER THIRTEEN

Upgrading Large Systems

PAUL E. COWDIN, CLIFFORD B. WHARIN, PAULETTE MERANDI, AND
GEORGE E. WATTS
Members, RESCAP, Eastern Airlines

Reservations call analysis project (RESCAP) is a joint Eastern Airlines
and IBM effort to examine, from the viewpoint of the telephone sales
and reservations agent (Res Agent), the various elements that influence
their productivity. While the immediate goal is that of accumulating
knowledge for developing hardware specifications for the next generation of agent hardware, it was recognized at the onset that the agent's
role is an integral part of a large and complex system and must be
analyzed in its proper perspective without inhibiting or degrading the
larger system in the process.

DEVELOPING A PERSPECTIVE
FOR CHANGE

As indicated by the Res Agents' official title, "telephone sales and reservations agent," this group of employees have a dual responsibility for
both selling the airline product and protecting the sale by reserving the
product for the customer. To develop a proper perspective of these dual
tasks and the impact of change, it is essential first to understand the
nature of the product. In simple terms, this product can be defined as "a
seat in motion." Equally basic is the concept that such a product is in-
stantly perishable, since a seat departing on a flight unoccupied represents a lost opportunity for selling the seat on that flight, and day. While
the obvious remedy for such perishability is to sell every seat on each

flight, the marketing task in reality is that of selling multiple units of seats, as dictated by the capacity of each aircraft. Thus to avoid perishability the airlines must focus upon matching units of "seats in motion," at a specific time, to a corresponding number of people who want to travel where and when the seats are going, and who are willing to pay for the service.

Compounding the selling task by a free market environment, stemming from governmental deregulation of the airlines, greatly expands the competitive challenge. In this climate, an oversupply of seats rapidly saturates the marketplace and heavy competition leads to innovative promotional and pricing practices. In many instances, innovation grows into proliferation accompanied by a variety of conditions and restrictions governing departure time, length of stay, and class of service. The result is apt to be a fluid product that is difficult to define and confusing for the customer to perceive. The Res Agents have the challenging task of selling, via the telephone, this complex airline product to the potential traveler, and also providing the link between the customer and the company's central site processor and data base for its aircraft seat inventory management system. These unique responsibilities require a careful blending of Res Agent intelligence, skill, and personality, with sophisticated hardware and software support systems.

At Eastern Airlines some 4000 Res Agents are working in 10 geographically dispersed reservations centers. They interface with the customer through an elaborate communications network that can automatically balance incoming call volumes by transferring between centers. The Res Agents in turn communicate with the company's master inventory control center (System One) through a terminal device and another complex communications system.

Although Eastern's System One is some 12 years old, it has always been maintained at the forefront of data-processing technology. Through hardware and software upgrades, the array of information available to the agent has been expanded and enhanced on a continuous basis. In fact, the array has grown to the point of becoming bewildering and confusing in scope for agents to cope with on their old terminal devices. Not only have these terminals become physically tired after 12 years of hard service, but they are significantly short of current terminal technology and inhibit agent performance.

INITIATING THE PROJECT

Management evaluation of the combined effects of traffic growth, terminal limitations, and product complexity upon Res Agent productivity led to a conclusion that future sales and reservations needs could be met either by continuing to follow the expensive practice of hiring more agents and building more reservations centers or by moderating this expense by undertaking a comprehensive productivity improvement program. The value of the latter course of action was reinforced when a preliminary analysis indicated an annual savings potential of approximately $4.0 million for each 5 percent gain in agent productivity.

It was recognized that there were many changes which could enhance agent and system productivity, including a vast array of current and emerging state-of-the-art hardware and software technology. Unfortunately, most changes would require either or both substantial system reprogramming or hardware investments before the magnitude of potential benefits could be determined. A priori evidence to substantiate which changes would be most advantageous was substantially lacking. Therefore, it was judged to be highly desirable to devise an approach which would permit systematic identification *and* evaluation of potential improvements before committing to systems modification and hardware investment. The decision to launch a joint investigative program, RESCAP, was formalized by Eastern Airlines and IBM late in 1979.

Project Strategy

The strategy devised for approaching the project was that of:

- Developing a broader understanding of *the problem(s)* from the viewpoint of the agent
- Devising technique(s) for collecting and analyzing agent performance data
- Developing method(s) for analytical evaluation of proposed ideas for improvement of agent hardware, software, and/or resource management
- Utilizing analytical input in the design and/or modification of agent support systems
- Continued operation of existing hardware and software systems, without degradation

Consistent with this strategy, the approach was further refined to create an experimental or laboratory reservations system that would support the testing and critical evaluation of a broad array of ideas relating to technological and resource management improvements. While experimental in nature, it was recognized that for data validity such a laboratory system would have to operate and have its performance measured in a real-world environment. To support this, project development efforts were concentrated upon first expanding project knowledge of agent performance requirements and problems, and then evolving operating criteria that would be consistent with the real world and nondegradation of existing systems strategy.

Agent Insight and Input

While the strategy and operating criteria were not sharply defined in the initial stages, they did evolve with surprising rapidity as key project personnel were assembled. The nucleus of this group consisted of a systems engineer and a marketing representative from IBM, a project coordinator from Eastern, and a consultant with a broad background in systems and industrial engineering. At the onset, the IBM and Eastern personnel attended the 4-week reservation agent training course. This exposure supplemented by consultant observations significantly enhanced project understanding of the reservations system, from the viewpoint of the agent. This, in turn, led to a three-element effort to expand project knowledge of agent performance requirements and problems. Briefly, these elements were:

- Random, but structured agent interviews
- Critical analysis of approximately 10,000 telephone calls
- A formal planning session with 19 expert agents

Interviews and data analysis   Although the interview effort was limited, it did include agents of varying experience and performance levels from three different reservations centers. The information gathered indicated specific areas of concern and provided impetus to expand the investigation. This led to the second step, in which a massive amount of agent and systems performance data was collected and analyzed. Not only did the data yield invaluable insights into which technological and resource management areas attention should be focused upon, but as a spinoff they also led to the development of an automated measurement system for continued measurement and analysis of agent performance.

Planning session   While the benefits derived from the interview and telephone call efforts were significant and lasting, neither had the overall impact or value of the planning session with the 19 expert agents. It was conducted at IBM regional headquarters in Atlanta, Georgia, and was patterned after one of their methods used for problem solving. In effect it was a major "brainstorming" session and utilized the bottom-up approach described in Chapter 2.

The 19 participants were selected by their respective reservations center managers for their expert knowledge of the capabilities and limitations of the hardware, software, and procedures in use throughout Eastern's reservations system.

The meeting was moderated by an IBM systems engineer and a marketing representative. There was no top management representation, again reinforcing the importance of uninhibited user input and knowledge. The session was broken into several phases, involving:

- Submitting of ideas from a user viewpoint that would support productivity improvement
- Prioritizing of those ideas in relationship to their degree of contribution to productivity effectiveness
- Developing of detailed descriptions of those ideas
- Emphasizing of problems associated with current methods
- Benefits that would accrue if the ideas were implemented

This led to a preliminary report which was transmitted to the agents for review, modification, and/or clarification.

The participants then resubmitted their final drafts, which led to the publication of a formalized document which became the basis for the development of the RESCAP laboratory.

The input from the three-phase effort provided solid project direction for formulating specific areas to be studied, and established a firm sense of agent participation and cooperation as the laboratory developed.

Conceptual Demonstration

IBM was impressed with the enthusiastic agent recommendations for development of a segment screen format, which would be capable of displaying a variety of information in various viewports. They responded by utilizing a combination of their latest hardware to create a conceptual demonstration for further analysis. The demonstration was structured around a mythical, but realistic, customer-agent telephone event. Typical agent input transactions were utilized, but the response information was arrayed in a segmented format that incorporated various highlighting techniques, scrolling features, and informational retention capabilities. Each of these enhanced agent productivity and served as a further stimulant for laboratory evaluation of an operational prototype.

LABORATORY DEVELOPMENT

Laboratorty development was continuously monitored to ensure that it would conform to operational criteria of:

- Operating in an environment of live customer calls
- Having access to Eastern's central reservation system (System One), but with transparency
- Being staffed and operated by reservations agents
- Being equipped with a flexible hardware/software combination between the customer and System One to facilitate a variety of studies
- Incorporating a terminal-oriented training system to instruct agents on the use of hardware-software developments
- Having a measurement system to collect and analyze performance data

- Having minimal adverse impact upon
  - Call production of the telephone sales and reservations department
  - System One

Within these criteria, implementation efforts were directed to areas of facilities, hardware, software, measurement techniques, and personnel and training.

Facilities

Facilities modifications affected primarily the user location. Because of the phased implementation, the old terminal hardware had to remain in place for a period of time, producing a crowded work station. The situation was relieved by installing shelves to hold reference material normally found adjacent to the terminal. There were no negative reactions to the relocation of reference material. The balance of the installation was completed without interruption of the day-to-day operation of the host system or its use.

Hardware

Hardware modifications consisted of installation of three distributive processors (see Fig. 13-1), with each serving a unique purpose:

- The development system was used to develop and test in a line environment. Because of the phased implementation concept, the development system remains a step ahead of the second (pilot) system.
- The pilot system offered the first opportunity to use experimental hardware and software in a limited but live environment. Use of the pilot concept allowed system testing prior to any introduction to the third (production) system.
- The production system offered the first opportunity to evaluate hardware and software in a live environment using a large volume of input and output.

All three systems used identical state-of-the-art intelligent terminals as input/output devices. The terminals incorporated screen segmentation and scrolling capabilities, as well as a nondestructive cursor, 80-character line, 43 lines of display, and other modern features.

While the physical configuration of the keyboard was dictated by the hardware selected for the laboratory, considerable flexibility as to character location and key functions was permitted. Again agent input was solicited, and through a survey of 120 agents a highly efficient keyboard arrangement was evolved and incorporated into the laboratory sets. The distributive processor technique allowed various concepts to be aired

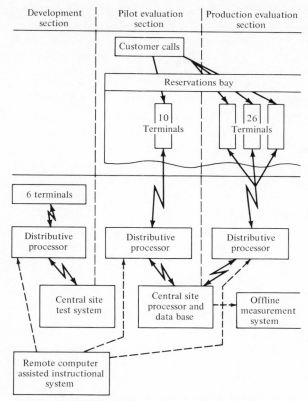

FIG. 13-1. A schematic diagram of the RESCAP laboratory.

with no impact on the host system. It also allowed step-by-step implementation of one study after another in an orderly manner.

Software

Software development was a joint IBM/Eastern Airlines effort. While IBM concentrated on systems (interface) programming, Eastern developed applications-oriented software.

The IBM-developed laboratory interface program was written to handle terminal-to-host linkup, a complicated procedure because of the disparity in system architectures. Other major systems efforts concentrated on response times, initial program load (IPL) procedures, and access to two host systems. The latter effort involved a linkup with the host reservations system and a computer-assisted instruction (CAI) package in a second (remotely located) host processor. The CAI package proved to be a valuable user-training tool employed as each new feature was implemented.

Eastern Airlines–developed software allowed for character conversion and/or insertion, causing messages sent to the host processor to appear as those sent from older equipment. Screen segmentation and output message scrolling management was also coded by Eastern, along with programs required to implement each new applications study.

Measurement Techniques

The measurement technique evolved over a period of time from a relatively simple straight time measurement program requiring a great amount of manual effort to an almost totally automated measurement program. The resultant program is interpretive in that it classifies events (telephone calls) based on agent input to the processor. The program then extracts data and provides a report on the time span being measured. This report is subdivided by call classification with attending statistics, such as:

- Number of calls
- Shortest call
- Longest call
- Average length of call
- Standard deviation
- Number of transactions

A further breakdown is provided which shows how many transactions were made by primary action code. Provision has also been made to extract data based on certain input transaction criteria. A side benefit of this feature is the ability to provide the marketing department with timely data relating to new service, fares, etc.

Personnel and Training

Agent indoctrination and training started in late 1980 and involved some 90 agents throughout the course of approximately 9 months of laboratory operation. Although each agent was trained through the remote computer-assisted instructional system and baseline performance information was established, no other special techniques were used in either personnel selection or training. Normal work schedules and administrative procedures of the center were followed at all times. This resulted in a normal turnover of agent population and a representative cross section of agent skill levels. It also yielded a broad base for subjective evaluations, as these agents endeavored to serve their customers in a normal manner.

LABORATORY OPERATION

A normal array of programming and human errors were encountered, as each study migrated from one laboratory section to the next. However, outstanding performances by both IBM and Eastern support personnel resulted in quick resolution of such problems, and acceptable levels of customer service were maintained. This was enhanced by a total absence of processor failures and the redundancy that had been designed into the laboratory system.

PRELIMINARY RESULTS

As the overall system reliability improved and the agents progressed along their learning curves, encouraging performance trends began to emerge and some preliminary conclusions formulated. Briefly these are:

- The laboratory concept is sound and proving invaluable for the evaluation of ideas in a fully operational environment.
- Agent acceptance of the training and operational systems under evaluation is enthusiastic and unanimous.
- Productivity gains in the range of 10 to 12 percent have been identified and are accompanied by a favorable improvement in agent selling performance.
- Conversion of all agent positions to an advanced terminal system, without adversely impacting System One or agent production, is feasible.

CONTINUING EVALUATIONS

Predicated upon current results, the joint effort will be continued, with the primary thrust being that of reducing the average hardware and software costs per agent station without degradation of productivity gains. This is to be undertaken by employing a modified strategy using more passive terminal devices and incorporating the productivity enhancements into the processor software. With the established laboratory resources, project confidence is high that identified productivity gains can be maintained or improved and a hardware/software design achieved that will yield superior cost benefit results.

IMPLICATIONS OF APPROACH

Evolution of the reservations call analysis project has been presented as a specific example of how large-scale, real-time, complex, computer-based, decision support systems can be upgraded without disturbing continuing operation of the basic system. The principal motivation for this effort was to determine specifications for replacement of the system interface device (terminal) which allows persons being supported by the system (reservations agent) to perform. The primary focus was directed to identification *and* evaluation of improvements in hardware and software, both currently available and emerging, which would be likely to have the most favorable impact upon efficient and effective performance of the persons being supported by the system, without modification to the basic system. Implications of the approach can easily be generalized to a wide variety of settings which involve large data-based systems with high-volume user input and output, such as in the banking, insurance, hotel, and car rental industries. Many organizations have large systems which can be upgraded to take advantage of newer developments and innovations, but they must be kept operational, and there is uncertainty about which specific changes are likely to be most advantageous in actual operation. An experimental approach such as RESCAP can serve as a model for development of a "laboratory" for identifying and evaluating various changes without disturbing the basic system and its ongoing operation. Those changes which are validated can subsequently be incorporated within the basic system or can be made operational using distributive processors while maintaining the same basic system.

PART SEVEN

Human Resources
Structure • People

The human resources structure is unique in many ways. Human resources perform work, and thus allow our organizations to function. Human resources permeate all the structures we have discussed, and are intimately involved in and affected by all the approaches to change directed toward productivity improvement within these structures.

Additionally, and most significantly, human resources are unique for their creative abilities. They are the key to productivity improvement—both directly by being more productive themselves and indirectly by being the agent which brings to bear innovation which allows other factors of productivity to operate constructively.

The reader is encouraged to review the human resources structure of Chapter 2 before continuing with this section.

We have singled out human resources for separate consideration as a structure mainly for emphasis, and to provide a vehicle for three separate approaches.

A few years back the concept of human asset accounting received considerable attention in the literature, particularly in academic journals. The premise was that human resources should be considered in much the same way as tangible assets, evaluated in terms of investment, depreciation, and change in value—and so reflected in the basic financial statements of an enterprise. Management should be accountable for wise use of both sets of resources and maintain their productive value on behalf of performance accountability. A few pilot applications were attempted, but the practical workability for using the concept never really developed.

Henry Dahl and Kent Morgan share their experiences and successes with the development and use of a somewhat similar, but uniquely different, approach by The Upjohn Company. Their significant work, presented in Chapter 14, represents a useful approach to management of return on investment in human resources.

Chapter 15 deals with approaches to reducing white collar staffing levels by shifting a significant portion of the white collar work effort from a fixed expense which continues even when not fully utilized to a variable expense which is directly related to variable work loads and to the upgrading of the quality of white collar work activity by eliminating dull, dead-end, and problem jobs.

Chapter 16 addresses issues which have been mentioned both directly and by implication many times in earlier chapter materials—participation and involvement by those who do work in developing productivity improvement of that work. It outlines basic considerations associated with success of such approaches.

Return on Investment in Human Resources

HENRY L. DAHL
Manager, Employee Planning and Development, The Upjohn Company

and

KENT S. MORGAN
Employee Planning Specialist, The Upjohn Company

The Upjohn Company has developed and implemented a process for measuring the return on the investment in human resources. With further development, this process has potential for measuring the impact of white collar productivity on organizations more effectively than the methods now in general use.

Traditional productivity measurements typically are aimed at separating direct and indirect human resource contributions. Upjohn's approach is to measure the return on investment (ROI) in human resources for the total company and by each business. Then, if needed, productivity is examined by job class within each organization. This approach facilitates the analysis of trade-offs between investments in human and capital resources. The following table illustrates common approaches used to measure return on investment in capital and in employees.

Level	Employee ROI	Capital ROI
World	$-^1$	—
Nation	—	+
Industry	$\times^2$	+
Company	$\times$	+
Division or group	$\times$	+
Business	$\times$	+
Functional units	$+^3$	—
Departments	+	—
Programs	+	—
Individuals	+	—

[1] $-$ Not being computed.
[2] $\times$ Being done by Upjohn.
[3] $+$ Being computed elsewhere.

Upjohn's measurement process is unique because it focuses on output in dollars versus input in dollars. It emphasizes the return the organization is getting on the dollars it is spending for human resources and capital rather than on the unit output per employee hour. The latter is inadequate for measuring total productivity in Upjohn, since less than 30 percent of our people are in manufacturing jobs.

This chapter describes the Upjohn system, its objectives, its rationale, its process, its measurements, its results to date, its problems, and the areas targeted for future development.

CONCEPTS

A business's capacity to generate earnings is determined in large part by its ability to effectively and efficiently use all the resources necessary to accomplish its objectives. The two major resources are capital and people. Scarce natural or physical resources (i.e., energy, raw materials) also have varying influences depending upon their availability. However, people and capital will continue to be the most significant resources managed by businesses. The discussion which follows describes some of the systems used by The Upjohn Company to advise management on the optimum use of these resources, especially the "human resource."

Because there is nearly universal agreement within business that people are a company's most important assets, it is reasonable to ask the following questions:

- How much is our investment in human resources?
- What return are we getting on this investment?
- What are optimum staffing levels?
- How can we improve the return on investment in human resources?

APPROACH

How Much Is Our Investment in Human Resources?

The term "investment" here is used in a nontraditional way. It refers to the commitment made when "positions" are created within an organization. People are hired to staff the positions; their salaries, benefits, and employee taxes and other employee costs are treated as "expenses." Even though people frequently join and leave organizations, the positions they occupy usually continue. For this reason the expense of the person in a given position should be considered as an "investment" in the same way we would consider the purchase of a printing press, machine die, or main frame computer.

The source of the funds used to acquire capital may be cash, debt, equity, or a combination of all. Unless the acquisition of the capital is made from available cash, the organization commits itself to a long-term series of annual cash flows necessary to purchase and maintain this capital.

Staffing a new position represents this same commitment. All the direct and indirect expenses associated with the position are committed for the duration of that position. It can be argued that employees can be laid off and positions can be eliminated; however, significant costs would be incurred with this action just as they would be for the removal of capital equipment.

Most companies are able to determine the major elements of the cost of employees through accounting for payroll, benefits, and employee taxes. Other related costs, however, such as for turnover, office space, hiring costs, training, and office equipment, are more difficult to measure. Human resource accounting (HRA) experts have published numerous approaches for measuring these. The conclusions from these studies may be helpful in justifying specific projects or in more accurately relating costs to their true source. But the HRA approach is more difficult to use in measuring the return on the investment of the total human resource for businesses or divisions of a company. The principal reason for this is that it is difficult to collect and assign all the costs and to assemble them accurately to a total business level. It is less complex and equally useful to adopt a measurement strategy which uses a deductive approach by working downward from standard financial statement information. The ratios and measurements used in Upjohn's employee planning model are derived in this manner.

The magnitude of the investment in human resources is significant and when measured accurately will illustrate the importance of managing this resource effectively. In recent years employee costs have increased dramatically and have grown as a proportion of many companies' total expenses. In the last 5 years at Upjohn, the average total cost of an employee has increased 40 percent while the number of employees has increased 20 percent. Obviously, getting a management "handle" on this growth is critical.

According to an Upjohn study, the total career investment in an individual is estimated to be 160 times the initial starting salary. The calculation of this multiplier is simple: an employee's annual starting salary is multiplied by a percent amount for an estimated annual merit and/or cost of living increase; this step is repeated for the expected number of years of employment; the final amount is adjusted by a percent factor for fringe benefits and employee taxes; and the result is an estimate of the total expenses for that employee. The correct multiplier is derived by dividing this number by the original starting salary. For an individual starting at $25,000 per year this is a $4 million commitment over the 30-year career lifetime of that employee. On a net present value basis, this would be comparable with a $1 million investment made today. Most companies thoroughly analyze capital investments of any significance ($100,000 or greater) and conduct detailed studies on the costs and potential returns of that commitment. It is doubtful that a similar analysis would have been done on the new position (employee) representing the $4 million investment. When the investment is viewed in these terms, the importance of measuring the return on the investment in human resources becomes obvious.

What Return Are We Getting on This Investment?

This question is likely to provoke much more thought and provide fewer answers than questions about the size of the investment. The difficulty in computing a return is complicated by the fact that most companies' income, balance sheet, and cash flow statements do not separate the major resource investments. Instead the expenses are combined under categories such as "marketing, research and development, administrative, sales, operations, and manufacturing expenses." It is much more effective to break out the investment in employees, capital, and purchased goods and services from these accounting categories and examine them independently. The table on page 283 illustrates this approach.

Sales per employee or earnings per employee are the traditional measurements often cited in corporate annual reports to reflect the productive use of employees. But a close look at these measures suggests they are of limited use. Partly, this is because they do not adjust for inflation; thus the figures almost always are positive. They also are subject to an apples and oranges metaphor by comparing a dollar of output with a unit of input. A simple analogy would be that of the owner of a taxicab company measuring the company's productivity as fares per taxicab. Over the

INCOME STATEMENT

	People	Capital	Purchased goods and services
Sales			
Cost of goods	×	×	×
Gross income			
Operating costs:			
Selling expense	×	×	×
Research	×	×	×
Administrative	×	×	×
Manufacturing	×	×	×
Net income			

years, fares would have increased because of inflation. Therefore, the ratio of fares per taxicab would be positive and also increasing. A very different outcome would result if the cost of operating each taxicab was considered in the equation (i.e., the dollar value of fares divided by the dollar value of the costs of gasoline, maintenance, insurance, etc.). In a period when costs increased faster than fares, a negative relationship would exist.

Measurements that relate the cost of the investment in human resources to the returns provide better indicators of a company's productive use of its human resources. The measurements which are shown in Fig. 14-1 with hypothetical data illustrate how these relationships might appear.

Comparison of human resource costs with the costs of a company's other investments (e.g., raw materials and services, capital) provides an improved perspective. The measurements in Fig. 14-2 might be pre-

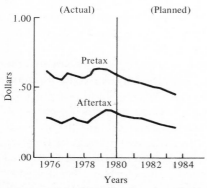

FIG. 14-1. Earnings for employee cost: pretax earnings/employee cost; and after-tax earnings/employee cost.

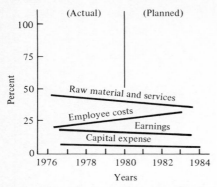

FIG. 14-2. Resource investments and earnings compared with sales: raw material and services/sales; employee costs/sales; capital expense/sales; and pretax earnings/sales.

sented to senior management.

The concept of "value added" can provide yet another improved perspective of a company's use of all the resources necessary to generate earnings. Value added is defined simply as the worth added to purchased goods and services through the addition of the company's research, manufacturing, technology, distribution, and/or marketing contributions.

Purchased goods and services + value added = sales

Value added may also be calculated as

Value added = sales − purchased goods and services

This concept provides a way of scrutinizing trade-offs between investments in capital and human resources. In addition, there are three major components of value added common to all businesses. These are employee costs, capital costs, and earnings (Fig. 14-3).

Comparing the proportion of each component with the total value added over time can highlight important trends. Comparing total value added with sales also provides valuable insight into the effective use of a company's combined resources. The ratios shown in Fig. 14-4 are suggested.

An additional use of the value added approach for projecting potential future returns is to calculate dollars of value added for each dollar

Distribution of sales dollars

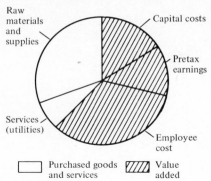

FIG. 14-3.

invested in a resource. Ratios used for this purpose are:

$$\$ \text{ value added per } \$ \text{ employee cost}$$

$$\$ \text{ value added per } \$ \text{ assets}$$

Management authority and writer Peter Drucker recognized the value added concept relative to employee costs when he warned that:

> It is rapidly becoming clear that both productivity and capital formation depend heavily on the "labor-income ratio"—the proportion of value added paid out in wages and fringe benefits—and that this is true whether we are

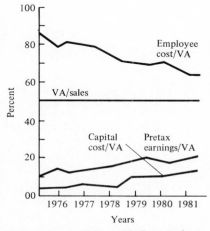

FIG. 14-4. Value added: employee costs/value added; capital cost/value added; pretax earnings/value added; and value added/sales.

DIVISION A
ALLOCATED EMPLOYEE PLANNING RATIOS

	1976	1977	1978	1979	1980	ANN.% GRTH.	1981	1982	1983	1984	1985	ANN.% GRTH.
A. NUMBER OF EMPLOYEES												
TOTAL EMPLOYEES	4561	4605	4822	4963	5261	4	5621	5811	5900	6158	6305	3
ADDITIONS	173	44	217	141	298	N.A.	360	190	169	178	147	N.A.
REPLACEMENTS	182	184	193	199	210	N.A.	225	232	239	246	252	N.A.
TOTAL TO HIRE AND TRAIN	355	228	410	340	508	N.A.	585	422	408	424	399	N.A.
B. EMPLOYEE COST												
EMPLOYEE COST/EMPLOYEE	22411	24112	26307	28344	31660	9	35474	39949	45022	50607	56739	12
PAY/EMPLOYEE	18139	19450	20302	22085	24548	8	27506	30976	34909	39239	43994	12
% OF TOTAL	81	81	77	78	78	-1	78	78	78	78	78	0
BENEFITS/EMPLOYEE	3261	3545	4501	4659	5205	14	5922	6669	7516	8448	9472	12
% OF TOTAL	14	14	17	16	16	5	16	16	16	16	16	0
EMPLOYEE TAXES/EMPLOYEE	1012	1117	1504	1599	1826	18	2046	2305	2597	2919	3273	12
% OF TOTAL	5	5	6	6	6	6	6	6	6	6	6	0
EMPLOYEE COST/TOTAL EXPENSE	.00	.47	.49	.51	.49	1	.52	.52	.54	.54	.56	2
EMPLOYEE COST/VALUE ADDED	1.00	.53	.53	.56	.52	-1	.56	.57	.58	.59	.60	2
NET ASSETS/EMPLOYEE	0	54397	51929	53274	57042	2	59278	66064	73161	80088	82649	9
C. ROI (EMPLOYEE)												
PRETAX EARNINGS/EMPLOYEE	0	21086	22957	21459	27010	9	25849	27534	30151	32218	33577	7
AFTER TAX EARNINGS/EMPLOYEE	0	13116	14392	15152	19008	13	18395	19773	20903	21074	22649	5
SALES/EMPLOYEE	0	72682	76172	77232	91142	8	94485	104509	114064	125300	134607	9
PRETAX EARNINGS/EMPLOYEE COST	.00	.87	.87	.76	.85	-1	.73	.69	.67	.64	.59	-5
AFTER TAX EARNINGS/EMPLOYEE COST	.00	.54	.55	.53	.60	4	.52	.49	.46	.43	.40	-6

DIVISION A
ALLOCATED EMPLOYEE PLANNING RATIOS

	1976	1977	1978	1979	1980	ANN.% GRTH.	1981	1982	1983	1984	1985	ANN.% GRTH.
D. SALES DOLLAR DISTRIBUTION												
PURCHASED GOODS & SERVICES/SALES	.00	.38	.35	.35	.34	-4	.33	.33	.32	.31	.30	-2
EMPLOYEE COST/SALES	.00	.33	.35	.37	.35	2	.38	.38	.39	.40	.42	3
CAPITAL EXPENSE/SALES	.00	.00	.00	.01	.02	N.A.	.02	.02	.02	.02	.03	11
PRETAX EARNINGS/SALES	.00	.29	.30	.28	.30	1	.27	.26	.26	.26	.25	-2
E. VALUE ADDED												
EMPLOYEE COST/VALUE ADDED	1.00	.53	.53	.56	.52	-1	.56	.57	.58	.59	.60	2
CAPITAL EXPENSE/VALUE ADDED	.00	.00	.00	.01	.03	N.A.	.03	.03	.03	.04	0.4	7
PRETAX EARNINGS/VALUE ADDED	.00	.46	.46	.42	.44	-1	.41	.39	.38	.37	.35	-4
VALUE ADDED/SALES	.00	.62	.65	.65	.66	2	.67	.67	.68	.69	.70	1
F. COMPONENTS OF RONA												
RONA	.00	.48	.28	.29	.35	-10	.33	.32	.30	.29	.28	-4
VALUE ADDED/EMPLOYEE COST	1.00	1.87	1.87	1.78	1.90	1	1.77	1.74	1.72	1.69	1.65	-2
VALUE ADDED/<NET ASSETS>	.00	1.66	.95	.97	1.12	-12	1.12	1.13	1.13	1.15	1.18	1
NET EARNINGS/EMPLOYEE COST	.00	.54	.55	.53	.60	4	.52	.49	.46	.43	.40	-6
EMPLOYEE COST/<NET ASSETS>	.00	.89	.51	.55	.59	-13	.63	.65	.66	.68	.71	3

FIG. 14-5. An example of employee planning model data, for a hypothetical company division.

287

talking about a company, an industry or a national economy. If the ratio goes above a certain threshold, apparently between 80% and 85%, productivity declines and capital formation falls too low to maintain present jobs, let alone create new ones.[1]

PROCESS

The employee planning model is an integral part of a formal, long-range planning process in use at Upjohn. It is one of four major components of the 5-year plan; the other major sections are financial, facilities, and strategic.

The data used as input to the model are derived by the various business planners. Their projections are consolidated in the Financial Planning department and provided to Employee Planning and Development for use in the model. Projections of future staffing needs also are provided. The information used as input to the model includes 5 years of history and 5 years of forecast data and is summarized below:

Sales
Pretax earnings
Net earnings
Assets
Capitalization
Depreciation
Payroll
Benefits
Employee taxes
Number of employees

Completed plans are presented to the five senior officers of the company in a 2-day session usually held several months before the first year of the plan will commence. All the measurements presented here, as well as others, are included in these presentations. The company's 17 businesses or profit centers are compared using these ratios. The most significant comparisons, however, are the ratios for each of our businesses over time. Positive or negative trends may be detected and management action initiated accordingly.

USING THE METHOD

Business-to-business comparisons by senior management may be used to allocate limited resources. However, it is important that in any business analysis, the varying nature of the businesses, maturity, market penetration, market potential, relationship to other businesses, emerging technologies, and new marketing strategies all must be weighed and considered. Figure 14-5, on pages 286–287, is an example of a report for a hypothetical division of the company.

Figure 14-6 illustrates a comparison between two divisions of a company using a traditional measure, sales per employee, and several of the measures from the reports in Fig. 14-5. Note the difference in conclusions that the additional measurements provide. On the basis of sales per employee, the performance of both divisions would be positive and improving. When the additional measurements are added, however, division II appears to have turned around a negative trend where the ratio of earnings to employee costs was deteriorating. Division I has not reversed that trend and may be heading for a serious economic imbalance.

What Are Optimum Staffing Levels?

Should we add people? Can we add them? These are the critical questions and decisions facing managers at budget review time. For this rea-

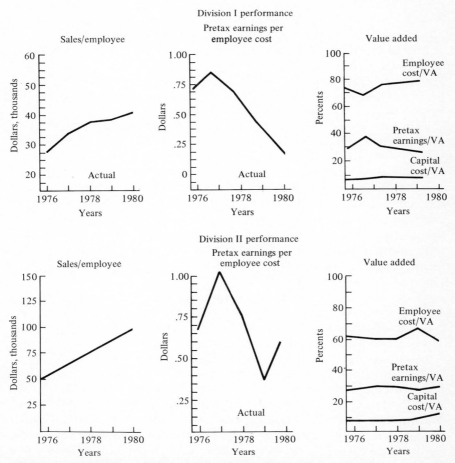

FIG. 14-6. Performance by divisions I and II: sales/employee and pretax earnings per employee cost are supplemented by value added data.

son, staffing options are generated for each of Upjohn's 17 businesses as recommendations for future hiring goals. In each case an assumption is made that employee costs should not increase faster than earnings for that particular business. In other words, the ratio of pretax earnings to employee costs should be held constant or improved for that division. Three alternatives are generated based upon this assumption.

The first alternative compares employee additions proposed by a division in its 5-year plan with the number of additions which will maintain or improve the pretax earnings/employee cost ratio. In this manner, senior management can review the proposed staffing recommendations of various businesses against a suggested goal. The second alternative uses the proposed additions but adjusts the cost per employee, again, to maintain or improve the ratio. The third alternative provides the division's proposed head count and average cost per employee but constructs a new earnings level high enough to support proposed staffing objectives and maintain the ratio of earnings to employee cost.

The first two alternatives emphasize control of employee costs, the denominator of the ratio, as a means of maintaining or improving the earnings to employee cost ratio. The first alternative establishes a goal for controlling head count and the second a goal for controlling cost per employee. Both impact total employee costs.

There are problems inherent in these approaches if they result in understaffing or noncompetitive wages. Both approaches eventually may increase long-term costs through higher turnover or reduced morale. In addition, the earnings assumptions in the forecasts are likely to be dependent upon the planned additions of people. Any suggested goal to maintain, reduce, or increase head-count levels from those in the plan will logically impact earnings. In our opinion, the last alternative—which emphasizes the goal to improve earnings—is the preferred approach, but realistically some combination of all three approaches probably will be appropriate. The report presented as Fig. 14-7 illustrates the presentation of the possible alternatives.

The choice of goals and means to improve the return on investment in human resources also must be closely aligned with the character of the individual business. Influences of the external market and economy also have an impact on the short-term results of the model's measurements. The ratio of pretax earnings/employee costs will decline with a decline in earnings (if employee costs have remained stable). If the decline is unrelated to employee productivity, the use of the ratio must include an analysis of the external influence. As mentioned earlier, the nature of the business, its maturity, market penetration, market potential, market strategy, emerging technologies, dependence upon economic conditions, dependence upon other industries, labor/capital mix, etc., all have some bearing upon the optimum strategies elected.

DIVISION A

ALLOCATED EMPLOYEE PLANNING RATIOS

	1976	1977	1978	1979	1980	ANN.% GRTH.	1981	1982	1983	1984	1985	ANN.% GRTH.
STAFFING GUIDELINES												
HOLDING PRETAX EARNINGS/EMP. CONSTANT							.85	.85	.85	.85	.85	0
(PLANNED 1981-1985)							.73	.69	.67	.64	.59	-5
A. GUIDELINE A												
PRETAX EARNINGS	0	97	110	106	142	13	145	160	180	198	211	10
TOTAL EMPLOYEE COST	0	114	129	125	167	13	171	188	212	233	248	10
AVG. TOTAL COST/EMPLOYEE	22411	24112	26307	28344	31660	9	35474	39949	45022	50607	56739	12
NO. OF EMPLOYEES *	0	4733	4919	4400	5277	4	4809	4712	4704	4603	4375	-2
(PLANNED 1980-1985)	4561	4605	4822	4963	5261	4	5621	5811	5980	6158	6305	3
B. GUIDELINE B												
PRETAX EARNINGS	0	97	110	106	140	13	145	160	180	198	211	10
TOTAL EMPLOYEE COST	0	114	129	125	167	13	171	188	212	233	248	10
NO. OF EMPLOYEES	4561	4605	4822	4963	5261	4	5621	5811	5980	6158	6305	3
AVG. TOTAL COST/EMPLOYEE *	0	24781	26838	25127	31754	9	30348	32393	35412	37827	39371	7
(PLANNED 1981-1985)	22411	24112	26307	26344	31660	9	356474	39949	45022	50607	56739	12
C. GUIDELINE C												
TOTAL EMPLOYEE COST	102	111	127	141	167	14	199	232	269	312	358	16
NO. OF EMPLOYEES	4561	4605	4822	4963	5261	4	5621	5811	5980	6158	6305	3
AVG. TOTAL COST/EMPLOYEE	22411	24112	26307	28344	31660	9	35474	39949	455022	50607	56739	12
PRETAX EARNINGS *	86	94	107	119	141	14	169	197	228	264	304	16
(PLANNED 1981-1985)	0	97	110	106	142	13	145	160	180	198	211	10

* INDICATES THE DEPENDENT VARIABLE WITHIN EACH STAFFING OPTION

FIG. 14-7. Analysis of three staffing alternatives, all holding the ratio of pretax earnings to employee costs constant: alternative I, guideline A, addition (or subtraction) of employees; alternative II, guideline B, employee costs needed to achieve pretax earnings; alternative III, guideline C, pretax earnings needed to support average employee costs at projected level.

How Can We Improve the Return on Investment in Human Resources?

Investments or programs which improve the productivity of employees will increase earnings without significant increases in employee costs. In fact, Dr. W. E. Deming, a national productivity expert, has observed that increases in productivity of any form are "pure profit."[2]

The following human resource investment guidelines suggest several objectives to be considered in optimizing our return in human resources:

- Invest in human resources only when a good return is expected.
- Consider human resource alternatives which generate optimum return.
- Investment in capital resources that improve the return on both capital and human resources.
- Improve the use and performance of currently employed human resources.

A positive first step in the direction of improvement is to measure the return on investment in human resources in a manner similar to that used in the capital review process. Just as questions are raised about investments in equipment so too can similar questions be asked about human resources.

The following might be asked as a means of justifying each addition in order to ensure each contributes to increased return on investment.

1. What purpose does the proposed new position serve?
2. What alternatives were considered to accomplish the same purpose?
3. Why was the proposed alternative selected over the others?
4. If the position is filled, what are the projected 5-year costs?
5. What impact will this position have on:
   a. Maintenance or improvement of sales?
   b. Maintenance or improvement in earnings?
   c. Improved utilization of purchased goods and services?
   d. Improved utilization of people?
   e. Improved utilization of assets?

PROCESS EVOLUTION AND BACKGROUND

The employee planning model described here has evolved at Upjohn over the last 10 years. It has grown out of a deep interest in optimizing the sizable investment the company makes in its human resource—the most significant expense to the company.

It was mentioned earlier that less than 30 percent of Upjohn's total work force is associated with manufacturing. The majority are knowledge workers, often with highly specialized training and backgrounds. Because traditional productivity measures are typically directed at the manufacturing environment or used in areas with measurable output, they are not as useful in an environment with a majority of knowledge workers. The lack of predictive measurements therefore became an initial incentive for us to develop a new approach.

Another characteristic of Upjohn which contributed to the development of the model is the existence of multiple profit centers or businesses reporting to major divisions of the corporation. Each of the businesses is significantly different in the nature of its work force. Upjohn Health Care Services, for example, uses little or no capital and is a very people-intense business. In contrast, the Fine Chemical division is highly automated and capital-intense. Attempts to draw comparisons between the two would be difficult (if not impossible) using traditional measures. Yet it is extremely important for senior management to make effective decisions regarding the allocation of scarce resources to each of the businesses. Measurements which relate the return on investment in both capital and human resources provide the best potential for guiding management to the best alternatives.

The development of the employee planning model has occurred as a result of the contributions of many individuals in several departments. The Employee Planning and Development unit coordinates the administration, direction, and presentation of the plan. The company's Management Science unit is responsible for the majority of the mathematical and programming contributions and for constructing a large portion of the model's logic and content. Individual business planners have provided valuable suggestions for improvements, and strong support has been provided by the Corporate Finance and Budgeting units.

Upjohn's centralized corporate services divisions have also had a strong influence on the development of the model. Divisions such as employee relations, financial services, and computer services all must allocate their expenses to the various businesses; therefore, considerable effort has been taken to allocate these expenses accurately. A recent improvement to the model was made to allow the ratios and measurements of the model to be shown on both an allocated and an unallocated basis. The conclusions are interesting; regardless of the version used, the trends over time are relatively unchanged.

FUTURE IMPROVEMENTS

There are several areas where efforts are needed to improve the planning model. Direct and indirect employee costs are not adequately considered for their impact upon the final measurements. Direct employee costs are those which can be directly related to sales or to the production of goods for sale. Examples include sales representatives, production workers, distribution center employees, and quality-control personnel. Indirect employee costs are those which can be related to service or support operations not directly impacting sales or manufacturing. Examples include accounting and finance jobs, marketing, advertising, employee relations, and public relations positions.

A second area which now is partially covered by the model but which has more potential for improvement is the use of value added. The contribution which the firm makes to the market value of its products is value added. A powerful analytical tool for use in planning would be the ability to identify the portion of value added that is contributed by people and the portion that is the result of capital investment. In lieu of this, it may be helpful to at least compare the total investment in each with the total value added. The investment in employees has already been identified to include wages, benefits, and employee taxes. The investment in capital is not as easily simplified. It may include depreciation, interest expense (the cost of financing capital), maintenance and service, some portion of dividends paid (also as a cost of financing capital), energy expense used to operate the equipment, some portion of employee expense necessary to support the capital, etc.

An attempt has been made graphically to present net value added compared with the investment in capital, human resources, and return on net assets as shown by Fig. 14-8. The result is complex because of the number of dimensions illustrated in the same analysis. However, once the chart is understood, it can point out some very important relationships and trends. First, as explanation, the X axis is net value added divided by total employee expenses and represents a form of return on that investment. The Y axis has the same numerator, net value added, this time divided by adjusted assets (assets less depreciation). A third axis, return on net assets, is shown increasing diagonally from the lower left to the upper right. The best position on the graph is in the upper right corner with high value added for both people and capital as well as high return on net assets. Each arrow represents a business or division. The base of the arrow is the current year position, and the head of the arrow is the business' position in 5 years (based upon their forecasts). The relative position of the arrows will show labor or capital intensity. The direction of the arrows will illustrate whether the forecast shows the business improving or losing ground. Because of the complexity of the graph and the limitation of time in presentations to explain it, it has not been effectively used. However, it has been included here as a means of summarizing some of the concepts presented earlier.

In this illustration, divisions 7 and 2 are both forecasting an improvement in RONA by increasing investment in both assets and people. However, the relative increase in investment in people is greater for

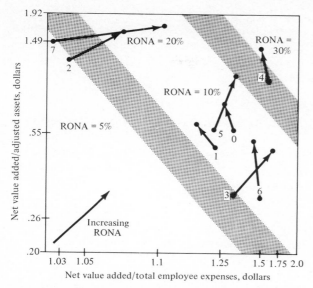

FIG. 14-8. Two components of return on net assets (RONA). Graphic presentation of net value added due to investment in capital and human resources and their combined impact on return on net assets. The third axis, return on net assets (RONA), is folded over to indicate increasing value as points move away from the origin and toward the upper right-hand corner.

division 7. Division 1 is maintaining approximately the same RONA by decreasing investment in people and increasing investment in assets.

CONCLUSION

The investment in human resources is one of the largest and most important investments made by a company. In order to effectively manage the investment, there must be a means to determine the size and trend of this investment and to measure the return received. The measurement system should be appropriately suited to the type of organization and to the level within the organization. Productivity measurements are not ends within themselves but are instead a means to determine where and how efforts are needed to improve the returns. It makes sense to target these efforts to those areas having the greatest potential improvement for the amount of additional investment required or to those areas already showing high relative return on investment. Areas of marginal return or negative returns should be carefully analyzed for their total contribution to the organization. The measurement systems presented in this discussion provide effective analytical tools for use in improving the productivity of human resources. This is particularly true for organizations with a high proportion of "white collar" or knowledge workers.

NOTES

[1] Peter Drucker, *The Wall Street Journal*, January 6, 1981.

[2] Statement from the NBC-TV "White Paper on Productivity: If Japan Can, Why Can't We?" June 1981.

CHAPTER FIFTEEN

Management of Human Resources

ROBERT N. LEHRER

Consultant

The subject of management of human resources is a vast one, drawing on work management, the behavioral sciences, and many other areas. We will deal with only a limited segment of this important and broad area: opportunities which exist within many organizations for improving work load/work force management and for enhancing quality of work life by use of variable-cost/variable-use human resources to augment a reduced size of work force.

This approach is used by few U.S. organizations but is used extensively in Europe and in Japan. The Japanese have achieved part of their oustanding productivity success by this approach, which allows them to enrich the working lives of their core permanent workers, who are regarded as being lifetime employees. It is an important and innovative approach which has considerable potential for improving clerical and, to a more limited extent, knowledge worker productivity. It also has potential for favorable impact on the entire white collar work force.

We will first review basic approaches to work load/work force management, and present the concept of *leased productivity*[1] to reduce the cost penalties associated with peak and lull periods of work load. We will then shift to consideration of the quality of work life, what it is, and some observations about white collar work life, particularly in clerical and entry-level activities. We will then discuss values and attitudes, and how work activities can either conflict with or reinforce these human dimensions. This then leads into processes for improving work activities to support the quality dimension along with the productivity dimension, and finally to leased productivity achievable by selling off dull, dead-end problem jobs.

WORK FORCE/WORK LOAD MANAGEMENT

The essence of work force/work load management is to plan the work and then work the plan. Work requirements are forecast and work-force resources are assigned such that necessary outputs can be accomplished in a timely and efficient manner, with no excess labor power involved.

In the factory production situation forecasts for products are translated into production quotas and then converted to labor power requirements by using job or production standards for each unit of work or operation. These performance standards, which are sometimes based upon past experience but usually are established by work measurement, specify the normal or standard time required to accomplish each unit of work according to a standard method and with defined quality requirements. The resulting work-force requirements are matched with available work-force resources, and the result is the final plan or work schedule. Work requirements and resources are matched, usually in a manner that views the available human resources as a fixed amount. Work load is leveled to avoid or minimize the need to increase or decrease the work force, frequently by producing for inventory when demand lags capacity to produce, and by drawing from inventory or by overtime operation when demand exceeds capacity.

The office situation is traditionally viewed as distinctly different from the factory production setting—and rightly so—but some of the same work force/work load management fundamentals still have useful application.

Most white collar settings are not as highly structured as factory production work. Job performance standards are usually not as formally developed. Work-load variations are frequently more difficult to forecast and even when they can be anticipated may not be manipulatable or controllable. Most white collar work results cannot be "banked" in inventory nor can they lag much behind the calendar time to which they are geared. Many white collar groups must perform with considerable workload fluctuations.

Work-load fluctuations for a department or company with 150 regular permanent white collar workers might well show a variation from peak load requirements of 220 workers to a valley level of 110, as shown by Fig. 15-1. Not only might the work load fluctuate week to week as shown, but variations may well occur on a much shorter basis, within weeks and days. Assuming that the general pattern and magnitude of likely fluctuations can be approximated, the size of the work force would be deter-

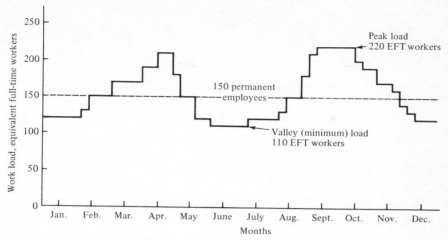

FIG. 15-1. A typical work-load pattern, with a low of 110 workers required and a peak of 220.

mined, probably somewhere between the maximum and minimum levels, perhaps at 150, as indicated in the figure. The heavy periods would be handled by overtime operation and extra effort, perhaps augmented by "borrowed" personnel, with the lull periods being used for relief, catching up, time off, vacations, and so forth.

Work-load fluctuations without matching work-force adjustments almost always result in inefficiencies. Overtime work is at a premium cost, and overtime efforts are often enervating, are directly less effective than comparable time during regular work periods, and for many individuals have substantial negative impact on morale. Lull periods are almost never used effectively, encourage letting up, stretch-out, and other unproductive work patterns, and frequently cause individual frustration and feelings of futility and lack of purposefulness. Not only does lack of work spawn inefficiency during the lulls, confirming Parkinson's law that work expands to fill the available time, but unproductive work practices tend to carry over to nonlull periods, causing additional inefficiencies, frustration, and undermining of morale.

The most basic of management precepts is to match the assignment of personnel to the requirements of the work available. Do not overassign, and do not underassign. The above situation can be cured by proper matching of human resources to the requirements for accomplishing the needed work. However, in many cases, matching the actual work force to the actual work load is almost an impossible task.

The use of formally established job performance standards, and monitoring of individual performance, can provide indication of stretch-out and extra-effort performance, and provide management with leverage to help control performance (as discussed in Chapter 7). This formal approach to work measurement and work management may not be workable in all situations because of the difficulty of developing adequate standards and control measures. Even in those white collar activities where it may be feasible, and also where it may not be, it is advantageous to first attempt to reduce variations in work load and then to consider alternative ways to accommodate the remaining fluctuations which cannot be removed.

Many organizations have improved white collar productivity by load leveling, formally analyzing cyclical work-load patterns, identifying the causes of fluctuation, and making structural changes in procedures and/or timing to reduce the difference between peaks and valleys. Further improvement can usually be achieved by use of more formalized approaches to planning and monitoring performance against plans, and by assigning personnel according to work-load needs—with additional needed people taken from other work and excess personnel assigned to other areas where loads require additional people. However, even when these things have been done, the reality of many white collar settings is that work loads still vary, and these load fluctuations must be dealt with, using a work force which is of a more or less fixed and inflexible size. The consequence is that peak loads must be handled by overtime, and lull periods result in underutilization and waste, as illustrated by Fig. 15-2.

There are other options which can be developed in most situations which allow staffing with permanent employees at a lower level and the use of a variable-cost/variable-use additional work force to handle load fluctuations on an actual as-needed basis. They may be part-time employees or individuals "leased" from organizations that specialize in temporary services. The following examples will be based upon the use of

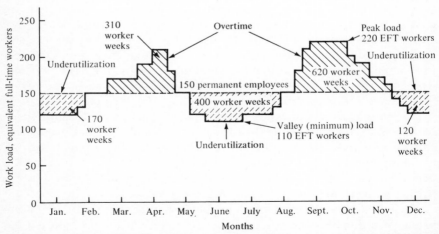

FIG. 15-2. Work load above 150 is handled by overtime. Loads below 150 represent underutilization of personnel.

temporary service personnel. We will return to the subjects of part-time employees and leased personnel later.

LEASED PRODUCTIVITY

Assuming that a suitable supplementary work force can be obtained by leased personnel from an appropriate temporary service organization, productivity can be improved and costs reduced potentially in three ways: by use of leased personnel to handle overtime work loads; by reducing the permanent employee group to the minimum work-load level and using leased personnel to handle all loads above the minimum or valley level; and by further reducing the permanent employee work force to eliminate dull, dead-end, problem jobs—which can be performed more efficiently by leased personnel. We will calculate the cost consequences of each of these three approaches, using typical cost values:

1. Average per hour pay rate of $5.00 for regular employees
2. Fringe benefits at 50 percent of regular payroll costs
3. Overtime at 1½ times regular pay rate
4. Fringe benefits and extra payroll costs for overtime at 15 percent
5. Temporary service personnel at $6.50 per hour, including indirect costs

The work load shown by Fig. 15-2 will be used to illustrate the potential for productivity improvement which can be achieved by use of leased personnel in a "typical" situation.

Selling Overtime Operation for a Profit

The two periods of heavy load peak at 210 and 220 equivalent full-time workers. The first period exceeds available workers by 310 worker weeks and the second by 620, for a total of 930. The total work load will require the 150 permanent workers for the full year, with an additional 930 worker weeks of overtime. Total payroll cost will be $2,660,850:

Regular time:
- 150 employees, $5.00 per hour, 52 weeks, 40 hours per week
  150 × $5.00 × 52 × 40 $1,560,000
- Fringe benefits, at 50%
  $1,560,000 × 0.50   780,000

Overtime:
- 930 worker weeks, 40 hours per week, at 1½ times $5.00
  930 × 40 × 1½ × $5.00   279,000
- Fringe benefits, at 15%
  $279,000 × 0.15   41,850

     Total annual cost $2,660,850

Regular time hours	312,000
Net cost per hour	$7.50
Overtime hours	37,200
Net cost per hour	$8.62
Total hours	349,200
Average cost per hour	$7.62

Using leased personnel for all overtime operation (see Fig. 15-2) at a total cost of $6.50 per hour will reduce annual costs by $79,050:

Regular time (same):	
▪ $1,560,000 + 780,000	$2,340,000
Leased productivity (selling overtime)—temporary service personnel	
▪ 930 worker weeks, 40 hours per week, at $6.50 per hour	
930 × 40 × $6.50	
Total annual costs	241,800
	$2,581,800

Cost reduction:	
Previous annual cost	$2,660,850
Costs with leased productivity	2,581,800
Potential savings or profit	$ 79,050

Employee hours	312,000
Net cost per hour	$7.50
Leased productivity hours	37,200
Net cost per hour	$6.50

Selling Idle Time for a Profit

The low work loads or valleys in Fig. 15-1 have a minimum value of 110 equivalent full-time workers. Reduction of the permanent employee work force to this level, from 150 to 110, would eliminate the three lull periods: the first of 170 worker weeks with a low of 120 workers; the second of 400 worker weeks with a low of 110 workers; and the third of 120 worker weeks with a low of 120 workers. The total idle time eliminated is 690 worker weeks.

In order to reduce the permanent employee group to the 110-employee level, and thereby eliminate the 690 worker weeks of idleness or underutilization, the work load which is above the 110 level will need to be covered by leased personnel. This work load totals 650 worker weeks in the first period, 740 in the third period. The second period has a low

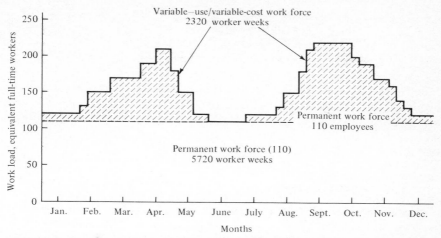

FIG. 15-3. The permanent work force has been reduced to the minimum work load (110). All work above this level is performed by variable-use/variable-cost temporary service personnel.

level of 110, which matches the lowered permanent employee level. An additional 1390 worker weeks of leased personnel services will be required in addition to the 930 for selling overtime for a total of 2320 (see Fig. 15-3). The total costs are now $2,319,200, with an additional reduction in annual cost of $262,600.

Regular time:
- 110 employees, $5.00 per hour,
  52 weeks, 40 hours per week
  110 × $5.00 × 52 × 40 .... $1,144,000
- Fringe benefits, at 50%
  $1,144,000 × 0.50 572,000

Leased productivity (selling overtime) 241,800

Leased productivity (selling idle time)—temporary
service personnel,
- 1390 worker weeks, 40 hours per week at
  $6.50 per hour
  1390 × 40 × $6.50 361,400

        Total annual costs $2,319,200

Cost reduction:

Previous annual costs, with leased
overtime coverage $2,581,800

Costs with 110 permanent employees,
additional leased personnel to cover work
load when and as needed: 2,319,200

    Potential additional savings or profit .... $ 262,600

Employee hours	228,800
Net cost per hour	$7.50
Leased productivity hours	92,800
Net cost per hour	$6.50

So far we have evaluated the potential savings or profit by the leased productivity approach from selling overtime (for a profit of $79,050) and from selling idle time (for a profit of $262,600). The next application is selling problem jobs. First we turn our attention to people considerations.

QUALITY OF WORK LIFE

Quality of work life (QWL) means that one receives psychic personal satisfaction from the work experience in addition to economic benefit. It is a highly individualistic matter. However, some common dimensions are generally applicable for all individuals, and relate to concepts of human dignity and self-fulfillment.

An interesting profile of white collar, mainly clerical, work life as it has existed within many organizations is outlined in the following quotation.[2]

White-Collar Companies

We've long had highly "people-intensive" white-collar institutions. Banks, utilities, home offices of manufacturing companies, insurance companies and the government have always employed large numbers of such people. In view of the expected heavy demand for white-collar workers, it would be worthwhile to examine the practices of these organizations.

Government agencies, banks, insurance companies and utilities once shared a number of similarities. First, in general they prided themselves on their reputations for job security and promotion from within. Second, they all had a great deal of routine work to process. Third, their staffs were composed of a small percentage of managers and professionals and a very large percentage of clerical workers. Fourth, they provided two broad career paths: one purely clerical, and the other managerial and professional. Over 90% of the clerical jobs were filled by young women, recent high school graduates. The majority of the managerial jobs were filled by men, mostly college graduates.

Until recently, this arrangement seemed to have the blessing of most interested segments of society. The young women had been conditioned by parents, relatives, friends and teachers to look forward to beginning their business careers with a bank, utility or insurance company. With few exceptions, they also expected their stay to be relatively short, perhaps two or three years.

This is how the scenario was usually acted out. The young 17- or 18-year-old female, for example, would join the XYZ Life Insurance Company as a messenger, file clerk or junior clerk-typist. Starting pay would be low, but the new employee could, with satisfactory performance, expect two or three small pay increases the first year, and at least one and possibly two promotions during the first two years. However, by the time she was 20 or 21, future advancement opportunities had been reduced sharply. This was an essential part of the system's ingeniousness. In effect, the insurance companies were running a kind of post graduate school, and "graduation day" took place after two or three years. By this time, some of these clerks had acquired their M.R.S. degrees and were ready to leave and start raising families. Others had now acquired enough business experience to take better-paying or more glamorous jobs elsewhere. A small percentage would stay on and might eventually become senior technicians, team captains or supervisors.

There were a few exceptions to this script, but the general practice was for the insurance company—or bank or utility—to hire a relatively cheap and docile female labor force which turned over every two or three years. Most of this turnover was voluntary, but company practices were designed to discourage too large a number from staying on. Whether the woman left to take a more exciting job or to get married, she could look back on her first place of employment rather warmly. She may not have been challenged or stimulated by her work, but no one had ever told her to expect that either. Instead, she had spent several years in a warm security blanket. . . . Assuming that this description of white-collar employment in the 50s and 60s is accurate, we must conclude that the differences between it and blue-collar employment were largely superficial. The point is that in both cases, a small number of decision-makers directed a large majority. Even if a firm happened to hire some people who didn't quite fit, it didn't make much difference since they'd either conform or leave in a relatively short time.

The New Knowledge Worker

Unfortunately for those companies, that orderly and predictable world exists no more. The typical applicant of today is simply not the known quantity of yesterday. A good number are more ambitious and independent, have less respect for authority, and generally are less willing to "do what they are told."

Mandt's description of the white collar world or work is, unfortunately, more descriptive of reality within many organizations than it should be. The white collar employee has been regarded as a temporary, exploitable commodity. "Workers should do as they are told and be happy about it." The general practice in many organizations has been to hire cheap and docile female office labor, with replacement after a relatively brief stay. Fortunately, modern management philosophy does not accept these views, and most organizations are sincerely interested in providing opportunity for white collar employment that is personally rewarding both psychically and economically. However, achieving quality of work life is difficult in many white collar environments.

Practices are changing, partly because of changing social values, which are affecting management thinking and modifying the values and attitudes of the work force, partly because of better understanding of behavioral dimensions of human beings and work stemming from the behavioral sciences, and partly because of economic realities, which indicate that other ways to organize work may offer economic advantage.

Attitudes

There are many well-founded analyses of the changing characteristics of our work force.[3] Changes in society have reflected a change in individual value systems, and people bring their value system with them to their jobs.

Contrasting the differences in work-force characteristics for the over 35 and under 35 years of age groups reveals marked differences in goals, attitudes, timing, and rewards. The over-35 group's goals tend toward upward mobility and material possessions or security. The younger group's goals center around duty to self, leisure-time activities, and meaning in life at work.

The older group's attitudes reflect conformity and self-denial or deferred gratification. The younger group evidences value attached to less uniformity in policies, flexibility, and entitlement to opportunity and benefits.

The outlook of the younger group is oriented to timing in the short-term and a focus on self, contrasted with a longer-term timing for the older group, and an orientation toward contribution to their family.

Both groups regard recognition and reward for accomplishment as important, with equity and fairness as critical requirements. Additionally, the older group places emphasis on respect and respectability, while the younger group tends to value leisure time, leisure-time activities, a "meaning" to their life, and money to support leisure-time pursuits.

Values and attitudes within groups are not entirely uniform. Individuals do differ, and some are not typical of their groups. However, the changes in values and attitudes mentioned above are regarded by most researchers as substantial, and significantly great that they should be addressed. The proportion of the younger group in the work force has, for many organizations, increased dramatically. Many younger workers have a strong distrust of "institutions," both in general and the one for which they work. Their personal value system is "obviously" correct from their view, and they have difficulty accepting different points of view. They feel economic pressures but react to them differently and for different reasons than the older group. Many believe strongly in social accountability for all organizations and have little understanding of and sympathy for the free enterprise system.

Most have a low tolerance for just doing what they are told, preferring to have a say in deciding the matter, and feel strongly that they are entitled to satisfaction and a sense of achievement from any activity in which they engage—play or work. Many are highly qualified, and if turned on are outstanding producers. If not turned on and challenged, they may well respond by being less than marginal employees, who are tuned out and who look elsewhere for challenge and satisfaction.

Social Values

One of the landmark contributions to enlightened management of human resources was made by Argyris,[4] about a generation ago. His observations had to do with the dilemma that results because the behavior required by the typical work situation is in basic conflict with the behavior judged by society as being desirable and correct.

Society places great value on mature or adult behavior, but the structure and management of work usually demand childlike or immature responses. Off-the-job social norms place a premium on individual assumption of responsibility, controlling one's environment, and growth from the infant stage to increasing maturity throughout life. These mature, adultlike behaviors were not only discouraged but were not tolerated in most job settings, as with those organizations described by Mandt. The human resource was regarded as a "commodity," to be used in conformance to tightly specified task assignments, with little or no opportunity for ingenuity, innovation, seeking of additional responsibility, or other aspects of maturity. Argyris forcefully indicated that conflict of values would eventually cause social disruption. We have seen some examples of this happening.

We have gradually come to believe that work experience should be satisfying and rewarding in more than economic terms—that the quality of life should include our work experiences. Jobs and organizations should provide opportunity for individual growth and mature, adultlike behavior, and not be dull, demeaning, or dehumanizing. Modern management philosophy would hold this to be correct because our own social conscience demands it—and also because the evidence of its economic advantage over other less humane approaches is persuasive.

Motivation

An equally significant contribution to enlightened management of human resources was made by Herzberg[5] about the same time as Argyris made his. Herzberg's contribution lends support to the economic advantages of organizing work such that mature, adultlike behavior is not only permitted but encouraged. It emphasizes the importance of structuring jobs in order to provide challenge, responsibility, achievement, a sense of accomplishment, opportunity for advancement, and recognition. It is the very nature of work itself which can provide motivation and stimulate superior performance.

However, Herzberg also documented the critical importance of "hygienic" factors, which if inadequately provided for can result in dissatisfaction, and by and large prevent motivational factors, even if present, from being effective. The dissatisfiers are potential disrupters and are inclined to be quite personal in orientations: a feeling that pay is not fair and equitable; inadequate or incompetent supervisory support; company policy which is viewed as interference with personal and job performance needs—or arbitrary, capricious, bureaucratic, oppressive; unsatisfying interpersonal relationships—particularly with supervision; and working conditions judged to be unpleasant or interfering with proper job performance.

Herzberg's insights have been confirmed by extensive additional research, dealing with almost all types of work, and in many different cultural settings. One can generalize from his findings. Basic hygienic factors should be provided for, to prevent dissatisfaction. If we desire to have motivated and productive workers, jobs should be designed to be challenging and satisfying. If we cannot do that, even emphasis on the hygienic factors will not result in motivated and productive workers for anything but short periods of time.

QWL and Productivity Implications

Changes in worker attitude, changes in social values, the concept of motivational and hygienic factors, and projection of future changes in the search for meaningful self-fulfillment are a confounding set of factors descending upon managers. One could conclude that worker productivity in the white collar area is a lost cause. Redesigning jobs to address the Argyris and Herzberg "requirements" has some intellectual and practical appeal. But will trends in values and attitudes toward work prevent achieving gains in productivity?

Daniel Yankelovich, a highly respected social value interpreter, provides optimistic assessment of opportunities for harnessing human desires on behalf of improving organizational productivity. He judges, on the basis of extensive data, that the self-centered "me" generation has been replaced by a widespread change in attitude toward need for involvement, commitment, and supportive interpersonal relationships. These forces can well be focused on external "worthy" causes, *or* they can be directed toward helping organizations become more productive.[6]

> I suspect that what is required of Americans in the eighties is not constant belt-tightening, nor punishing our institutions (we need to improve them, not cripple them), nor the defeatism that "accepts reality" and settles for less, and certainly not abandoning the high goal associated with the search for self-fulfillment. What is required is to accomplish the one great task that has eluded Western civilization since the age of science and technology began— breaking through the iron cage of rationalization and instrumentalism in order to make industrial society a fit place for human life. . . .
> My surmise is that the social signals we receive in the next few years will communicate confusion, faltering leadership and disarray, but that beneath

the surface many elements of health and strength needed to take the crucial second step in building a new social ethic or commitment will be at work.

Taking Constructive Action

Developing a white collar working environment which is more responsive to individual human needs, which develops commitment, productivity, and quality of working life, is evolutionary. Some organizations are further along than others. Even those that are advanced in their development have further to go. Each must progress from where they are by following a well-thought-out, step-by-step, nonthreatening, and largely self-directed plan.

Organizations with human resource development staffs are likely to have good supportive resources available to help supervisors and managers develop and implement plans. Organizations without such resources can proceed on their own on a do-it-yourself basis. It is not difficult and is a low-risk venture, provided that it is done in a reasoned manner.

The keys to success are:

- Involvement and participation, gaining consensus (or at least substantial unanimity) concerning the direction of desired change
- Identifying reasonable steps which are likely to bring change in the desired direction
- Evaluating the pros and cons of these steps
- Establishing priorities
- Testing the most promising steps by actual use
- Evaluating: did the change move us in the desired direction?
  If so, consolidate and incorporate the change as normal work practice
  If not, back up, abandon the change, and test out the next most promising one
- Repeat the cycle

If one follows this procedure, which has been called *systematic muddling through* or planned incremental change for improvement, common sense and good faith almost always guide one to continual incremental, no-risk (or low-risk) changes which are favorable and which add up to substantial improvements. Any supervisor or manager can use it.

Earlier in the chapter we presented the concept of leased productivity, the use of variable-cost/variable-use human resources so that the permanent work-force size could be reduced. If work-load fluctuations are a reality and the economics favorable, this is likely to be an attractive and viable opportunity—provided that it can be constructively integrated with the needs of the organization. The needs of the organization are (or should be) very heavily influenced by the need to move in an evolutionary way toward a better quality of work life. This should not be done just to be nice to people. It should be done with recognition that quality of work life improvement can yield substantial improvement in productivity. This really is the objective. Being nice to people, providing dignity, challenge, and satisfaction, developing commitment, being involved in improving work activities, having a chance to "grow," having influence in matters which affect work activities—all are related to QWL *and* productivity.

Adoption of the leased productivity concept can be a unilateral management decision, and this may be appropriate in some situations. However, in most cases it will be advantageous to proceed with at least some direct involvement and participation of the employee group in planning how to proceed.

Decreasing the size of the permanent work force provides opportunity for enriching the work activities and upgrading the "quality" of the remaining smaller permanent employee group. The reduction in size should be approached in a humane way, concentrating on providing better and more satisfying work activities for the "core" group of the best and highest-potential employees. Job duties should be analyzed so that enrichment is achieved and so that work assignments for temporary personnel are well structured and matched to skills that can be provided by these personnel. This is not a difficult matter, but it does deserve reasoned consideration, and in most cases should be done with substantial involvement of core-group employees.

Further reduction in the size of the permanent employee core group can be achieved by "selling" problem jobs. This can be done, potentially, at a profit by the leased productivity approach. In addition to the cost benefit, substantial improvement in the quality of work life for the reduced size of core employee group can be achieved.

LEASED PRODUCTIVITY—CONTINUED

Selling Problem Jobs for a Profit

Most organizations have problem jobs, and often problem employees as a consequence of dull, dead-end, nonchallenging work which must be done. These problem jobs frequently (but not always) are entry-level positions, which are difficult to keep filled, are performed inefficiently, and require an inordinate amount of supervisory time, attention, care, and effort to maintain even a minimum level of performance. In our example it would be reasonable to assume that 10 or so of these jobs exist and that 10 positions could be covered by leased personnel, properly selected, who could perform these jobs more efficiently than the 10 unhappy problem-job employees. Productivity increase of 15 to 25 percent would be a reasonable experience-based expectancy.

Covering 10 problem jobs with leased personnel (see Fig. 15-4) with a 15 percent productivity improvement, working only when needed,

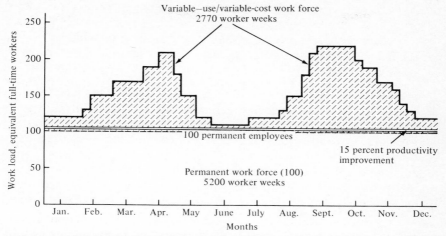

FIG. 15-4. **The permanent work force has been reduced to 100, with all load above this level handled by work-only-as-needed short- and long-term temporary service personnel.**

would require 18,000 leased personnel hours (10 jobs, 52 weeks, 40 hours a week at a 15 percent better performance rate). The permanent employee work force can now be reduced to 100, problem jobs have been eliminated, and total annual costs can be reduced by an additional $39,000:

Regular time:
100 employees, $5.00 per hour, 52 weeks, 40 hours per week

100 × $5.00 × 52 × 40	$1,040,000
Fringe benefits, at 50%	
$1,040,000 × 0.50	520,000
Leased productivity (selling overtime)	241,800
Leased productivity (selling idle time)	361,400
Leased productivity (selling problem jobs)— temporary service personnel, 18,000 hours at $6.50 per hour	
18,000 × $6.50	117,000
Total annual costs	$2,280,200

Cost reduction:

Previous annual costs with leased overtime and leased coverage of work load above 110 employee level	2,319,200
Cost with 100 employees, 10 problem jobs done by leased personnel	2,280,200
Potential additional savings or profit	$ 39,000

Employee hours	208,000
Net cost per hour	$7.50
Leased productivity hours	110,800
Net cost per hour	$6.50

In addition to the $39,000 profit from selling 10 problem jobs, benefits and savings will result from elimination of the efforts required to keep these jobs filled. Recruiting, hiring, and indoctrination efforts would be appreciable, as would the supervisory efforts and lost time associated with staying on top of the problem employees. Saving these efforts, and eliminating the headaches associated with them, would be of value but is not easily expressed in absolute dollar terms. A value could be approximated and perhaps would be in the range of $1000 to $15,000 a year.

VARIABLE-USE/VARIABLE-COST HUMAN RESOURCES

Our example of leased productivity has been based on the concept of reducing the size of our permanent work force below the valley or minimum load level, and using a variable-use/variable-cost worker pool to perform all work above this point. We have assumed that this worker pool would be supplied by a firm which specializes in furnishing temporary service personnel. However, part-time employees may be used, perhaps by directly employing a group of individuals for on-call part-time work, using retired employees, variations of flexitime, job sharing, undertime, etc. There are many options.

Both the use of leased personnel from firms specializing in providing temporary service personnel and the use of part-time employees have advantages—and disadvantages. The cost differences are fairly easy to analyze, provided that the real cost of indirect and fringe expenses can be determined. These costs are usually underestimated, for both full-time and part-time employees. When indirect and fringe costs are realistically included, and when an organization is paying somewhat the going rate for the area, the cost per regular hour a firm pays for one of its own permanent employees is usually a bit higher than the net cost per hour for a comparable temporary service person, and considerably higher per overtime hour. This cost differential tends to get smaller for part-time employees.

In addition to potential cost advantages which may favor the use of either leased personnel or part-time employees, depending upon the specifics of the situation, there are both advantages and disadvantages which are not easy to express directly in cost terms. Leased personnel do not obligate the user organization beyond the direct charge for time needed and worked. The temporary service firm provides for all other obligations. An arm's-length relationship of this sort may be quite advantageous.

Temporary service firms vary considerably in their capability and performance. The industry is still a young one and in the process of maturing. It presently furnishes about 2 percent of our national labor force and is projected to expand to about 10 percent.

Some firms are very professional and can help an organization analyze its situation to identify ways to use the leased productivity approach profitably. Such organizations can furnish experienced, qualified, bonded, use-as-needed or long-term-assignment personnel for a variety of office assignments. A range of skills can be provided, including some at quite high professional levels. They usually provide for supervision, monitoring, and performance evaluation for their people.

SUMMARY

Use of the leased productivity approach in a situation with the workload fluctuations of our example resulted in reduction of annual costs from $2,660,850 to 2,280,200, for a savings (or profit) of $380,650. Annual payroll costs have been reduced from $2,660,850 to $1,560,000, and leased personnel services of $720,200 have been purchased. The total savings (or profit) is composed of:

Selling overtime, for a profit of	$ 79,050
Selling idle time, for a profit of	262,600
Selling problem jobs, for a profit of	39,000
Total profit from leased productivity	$380,650

In addition, relief from the hassle of dealing with and keeping filled selected problem jobs results in savings somewhere in the range of $1000 to $15,000 annually.

The permanent employee work force has been reduced from 150 to 100, which represents a significant improvement of perhaps more potential value than the almost $400,000 savings. The smaller-sized permanent or core employee group can be "elite," composed of the best—the most capable, loyal, ambitious, and productive. They can have their work upgraded and their working lives enriched. It is likely that some of the savings from leased productivity would be invested to further develop their value and to upgrade their salary levels.

How profitable the leased productivity approach will be for a given organization depends upon the specifics of the situation. Work-load fluctuations, pay rates and fringe/indirect costs, problem jobs, costs and availability of temporary service personnel, and a host of other factors must be considered. It is rather easy to make a rough-cut analysis to gauge the magnitude of potential benefits. If they are sufficiently attractive, detailed analysis and planning would be worth the extra effort. In our example, the benefits were almost $400,000 per year and a one-third reduction in size of the permanent work force. Considerable effort to remove barriers to use of the concept would be merited. It can be done in many situations, and it is being done.

Our example has implied that mainly low-level clerical personnel are involved in leased productivity. This may or may not be the case. Again, the specifics of the situation are in control: the specific organization, its people and its work; and the capability of available temporary service firms. In some cases the approach may include higher-level "professional" personnel, and it may be extended to encompass off-shift use of facilities and equipment.

NOTES

[1] I am indebted to Robert Gallagher of Norrell Services, Inc., for this terminology, based on his presentation, "Profits Are for Everyone."

[2] Edward Mandt, "White-Collar Workers in the 80s Will Demand a New Style of Management," *Personnel Journal,* March 1978, pp. 140–141.

[3] Based upon material prepared by the American Productivity Center.

[4] C. Argyris, *Personality and Organization Theory,* Harper, New York, 1957.

[5] F. Herzberg, B. Mausner, and B. Snyalerman, *The Motivation to Work,* Wiley, New York, 1959.

[6] Daniel Yankelovich, *New Rules: Searching for Self-Fulfillment in a World Turned Upside Down,* Random House, New York, 1981, pp. 262–263.

CHAPTER SIXTEEN

Quality Circles*

ROBERT N. LEHRER
Consultant

No book dealing with white collar productivity would be complete without some coverage of quality circles (QC), for the QC movement is probably the "hottest" management topic of the decade. Impressive improvements in white collar productivity and quality of work life have been achieved by QC, and it is a substantial and proved approach. However, it is not a panacea, and it should be used with full knowledge of what it is.

Quality circles involve some 8 million Japanese workers in participative problem solving. Some millions of U.S. workers are likely to be similarly involved in QC activities during this decade. Interest in QC is intense and widespread. The business press has given it broad coverage, and a number of consultants are promoting it. Unfortunately, a great deal of the available information is misleading and does little to help the potential user understand what QC really is, and how it can be used successfully. The objective of this chapter is to set the record straight on circles and to provide guidance to help improve the odds of successful application of this uniquely Japanese innovation.

* Based upon material published in R. N. Lehrer, *Participative Productivity and Quality of Work Life,* Prentice-Hall, New York, 1982, with permission of the publisher.

BACKGROUND

The concept of QC was born of necessity and ingenuity. The necessity was to enhance the quality of Japanese products during post–World War II redevelopment so that Japanese industry could compete in international markets against other producers who had already established their reputations for quality products. The ingenuity was integration of "quality" technology with the Japanese style of management.

U.S. decline in productivity, and problems associated with quality of work life, may well be the necessity for our adoption of QC, but do we have sufficient ingenuity to emulate Japanese success?

American leaders, shortly after the end of World War II, with considerable wisdom and generosity, embarked not only on programs of rehabilitation for their war-ravaged allies but also on programs to rebuild the productive capability of their defeated enemies. In addition to providing capital goods, the United States shared its experience and expertise in productivity enhancement, and provided technical assistance and educational programs. Productivity centers were established to coordinate industrial redevelopment and to provide educational and advisory services in productivity subjects.

Japan, in particular, rapidly learned the fundamentals of cultivating productivity, and has put them to use in ways which would make any teacher proud of a student. It has come from devastation to among the first-ranking industrial powers in less than 30 years and has consistently been the world leader in rate of increase in productivity improvement. It has been able to do this mainly by integration of productivity enhancement with national and individual goals.

Japan has implanted American productivity know-how into its own unique way of doing things. One significant result is quality circles, which are remarkably similar to, but also uniquely different from, the *participative* work simplification approach to worker involvement in solving work problems and developing better work methods.

Japanese leaders recognized at the start of the redevelopment efforts after World War II that if Japan were ever to compete in international markets the poor quality image associated with prewar products must be overcome. Along with productivity technical assistance, assimilation of U.S. quality technology was targeted as being of paramount importance. U.S. experts, particularly Dr. Edward Deming and Dr. Joseph Juran, were made available, and the Japanese rapidly mastered the technology. They integrated the technology with their own style of management.

Japanese custom leads to a strong conviction that all members of an organization have personal obligations to the organization, to other members of the organization, and to society—to help their organization become economically successful and thus to help their country become a leading economic power.

Japanese custom also provides job security, lifetime employment, favorable levels of trust between management and labor, a competent engineering community willing and able to share its knowledge, and a national motivation to improve the economy of the country.

Japanese organizations are inclined to involve their people in deliberations concerning problems and plans, and to encourage consensus decisions on important matters. The integration of quality technology was approached on the basis that each individual had responsibility for quality and should be provided with technology skills so that he or she could help solve quality problems.

Dissemination of information on quality technology and guidance in involving workers was fostered by the Japanese Union of Scientists and Engineers (JUSE) in 1962, and thus the quality circles approach began. Workshop discussion groups (circles) were started within a number of organizations, and supervisors and workers were provided training in basic problem-solving methods and elementary quality-control techniques. They then were invited to form small groups (circles) to search for and solve quality problems.

The success of the Japanese with establishing high-quality, low-cost products has been noted in the United States for many years, first with optical products, then with electronics, and on with other lines. The U.S. reaction for many years was one of ignoring the accomplishments, then attributing achievement to low wage rates, with slow acknowledgment that unique innovative approaches were being used to involve thoroughly all members of organizations in participative efforts to improve individual and organizational performance. This acknowledgment not only came slowly but tended to be dismissed—that may work in Japan, but never in the United States. "What can we learn from Japan? We *taught* them what they know."

U.S. management finally became interested, in the 1970s, in the Japanese way of doing things so successfully. It was slowly recognized that Japanese wage rates were not low but were among the highest for total employee costs among major industrial nations. Obviously, something other than low labor costs must have been responsible for Japanese success.

Several Japanese companies established U.S. production facilities with interesting results. Plants producing similar products achieved productivity levels in the United States under Japanese management which were better than in Japan. Several U.S. manufacturing facilities which were experiencing high costs, poor quality, and low productivity were acquired by Japanese companies. The Japanese style of management was installed, largely implemented with "reeducated" U.S. managers and supervisors. The results were outstanding. The Japanese way *could* work in the United States—an open style of management, with involvement and participation of all workers in improving their jobs, developing better ways to do things, and solving work problems.

The Japanese are acquisitive people when it comes to knowledge.

They are also open in sharing their knowledge. Their success with quality circles was generally known, openly shared with U.S. visitors to Japan and by visitors from Japan to the United States. Finally a few U.S. companies became interested. Lockheed Missiles and Space Company was one of the early ones to seriously pursue the potential use of quality circles in the U.S. setting. They sent a study team to Japan to learn about Japanese methods, and "Americanized" the program for use in their facilities—in 1974. Success was rapidly achieved, and the quality circle movement in the United States was started—and has since expanded.

SCOPE

Quality circles were originally motivated by the necessity to improve product quality, but in practice the focus quickly broadened to include almost all considerations which have a bearing on people doing their jobs.[1] One analysis[2] indicates the following types of problems as typical of QC programs:

Area of impact	Percent of activity
Quality	22
Efficiency	12
Cost	11
Equipment	10
Morale	10
Process control	9
Missed work	8
Safety	4
Learning	3
Other	11

The term "quality" is not really descriptive of the range of problems addressed. Even though quality is still important, only a bit over one-fifth of typical projects are restricted to quality considerations. The term "productivity and quality of work life circles" would be more descriptive—but QC is the terminology most frequently used, even for white collar improvement activities.

DOGMA

As with any programmatic approach, dogma concerning "correct" practices, procedures, and approaches does develop. This is particularly true of the QC movement. Examples of dogma are: "To be effective, the QC must be limited to a group of three to twelve members," "No step can be left out and they must be followed in a given sequence." "All the circle concept means is that management 'pays attention' to the workers and the workers produce more." "Interdepartmental circles are not allowed in Japan, or in well-run circle programs here." All these declarations are lacking in substance. They are dogma: "Points of view or tenets put forth as authoritative without adequate grounds."

Quality circles are constrained and aided by the very same forces which aid or constrain other approaches to participative problem solving which are intended to enhance productivity and the quality of work life. The most significant principles underlying successful QC use are those associated with the open style of management which provide the *climate* within the organization for all individuals to do their jobs well *and* to search for improvements. The QC approach is a way to encourage and facilitate group activities on behalf of involvement in improvement of work activities, both enhanced productivity (which includes the "quality" dimension) and enhanced quality of work life.

Circle size depends upon many factors, such as personality of the members and the leader, their abilities to interact effectively, the leader's style and ability, and the nature of problems. There is no set step-by-step procedure which has universal validity—other than a joint effort to identify improvement opportunities, to evaluate among the options, to set priorities, to systematically develop and test improvements, to obtain necessary agreement and authorization for implementation, and to effectively implement improvements. The concept is far more than just "paying attention" to the workers. Just paying attention to the workers *does not* necessarily cause workers to produce more. Circles may be structured to cross organizational lines, and even to cross entire organizations.

Other examples of dogma are many, and equally misleading. They include such things as regarding statistical techniques as essential or a given training program and specific topical coverage as necessary, and they frequently imply that QC activities should have high visibility and receive much publicity within the organization. All these things may or may not be appropriate. None of them is essential. What is appropriate depends upon the specific setting.

MANAGEMENT SUPPORT

The QC approach requires a conviction on management's part that participation by employees in identifying and solving work problems is desirable, and that such participation will be supported as required to achieve the desired involvement. It is far more than a passive commitment, and far more than just paying attention to the workers. The organizational climate must be supportive, which means that management *sincerely desires* involvement of workers, and that the entire organization supports such involvement. Even if this is so, the perception by those affected of the opportunity being desirable, with little or no risk, and as a nonexploitive approach which will be of benefit to them, is critically important.

The assumption is either that management use of QC is the result of shifting to a more open management style than has been the case or that QC is being used as a means to further implement an open management style already in existence. It is also assumed that management wants their workers to deal with issues and problems which may be currently handled by staff people, and which supervisors and middle managers may regard as being their prerogatives to control. Many managers, supervisors, and staff people are threatened by such changes, and unless the issues are dealt with "up front" and on a proactive basis, difficulties are likely to be encountered.

POLICIES

After management has decided that they wish to shift to a more open style of management and that a QC approach might be useful, a number of issues must be considered. First in priority should be preparing the organization, with particular attention to middle management, for sharing responsibilities and prerogatives, as required by the open style. This can seldom be done by directive, and it may require considerable effort. Next in importance is to develop a policy structure to support the efforts.

Decisions should be made concerning what problems are not appropriate for circle efforts. Focusing only on work-related issues which directly affect the circle and excluding all matters relating to pay, promotion, and other "industrial relations" issues is a common approach. When a union is involved, all issues which directly affect bargaining and contract provisions are usually excluded from circle consideration.

Policies for processing, evaluating, and acting upon circle recommendations should be specifically defined, as should the procedure and timing for feedback to circles of evaluation and decision about recommendations.

Reward and recognition should be dealt with in a proactive manner, considering policies and practices which already exist, as well as the formulation of new or integrated approaches. Few short-term direct financial incentives are used with quality circles in Japan, but extensive indirect incentives and generous use of recognition of team contributions to the organization are common.

In addition to team and individual recognition, some sharing of benefits is appropriate. This "gain" sharing may be in many forms, long- or short-term, and addresses the question "What's in it for me?" How these issues of recognition and reward *should* be handled depends upon the specifics of the individual organization. There is no "pat" answer. The Japanese do cultivate awareness of long-term financial benefit being associated with productivity improvement and circle accomplishments.

Management, and the union if one is present, should understand the program, policies, structure, and operation. Perhaps even more importantly, middle management needs to be thoroughly informed and supportive.

CIRCLES

QC involvement is typically voluntary, and the problems which are dealt with are selected by the circle. Potential circle members may be exposed to QC training and then formed into teams or circles as they desire to be involved, or those who desire involvement may be grouped into circles and then provided training. In some situations a few interested individuals may "recruit" fellow workers in order to form a circle.

Circle composition may be based upon involvement in similar work activities, location, organization unit, or commonality of responsibility and problems dealt with. A common approach is to organize circles as an adjunct of the existing organizational structure, with voluntary membership drawn from areas with common work concerns within one supervisory unit, and with the supervisor as the circle leader. The supervisor may have several circles, depending upon the number of people supervised, the number who want to be involved in circle activities, and their commonality or divergence of work-related interests.

Circles can also be organized across lines of responsibility and need not be restricted by organizational structure. They also can be organized at higher levels of the organization, either following the organizational structure or cutting across it. Circle leadership may be organizationally determined, or the leader may be elected by the circle members.

LEADERS

When circles are organized as voluntary activities within the normal organizational structure, the supervisor (or manager), as leader, is provided with additional leadership tools and opportunities for developing his or her people and for facilitating their meaningful involvement in solving work problems. He or she, ideally, would exercise full leadership for circle activities, including training, conduct of circle meetings, coordination of obtaining resources (information, data, expert advice, etc.), interfacing with other organizational elements, submission of recommendations, obtaining authorization and resources for implementing recommendations, etc.

These responsibilities may weigh too heavily, requiring that assistance and support be provided. This is usually done by a QC coordinator or facilitator, who trains the leader and may help the leader develop training abilities and assist the leader in training circle members. The facilitator also provides other supportive services, and attempts to make the leader's role as effective and easy as possible, evolving toward participative leadership being normal managerial style.

FACILITATOR

The QC coordinator, or facilitator, is a key individual who provides not only training and support for the circle leaders but leadership and support for circle activities throughout the organization and for development of the program. The coordinator is frequently a staff person and may be assigned to QC on a part- or full-time basis—depending upon the scope of program efforts.

STEERING COMMITTEE

Many organizations include a steering committee in their QC efforts. The objective is to provide guidance and policy direction for the development and operation of circle activities—and perhaps more importantly, to obtain management involvement in the process of planning for productivity and quality of work life changes within their own areas of responsibility. By such involvement, they hope, a sense of ownership of the program is developed and management support results from their integration of improvement responsibilities with their other normal responsibilities.

The steering committee has two basic concerns in planning and guidance: (1) strategic, in identifying appropriate need/opportunity areas where QC activities would be particularly beneficial and successful, and to encourage development in these areas; and (2) to provide tactical support, guidance, and encouragement. They are concerned with coordination of the overall QC effort, integration with other improvement endeavors, removing barriers, and providing inspiration, guidance, and support—particularly for, but not confined to, the coordinator.

TRAINING

QC training seeks to provide the ability to be involved, effectively, in participative problem solving, and to support involvement. Usually, four levels of training are involved: (1) management and union, (2) the facilitator, (3) the leader, and (4) the QC members.

Management at all levels should be informed of the nature of the QC effort, how it will operate, their role in the program, the need for their support, and how they can benefit from the endeavor. This may be accomplished informally as the program is structured, or by formal training sessions. It may include involvement of managers in a real or simulated QC meeting in order to demonstrate problem identification, solution, and presentation of recommendations.

The QC coordinator or facilitator requires much more extensive training and/or experience, for program execution and development will rest on his or her shoulders. Complete familiarity and facility with training materials and group leadership, as well as with program structure and policies, is required. The facilitator provides formal training for leaders so that they are prepared to train circle members and may assist them by sharing the instructional activities. He or she also provides instruction for the circle leaders on how they can initiate and operate circle activities, and how to avoid or resolve conflicts. The facilitator's role is to develop the QC leadership capability within the organization, to support circle activities by assisting and encouraging the circle leaders, and to coordinate and facilitate the development of the QC program throughout the organization.

QC leaders are provided extensive exposure to the instructional materials which they will use to train circle members, and to additional background instruction to enhance their confidence in and facility with program philosophy, procedures, policies, and instructional activities. They are usually provided with "packaged" instructional materials and additional supportive information.

Training for QC members usually concentrates on:
1. Background and motivational aspects
2. Creativity
3. Problem identification and problem scoping techniques
4. Problem analysis and problem-solving techniques
5. Management presentation techniques
6. Case examples and experience in using techniques

The exact content of QC training will vary, depending upon the nature of the work problems involved, previous training and experience of members, etc. Most programs make use of the Pareto or A-B-C technique for identification of the significance in frequency of occurrence or magnitude and importance of problem elements, and cause/effect or fishbone diagrams for analysis of problem elements.

The QC process makes use of creative thinking to identify potential problem/opportunity areas, and may use Pareto analysis and cause/effect diagrams to aid in defining appropriate problems/opportunities on which to work. Creative thinking, supplemented by Pareto analysis and cause/effect diagraming may then be used for analysis and solution of the selected problems/opportunities.

Instruction, in gross terms, is intended to develop awareness of work problems or opportunities, ability to develop priorities for attention to problems and opportunities, ability to develop creative approaches to them, ability to systematically analyze and solve problems, and the ability to organize, justify, and present the recommendations to management for decision and/or recognition.

Training materials can be individually developed without much difficulty. Or they can be purchased from various organizations and consultants.

KEY CONCEPTS

Dr. Kaoru Ishikawa, formerly of Tokyo University, was instrumental in providing leadership for quality circle development in Japan. He describes the key concepts associated with QC as:

- Self and mutual personal development
- To develop an increased quality awareness
- To capture the creativity and brainpower of the work force
- To improve worker morale
- To develop managerial ability, particularly of circle leaders

These same concepts are "main-line" for all participative problem solving programs. They are all based upon the conviction that satisfaction can be derived from doing one's job well *and* from the process of devising ways in which one's job can be done even better. Also, they are based upon the conviction that people are, at least potentially, creative and responsible, and that given a nonthreatening and risk-reduced environment with encouragement, training, and leadership, they will become involved in improving personal and organizational performance—they will work *smarter*.

QC philosophy tends to be somewhat distinctive in regard to the voluntary nature of becoming involved. If it is to be completely a voluntary matter, an environment which clearly indicates the benefits of becoming involved and continuing to be involved must be developed. This is quite a challenge, but a healthy requirement.

Full involvement of all members within a circle, and mutual, supportive interaction are also QC characteristics. Each circle member has obligations and responsibilities to the circle and its members. The leader has heavy obligations and responsibilities to the circle and its members. The leader has heavy obligations to lead and facilitate, to avoid domination, and to foster individual, personal growth and development of each and every member. Circle projects and recommendations represent team endeavors, and the entire team receives recognition and credit for accomplishments.

Suggestions for circle projects may originate from any source—from circle members, the circle leader, other circles, management, staff, etc. However, the circle members usually are responsible for selecting the projects which they, as a team, will pursue. Selection is based upon evaluation of the significance of a range of problems or opportunities which have been identified by the circle along with suggestions furnished from other sources, and a systematic development of priorities by the circle. Considerable faith in the ability of circle members and their leadership may be required for many managers to accept the concept that the circle decides for itself what projects they will pursue. But experience clearly indicates that people are responsible beings. Given the "tools" and the opportunity and leadership to grow, they do measure up.

Circle activities must be supported not only by training and leadership, but with time and encouragement for project work. Time is usually provided, during working hours, on a regular schedule, perhaps one hour every week or so.

Many QC participants feel strongly that one of the most powerful means of recognition and reward derives from the process of being involved in improving the productivity of their activities, and thus improving the quality of their work lives. Being directly involved, being consulted, and participating in decisions which affect them provides recognition and reward *only* when the Herzberg hygienic factors are adequately satisfied. A sense of being treated fairly and of not being exploited is critically important.

ARE QUALITY CIRCLES FOR YOU?

We have outlined the main features associated with quality circles, and mentioned that conceptually the key philosophy is basically one of an open style of management. It is essentially the same as other approaches to joint problem solving, which have been around for some time.

All these approaches are similar in that they are a *sharing* of responsibilities and prerogatives, directed toward participation and involvement in solving work problems. Management must sincerely believe in the "properness" of involvement and participation, and accommodate adequately to them if any participative program is to succeed. Experience has furnished many examples of failure where various levels of management or individual managers have not had sufficient conviction or have not been aided in accommodation, even when "lip service" has been given. Top management decision to go the participative route is necessary, but not sufficient to gain understanding and commitment. A frequent cause of failure is that top management made the decision to go the participative route *but* middle management was never really back of it.

Once the matter of organizational commitment, understanding, and support is taken care of, the issues of *desire/opportunity, ability,* and *mechanism* should be dealt with—before proceeding.

Desire

Any participative program is based upon the assumption that people have the desire to be involved in decision making which affects them and that an opportunity for such involvement does exist. Most people are inclined in the direction of wanting to be involved. The strength of this inclination will depend greatly on the individual, his or her basic value structure, personality, and most importantly his or her perception of the climate for involvement which exists within his or her organization and unit of the organization. If management is not inclined toward a participative and open style, individuals perceive this and are likely to be resistant to involvement. Anyone who perceives risks or unpleasantness associated with involvement is likely to avoid being involved. If being involved is, or is thought to be, personally counterproductive, one will avoid involvement. This is so for the "worker," for supervisors, and for all individuals within an organization.

In order for *desire/opportunity* to be a positive factor in support of participative problem solving the climate must be supportive, *or* the participative activities must be shielded from negative forces until sufficient strength develops to overcome and remove barriers. The individuals to be involved, their leader or supervisor, middle management, top management, and the union if one exists, should *all* share common values concerning the desirability of involvement, and conviction that opportunities can and will be made available. Trust, responsibility, high expectancies, mutually supportive relationships, recognition, reward, personal growth, openness—these are all important.

Ability

If people within an organization have a desire to be involved in solving work problems, and the climate is supportive for involvement, the next prerequisite for successful participation is the ability to participate—the skills for recognizing *and* solving problems. The "tools" must be made available. It is not sufficient just to have involvement.

Appropriate participative skills include many associated with leadership and interpersonal relationships, techniques for "scoping" problems and/or opportunities, techniques for problem analysis, procedures for gaining access to useful supportive resources, evaluation of alternatives, skills, and techniques for presenting recommendations for problem solution, techniques for presenting justifications in support of change, and techniques for follow-up and postchange monitoring.

Most participative problem solving programs provide *some* of the necessary abilities by formal training. Quite frequently additional abilities are provided in an informal way by coaching and staff assistance, introducing additional tools and techniques on a selective basis when it becomes apparent that additional abilities are needed for dealing with problems and projects.

Tools and techniques which are useful and appropriate for inclusion in formal training sessions will vary quite widely, depending upon the types of problems likely to be encountered and the goals and objectives which are being pursued.

Mechanism

Assuming that the *desire/opportunity* and *ability* factors have been adequately addressed, the final prerequisite for effective involvement is the mechanism for involvement. One might naively assume that desire/ opportunity and ability are sufficient, but this is not so. Many issues must be considered, decisions made, support and commitment obtained, and policies formulated:

1. How do participative efforts relate to the "normal" organizational structure?
2. Who provides the leadership?
3. Who initiates participative efforts?
4. Are efforts entirely group endeavors, or are solo efforts also desired?
5. Who provides training?
6. Who coordinates the efforts, provides access to other resources, crosses organizational lines?
7. How are problems and/or opportunities identified?
8. How are these evaluated and prioritized?
9. What areas, issues, or problems are excluded?
10. Who decides on projects to be worked on?
11. What time is provided for problem solving? How much and how often? On paid time? Regular time or overtime? Who is eligible?
12. How are recommendations handled? Who decides? What are procedure and timing of feedback?
13. Strategy and policy for recognition and reward? Alternatives?
14. Provisions for "educating" management? What levels? How? How do they get involved? Are they supportive?
15. Is *desire/opportunity* positively reinforced and supported?
16. How will results versus costs be evaluated?
17. What are future objectives and expansion plans?

The above listing, by no means an exhaustive one, is intended to indicate that the *mechanism* for supporting participative problem solving is complex and merits considerable and continuing attention. Thorough planning before getting into formal participative programs is prudent. Evolutionary development is also desirable, step by step, with evaluation and refinement to improve effectiveness based upon experience and additional insight.

The three prerequisites are sequential, and fold back on one another in a closed cycle:

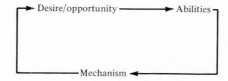

Continuing evaluation and replanning is necessary.

What Next?

Once the four fundamental issues (open style of management and organizational commitment; desire/opportunity; ability; mechanism) have been addressed, one should be in a position to make a meaningful decision about using quality circles—or some other participative approach. The next steps should concentrate on a *strategic* plan and the necessary *tactical* support.

QUALITY CIRCLES: THE ULTIMATE SOLUTION?

Many knowledgeable experts, including those who are intimately familiar with both Japan and the United States, flatly state that quality circles *will not* work in the United States. Our cultures are too different, our social values quite dissimilar, our organization mores not comparable, and the Japanese are a homogeneous people and we are not. They are correct! QC will not work *the same way* in any other setting as in Japan.

However, quality circles in non-Japanese settings have been successful!

Unfortunately, most non-Japanese applications of QC are not as successful as they could and should be. Some organizations are using QC as a means of exploitation and are not addressing the fundamental issues which support QC in the Japanese setting. QC is frequently used only for first-line activities and not throughout the organization. Many organizations are using QC in a nonexploitive way but with no attempt to modify the organizational culture to achieve a truly participative and open style of management.

Quality circles are not the explanation for Japan's productivity success. QC is but one element in a complex of many contributing factors. Our use of QC can be beneficial, as has been demonstrated by many successful applications. But we should strive for more than a transitory benefit, which is likely for many organizations. We can learn from the Japanese how we can go beyond this one element of their success.

QC programs, or even the concept of systematic muddling through which was discussed in the last chapter, can be useful and can help move an organization toward further improvement in productivity and quality of work life. But we can learn much more from the Japanese than just the program concepts of quality circles. As discussed in the last chapter, we can, in some settings, reduce the size of the permanent work force, level work-load fluctuations by a variable-use/variable-cost work resource, do away with some problem jobs, and enrich the work lives of the remaining and smaller "elite" core employee group. We can approach the Japanese practice of lifetime employment and can afford to invest in and reward our most effective, loyal, and productive employees. Imaginative study of the Japanese setting will provide many useful insights for improving the opportunity for successful use of QC and will help to provide the understanding which will allow any participative and involvement approach to successfully evolve from a program approach to a way of life for an organization.

If we desire the ultimate solution to productivity and quality of work life, quality circles should not be a *program* but should only be activities which reflect basic organizational values, values which are dedicated to a truly open style of management, values which permeate the entire organization, values which place a premium on individual growth and security, values which elicit individual and group dedication to outstanding organizational performance and continual improvement.

NOTES

[1] In conversations with Japanese friends and visitors, both here and in Japan, I have been impressed by the strength of their reactions to comments about U.S. interest in quality circles. They generally say that quality circles are passé. Only smaller and not very progressive Japanese organizations use quality circles. Considerable conversation has been required to find out exactly what they are saying—which is that circles have progressed far beyond concentration on quality and the use of quality-control technology. "Progressive" organizations focus on any and all issues which can lead to improvement in productivity and quality of work life.

[2] D. N. Amsden and R. T. Amsden, *QC-Circles: Applications, Tools and Theory,* American Society for Quality Control, Milwaukee, Wis., 1976.

REFERENCES

Konz, Stephan: "Quality Circles: An Annotated Bibliography," *Quality Progress,* April 1981, pp. 30–35. (A useful listing of English language QC-related publications, from 1966 through 1980.)

"Comment on Quality Circles," *Grid Update,* summer 1981, pp. 4–5. (Editorial comment by Blake and Mouton: cautions about the dangers of QC becoming a fad; differences between Japanese and U.S. organizations; and need to view QC, not as the reason for Japanese success, but as perhaps among the least important aspects of the Japanese productivity situation which may be contradictory when extracted from one culture and applied mechanically in another. Their conclusions stress the importance of organizational culture as a precondition for successful use of QC.)

Ouchi, William: *Theory Z: How American Business Can Meet the Japanese Challenge,* Addison-Wesley Publishing Company, Reading, Mass., 1981. (Analysis of Japanese and American management and the American version of Japanese management. Contains an interesting appendix discussing QC.)

Pascale, Richard Tanner, and Anthony G. Athos: *The Art of Japanese Management: Applications for American Executives,* Simon and Schuster, New York, 1981. (An excellent comparison of Japanese and American management and organizational culture, which makes clear why QC has been so successful in the Japanese setting and why some difficulties are likely in other cultures.)

How the USA and Europe Can Increase Productivity and Enhance Quality Control: An In-Depth Japanese Industrial Survey, The International Technical Information Institute, Tokyo, 1980. (Lessons from Japan, offered by the Japanese, which provide a comprehensive view of the Japanese setting, organization, and management.)

PART EIGHT

Summary

CHAPTER SEVENTEEN

Using the Concepts

ROBERT N. LEHRER
Consultant

The need to improve productivity of the white collar work force, particularly the knowledge worker sector, is obvious. We have elaborated upon this theme with a variety of illustrations of how to do it. The tools, techniques, procedures, and programs for productivity improvement which have been discussed are only a sampling of what is available.

We have presented specific approaches primarily to elaborate our conceptual framework, and secondarily to illustrate selected and already available techniques. Some readers will find these techniques directly applicable to their situation. However, most will find them points of departure for gaining insight into how the conceptual framework can guide one to visualize other analysis techniques which would be more useful and more sensitive to addressing their own unique needs. These innovations may borrow from concepts already illustrated or they may be substantial departures. Their common characteristic will be assessing the opportunities for constructive change within an organization and developing appropriate strategic and tactical approaches which are responsive to the individual setting.

Some readers will have completed their assessment of opportunities for improving white collar productivity within their own organizations as they have read the book, and at this point have a plan of action in mind. Others will need to reflect on the matter. Leverage points will need to be more clearly identified. A strategy will need to be developed. Where should one start? With one focus, or a multiple thrust? What should be the timing? What first? How should strategy and approach be balanced? How much reliance should be placed on participation and involvement? How much emphasis on office automation?

These are not easy questions to answer. However, they deserve serious consideration.

PERSONAL COMMENT

This book has been a challenge to organize and produce. But the endeavor has been quite satisfying, and it encourages me to be very optimistic about opportunities which exist within every organization for systematically enhancing white collar productivity and quality of work life.

The book is a departure from the usual approaches to white collar productivity, particularly in the conceptual framework for viewing various interdependent structures within an organization. By assessing the opportunities for improvement within each structure, specifically related to the unique characteristics of the organization or organizational unit being considered at a particular time, one can evaluate the potential benefit from further effort devoted to analysis within each structure and determine the characteristics of useful improvement techniques.

Each structure and structural element has been presented in terms of concepts and generalities and has been elaborated upon with presentation of specific analytical improvement techniques. Not all possible analytical techniques have been presented, and even those which have been are not suggested as *the* ones which should be used. They are illustrations of how one might go about cultivating improvement opportunities which exist, and they will serve as examples of proved approaches which have been effective for specific settings. The contributing authors have been generous in sharing their experiences and insights, and have provided guidance sufficient to allow use of their approach, or modification to meet the unique requirements for other settings. The fundamentals for improvement apply equally well to all organizations, small or large, for-profit or not-for-profit, service-producing or product-producing. The degree of appropriate formalization of approach will vary, depending upon the specific organization, but the fundamentals remain the same.

All the structures which have been presented are uniquely important in our quest for improvement. However, the human resource structure is signally important and should receive primary attention. The ultimate in white collar productivity will be achieved only when each individual within an organization is provided with the setting that allows, even demands, maximum volitional performance and improvement on behalf of contribution to organizational mission and which provides both tangible and psychic reward and satisfaction from doing so.

We have discussed the concepts of efficiency and effectiveness and have indirectly emphasized the truism that *efficiency* is not sufficient. We further emphasized the importance of effectiveness by designating the contribution to organizational mission as a special sort of effectiveness, *validity*. The overriding concern in white collar productivity should be in devising ways to enhance the validity of individual, group, unit, and organization efforts.

Measurement

Two views of measurement as a necessary element to support productivity improvement were presented by Carl Thor and Marvin Mundel. Both authors emphasize measurement as a means to an end; the end is improvement. Measurement is a useful base for cultivating improvements which enhance productivity.

Measurement can be approached in a variety of ways. Carl Thor provides the background of basic concepts for *productivity* measurement, which can be as comprehensive as the APC total productivity measurement system at the firm level or as uncomplicated as multiple-factor measures developed by the nominal group technique (NGT).

Total productivity measurement provides for an inflation-free look at overall business performance with identification of contribution to profitability which is due to both productivity and price recovery associated with various input factors or resources used. Such schemes can have direct relationship with financial accounting records and can serve the needs of both top-level and operational-level management. The use of specific company cost-price experience is recommended for removing the effects of inflation, and to fully link productivity and profitability within an organization.

The nominal group technique was presented as an example of an approach for facilitating identification of appropriate measures for evaluating white collar and knowledge work by those who are involved with doing the work.

The NGT approach provides opportunity for individuals assembled as a group, which may be a normal working group or a group assembled in name only, to address improvement or measurement issues creatively and judiciously without undue influence or domination from individuals of unequal power and influence. The process provides for individual and private development of concepts and ideas, a nonthreatening sharing and further development of them, and nondisclosed individual evaluation of the best, which are then pooled to reflect the combined evaluative judgment of the entire group. It is a useful device for involving individuals in meaningful group activity while providing each individual a shielding from group and individual pressures which inhibit participation and interaction with most group approaches. The resulting measures represent the best insights of those affected, those who are in the best position to know what is most appropriate. The approach is recommended as an easy one to use in the white collar, knowledge work area, for it respects the unique characteristics associated with such work and its environment.

Marvin Mundel approaches measurement from a different point of departure, concentrating on a logical structure of work-units, starting with the highest level being associated with the results achieved from the various service outputs provided by a group, organizational unit, or organization (the 8th-level work-unit). He is directing attention to evaluation of *validity* at this level, and progresses to each lower level of work-unit to define, evaluate, and measure the necessary component outputs which are required at each level—until one has arrived at a level of detail which is appropriate for measurement and analysis sufficient for cultivating improvement in the direct use of various input resources, and for meaningful forecasting, planning, and control.

Various "measurement" techniques may be required to use the hierarchy of work-units approach: time study (intensive sampling), predetermined time systems, standard data systems, direct time study (extensive sampling), fractionated professional estimates, standards established by "fiat," and mathematical analysis. Some of these techniques are easy for the nonexpert to use, while others require considerable skill and experience. Participation by those doing the work in the analysis and measurement is implied and appropriate. Involvement approaches, such as NGT, may be used for some measurements, while expert assistance is required for others.

Mundel presented two examples of the use of work-unit analysis, one for a plant engineering organizational unit, and one for various organizational units within a municipal government. Only a bit of imagination is required to visualize the use of his approach for analysis of *any* "service" unit within any organization. He provides further elaboration and application to a variety of service activities in his forthcoming book, *Improving Productivity and Effectiveness* (Prentice-Hall, Inc.), which is scheduled for release later in 1982.

Organizational Structure

Two approaches to enhancing productivity by analysis within the organizational structure were presented, one from the top down, and one from the bottom up. Both are concerned with improving the relationship between individual effort and contribution to organization mission; that is, they are both concerned with improving validity.

Ralph Johnson presented INTROSPECT as an example of a well-developed and highly successful approach to an abbreviated organizational analysis. Similar results can be achieved by various other approaches. However, INTROSPECT is a good model to emulate or to use as a pattern for critical analysis of organizational structure and allocation of effort in order to simplify the formal structure, reduce the number and layers of management, and better focus managerial and individual efforts toward those things which contribute to organization missions.

Experience with INTROSPECT within some 125 organizations of various types leads to the conclusion that most organizations have more managers than they need—40 percent too many is not unusual, and typically the excess is greater than 25 percent! These conclusions are supported by Japanese observations that U.S. organizations are much "deeper" than those in Japan, with comparative figures of about 11 organizational layers for U.S. organizations in the same industry which has only 7 in Japan.

In addition to potential economies in white collar, management, and knowledge worker employees which can result from an organizational analysis, the potential benefit from reemphasizing organization mission and efforts which support achievement is of equal potential value. A critical analysis of organizational structure from a *validity* improvement point of view is a high-priority need for overall enhancement of white collar productivity, particularly for the knowledge worker. Structural barriers which restrict individual, group, and organizational productivity by reducing validity of efforts should not be permitted to exist. But, unfortunately, they do exist within most organizations.

George Odiorne reviewed basic concepts and benefits associated with management by objectives (MBO), our second approach to productivity improvement within the organizational structure, and provided recommendations for its successful use. I have called this approach a bottom-up one, for it emphasizes the development of individual goals and objectives. However, it is also a top-down approach which develops individual goals and objects against a background of organization objectives and strategy. When done well, it helps to assure that individual objectives have high validity relative to organizational mission.

The basic concepts associated with management by objectives are fundamental characteristics of enlightened and effective organizations. Organizations now using MBO are encouraged to assess their process and method in order to develop more effective integration of the concepts with their style and way of managing. Organizations not using MBO are encouraged to devise ways to incorporate MBO *or* its basic concepts into their organizational modus operandi.

Many things which I refer to as basic concepts associated with MBO may not be considered by others as part of MBO. The formal use of goal setting, integration of individual and organizational goals, the concept of all employees being managers having dual managerial responsibilities (to do, and to improve), group problem solving, dual budgeting (operational and improvement), continuous feedback of performance, individual self-control and self-direction, and many other behaviorally based managerial concepts may be used independently of a formal MBO program. For example, many of these concepts are involved in the approach of Lefton, Buzzotta, Sherberg, and Karraker as presented in their book *Effective Motivation through Performance Appraisal* (Ballinger Publishing Company, Cambridge, Mass., 1977).

The full potential for organizational productivity, with particular reference to the white collar work force, cannot be achieved without attention to purpose on the part of the entire organization. MBO, and/or its basic concepts, provides a way to do so.

Functional Activity/Work Structure

Measurement is not an end in itself but is a means to the end of facilitating productivity enhancement. Measurement can be done in many ways. Which approach or approaches are appropriate depends upon what is to be measured and for what purpose. We have defined the functional activity/work structure as an elaboration of the functional organization in order to have a framework for measurement.

Various functional "things" must be tended to in order to achieve organizational goals by the strategic approaches which are considered to be appropriate in order to fulfill organizational mission. Measurement can be approached in terms of the various necessary functions by measuring the resources which are consumed on behalf of defined functional categories and relating these to various output indicators. A group of partial productivity measures will be the result. These gross, function-based partial productivity measures can be tracked over time or compared with similar measures for other organizations. They can be quite useful, even though they are very gross and aggregate measures, for gaining insights into where productivity improvement efforts might be beneficial. Many organizations use measures of this sort, and while they are useful, they are not sufficiently detailed for many diagnostic purposes.

Going beyond the use of functional categories, various activities within each function can be defined as input resource categories and related to appropriate output indicators in order to develop a set of more detailed partial productivity measures which are more useful for diagnostic purposes. How many activity categories are desirable? Is it useful to have 20 or 200, or somewhere in between? Are the needs for measurement only in selected areas, functions, or activities—or does the need for measurement extend to *all* indirect activity? It depends. It depends upon the situation and the intended use for the measures.

All functional activity within an organization can be measured. David Conway has provided one example of a proved approach to measuring all functional activity using only 115 categories. His approach, the Common Staffing System (CSS), has been specifically tailored to the measurement needs of the IBM organization but can be used either "as is" by others or as a conceptual basis for the development of other approaches.

The resulting measures are regarded by IBM as approximate measures, which measure activities and not individuals, which are useful for diagnostic purposes. The success achieved by IBM with CSS should provide inspiration for other organizations to approach white collar measurement for the purpose of facilitating productivity enhancement from the top of the functional activity/work structure. If the reader has concluded that the top-down approach is useful only for large, multifacility organizations, the point has been missed; the fundamentals embedded in the CSS example have been obscured by the specifics associated with the application environment. Top-down measurement can be useful for white collar productivity enhancement within any organization. The specific approach should be designed in light of the intended use for the measurements.

Robert Nolan has approached measurement from the opposite end of the functional activity/work structure, dealing with work activities which are well structured and repetitive and for which given actions are required for completion of units of work. Measurement is for the purpose of productivity enhancement—work management. The area of application is primarily clerical. Work measurement and work management are useful approaches to enhancing white collar productivity, but the overall needs for measurement extend well beyond the clerical area. Work measurement and work management merit consideration as useful approaches to white collar productivity, but only after other measurement approaches have also been carefully evaluated. It may be an appropriate approach, or other approaches may be more useful.

The in-between approach to white collar measurement as presented by Douglas Crocker fills the gap between very detailed and very broadly based partial productivity measures. His approach provides many options for analysis and measurement in support of productivity enhancement, particularly when dealing with aggregations of tasks and activities which are ambiguous and not highly structured. He has presented the basic concepts of multiple linear regression (MLR) along with considerable guidance on how the concepts can be usefully applied, and has provided extensive references. These references are recommended reading, particularly for the analyst who is likely to be involved in application of MLR to the white collar area.

We have concentrated on measurement with this part of our conceptual framework. The earlier presentations on measurement are also pertinent, and along with the presentations in this section of the book provide a reasonably comprehensive overview of measurement as applied to the white collar area. Most of the many measurement options which are available have been described. This background, along with assessment of a specific organization, should allow appropriate selection of useful measurement approaches, if one keeps in mind that measurement is only a means to an end.

Service Interchange

The third vertical structure in our conceptual framework for viewing white collar productivity deals with service interchange. Each unit within an organization can be considered as a service interchange mechanism, furnishing services to other units and requiring services itself. All services can be identified, and priced in terms of their cost to produce and in terms of their value to the user. Benefit/cost relationships can then be used as a point of departure for identifying alternative ways to improve the benefits, reduce costs, and enhance the productivity of the organization. Analysis may be confined to one unit or may include all overhead activities.

Overhead value analysis, developed by the McKinsey consulting organization, was presented as a mature and comprehensive example of service interchange analysis. Two other approaches were briefly discussed: operation function analysis, which is less comprehensive and concentrates on the interactive demands across organizational units associated with selected functions, and BODCA, which analyzes decision patterns and costs.

In addition to these approaches, Mundel's work-unit analysis can be useful, for it analyzes services starting at the results level with 8th-order work-units and sequentially defines lower-level inputs required to produce them.

Opportunities for substantial white collar productivity enhancement result from service interchange analysis, for attention is directed to the interactive consequences resulting from individual and unit demand for specific services which are usually not well evaluated as to their value or cost.

Horizontal Structures

Three supportive horizontal structures were presented, each of which focuses on specific resources which permeate the entire organization: information, physical/technology, and people. Each is a critical resource, intertwined with the vertical structures. However, considering them separately is advantageous.

Information

There are many approaches to analysis within this structure. We have elected to concentrate on a "people-based" approach, paperwork simplification. Ben Graham has shared his experiences with the basic process associated with involving people who are doing the work with analysis and improvement of their work, by providing them a broader perspective of their activities and the interrelationships of their efforts with those of others.

Obviously, elements of the other two horizontal structures are also involved. Technology, particularly office automation and computers, is a necessary resource. Proper interface is provided by education and advice, to allow the users of the technology to develop the design in keeping with their needs and with advice from the technologists concerning technological capabilities and potential. The human resource interface is provided for by the participative approach.

Physical Resources /Technology

Technology has been the driving force for productivity growth from a historical perspective. While the overall impact of technology is favorable, its impact on white collar workers beyond the clerical area has been marginal at best. However, the potential benefits associated with information technology applied to the knowledge worker area are very attractive. These potential benefits have not been realized, largely because of lack of *management* of office technology. Lessons learned from management of product, process, and manufacturing technology provide a useful pattern. In addition to the technology dimensions, keen attention to the human and effective application dimensions is required.

Every organization can benefit from more formalized approaches to their management of this high-potential resource. Various aspects of doing so have been presented and should serve as a basis for developing more formalized approaches which are appropriate for any specific organization.

Paul Cowdin and his RESCAP associates have presented an example of managing technology where a large-scale computer-based decision/operation support system is already in existence. They have demonstrated an effective methodology for identifying and validating systems upgrading alternatives in a live operational environment while preserving the integrity of and transparency to the existing system. Proved improvements eventually can be incorporated into the host system or continued in use via a distributive processor interface.

It is doubtful that the same approach as presented would be appropriate for any other organization. A joint manufacturer/user project is not needed, for the basic methodology has been developed and proved—and can be adapted to the needs of others. The experimental laboratory approach and the involvement of "users" along with user-sensitive technologists in the entire process are elements of potential utility to many organizations for upgrading their own large-scale systems.

Human Resources

The human resource structure transcends all the others we have considered. Adequate development of this resource will lead people to cultivate improvement opportunities associated with all the other resources and structures as a normal course of events.

We have presented several specific approaches to this structure, starting with Henry Dahl and Kent Morgan's approach to evaluation of rate of return on investments in human resources, and evaluation of interactive benefits associated with substitution of human and capital investments. Their approach is a sophisticated one, of particular potential for large organizations. Their conceptual approach is also useful for any organization.

We then presented the concept of leased productivity, which can be applied easily to many clerical situations in both small and large organizations, with considerable economic benefit. The concept has potential for application to knowledge worker areas where adequate skilled personnel are available on a part-time or leased basis. The approach also can be extended so as to eliminate selected "problem" jobs.

Quality of Work Life and Quality Circles

The above two approaches to human resources tend to imply that human resources are treated as a commodity and in a mechanistic way. This, of course, is not the intent. Individual and human values are significant, and are an integral part of the approaches.

The concept of quality of work life (QWL) was developed in Chapter 14 as background for selling problem jobs. QWL is far too important to be associated *only* with this application. It is fundamental for *all* working people, both from the quality standpoint and from the productivity standpoint. People, the knowledge worker, the manager, the clerk, are all motivated by the same basic things. Being productive, searching for ways to enhance productivity, having opportunity to grow and to be creative, developing mutually supportive relationships with one's work group—are all associated with QWL and with productive individuals and organizations.

People are provided a sense of psychic satisfaction and well-being from work life experiences, from being productive, and from being involved in searching for ways to be *more* productive. Improving the quality of work life is a major social concern and is also being recognized as a significant need for their organizations by many managers. QWL can be substantially improved by involving people who are doing work in improving their work.

One of the most popular current approaches to improving QWL and productivity is quality circles (QC), which were discussed in detail in Chapter 16. The QC approach has been effective for many organizations but has become somewhat of a fad. Continuing success will require going beyond a faddish program approach in order to deal with the basic culture of the organization and to develop a truly open style of management.

There are many approaches to developing QWL through participative activities. Paperwork simplification is somewhat similar to QC in some respects, and also somewhat different. QC is somewhat unique in its voluntary nature, in the vesting of prerogatives for project selection with the circle, and in the provision for continuous involvement and concern for improvement of individual and group performance. The concepts of participative work simplification, task forces, matrix organization, and QC can all be used, combined, and recombined to respond to specific opportunities and needs.

PRODUCTIVE ORGANIZATIONS

The Ruch and Hershauer Study

One of the few in-depth studies of organizational characteristics associated with highly productive and successful organizations was conducted by Ruch and Hershauer,[1] who studied and evaluated 32 organizational characteristics for 12 organizations noted for their reputation as highly productive. The results indicated:

1. "The particular combination of variables that leads to high productivity in one firm may not work for another because of differences in technology, type of employee, company history, location, and a multitude of other confounding factors."

2. "Great diversity exists among them in the dimensions evaluated."

3. "The most uniform and extreme evaluation is with respect to 'Beliefs Regarding Productivity.' . . . (with the exception of one firm with an unusual union situation at the time) the twelve firms are characterized as strongly believing that low productivity need not be accepted as a 'fact of life' or a 'product of our time.' . . . Productivity is definitely considered an organizationally controllable variable capable of being very high if properly managed."

The message coming from this study can be generalized, reinforced by many experiences from other organizations and their productivity efforts. Those who succeed have conviction that productivity can be "managed." This conviction is not confined to a few managers but is a shared value which permeates the entire organization. It is a shared value which is given substance by commitment, usually incorporated in the value structure of organizational mores, but also often formalized as part of the basic business objectives and strategies of the organization. Productivity improvement is consciously planned for, and supported.

We discussed in Chapter 12 the desirability (or necessity) for a formal commitment to office automation on the part of the board of directors and top management. A broader approach to white collar productivity is called for, one which includes technology as a component but not as the whole of the matter.

While most of the organizational characteristics which were measured by Ruch and Hershauer showed no particular pattern, four in addition to "beliefs regarding productivity" did show some indication of a pattern. These are:

1. A supervisory leadership style tending toward "participative" and away from "autocratic." First-line supervision involved their people in decisions and problem solving, even though upper management may have been less inclined to do so.

2. Extensive and open communication, particularly in regard to performance feedback. People knew how they performed, and how well they did or did not measure up to expectations. There was a strong emphasis on mutual trust and openness.

3. Technology was exploited, on a cost-justified basis.

4. Job security tended to be fairly strong.

Again we can generalize, and add to the insights provided by the study some observations from other organizations. In addition to conviction and support for the conviction that white collar productivity can be managed constructively, organizations that are particularly successful in improving productivity tend to have a high regard for human values, provide opportunity and reward for their people to be involved in innovation for improving productivity, and view technology as something to be exploited for individual and organizational benefit. An open style of management is typical, either in being or as an evolutionary goal which is being pursued.

There is no "one right way" to pursue white collar productivity—no pat answer or program for doing it. However, there are approaches which are effective, geared to the individual organization and its own unique setting. White collar productivity can be managed—and consistently improved.

The Kearney Study

A more recent analysis of factors associated with highly productive organizations was made in 1981 by A. T. Kearney, Inc.[2] Sixteen companies with acknowledged, successful productivity programs were selected and compared with 24 other companies, matched by industry but randomly selected.

The highly productive organizations neither grew faster nor were more efficient in the "classical" definition of productivity, sales per employee. However, they outperform the matched group in earning higher return on equity and on total capital. The leaders outperformed the matched sample by nearly four to one. They consistently earned 30 percent more on sales than others in their industry. A large share of their success is associated with their approach to managing productivity improvement. The common elements were:

Commitment and involvement throughout the organization All the leading companies believed that they had firm top management support, but only 6 percent of the matched sample had it. All areas and levels of the leading organizations were typically involved in productivity improvement efforts. Some of them used steering committees to provide guidance and encourage involvement. Others handled productivity improvement as a regular agenda item for their management or executive committee meetings. Many also used a hierarchy of productivity committees, with responsibility at the function and department levels for establishing goals for improvement, priorities for efforts, commitment of resources, monitoring of results, and assurance that needed decisions were made.

A broad perspective   Productivity is viewed broadly by the leader group. The basic definition of productivity, output divided by input, is expanded to include more elements and to focus on results:

$$\text{Productivity} = \frac{\text{product} + \text{quality} + \text{service} + \text{image}}{\text{people} + \text{tangible assets} + \text{money} + \text{information} + \text{technology}} = \text{results}$$

Work on the right things   The leaders understand the difference between efficiency and effectiveness, and the concept of validity. They search for project and improvement opportunities which will have impact, and are sensitive to the strategic nature of constructive change.

Know where you are going and if you are getting there   Planning for productivity improvement and measuring progress against plans is routine for the leaders, with thoroughness and clarity of understanding of company direction throughout organization levels. In many cases productivity efforts were formally tied in with basic organization goals and strategies.

Singularity of responsibility and accountability   The leaders are dedicated to improving performance, and provide a framework for formally managing productivity improvement efforts. Formal goals and objectives for performance *and* improvement are used together.

Summary

The insights developed by the Ruch and Hershauer and the Kearney studies provide guidance for those who are not yet certain how they should approach the broad area of enhancing white collar productivity within their organizations. Plan, assess, involve, commit. Manage productivity improvement as a basic function within the organization, one which should involve everyone, at all levels, in seeking improvement.

NOTES

[1] William A. Ruch and James C. Hershauer, *Factors Affecting Worker Productivity*, Arizona State University, Tempe, Ariz., 1974.

[2] The following comments are paraphrased from the report *Managing for Excellence: A Research Study on the State-of-the-Art of Productivity Programs in the United States*, A. T. Kearney, Inc., Chicago, 1981.

Index

About the Editor
in Chief

ROBERT N. LEHRER, a consultant in Atlanta, specializes in helping organizations improve productivity and the quality of work life.

He holds a Ph.D. from Purdue University and was designated a Distinguished Alumnus in 1964. He is also a Fellow of the American Institute of Industrial Engineers and the American Association for Advancement of Science.

He has written three books on productivity and work problems: *Work Simplification: Creative Thinking About Work Problems,* 1957; *The Management of Improvement,* 1965; and *Participative Productivity and Quality of Work Life,* Prentice-Hall, 1982.